CONTENTS

Directory of Maps

INSIDERS' GUIDE® TO

BALTIMORE

SIXTH EDITION

JUDY COLBERT

INSIDERS' GUIDE

GUILFORD, CONNECTICUT
AN IMPRINT OF GLOBE PEQUOT PRESS

All the information in this guidebook is subject to change. We recommend that you call ahead to obtain current information before traveling.

INSIDERS' GUIDE ®

Copyright © 2010 by Morris Book Publishing, LLC

In the Getting to Know Baltimore Architecture Close-Up on pp. 34–35: Thanks to Mary Ellen Hayward and John Dilts for information about Baltimore's architecture and to John and his coauthor John Dorsey for *A Guide to Baltimore Architecture,* 3rd edition (Tidewater Publishers, Centreville, Maryland, 1997). Thanks also to John C. Poppeliers, et al., for their book, *What Style Is It? A Guide to American Architecture* (John Wiley & Sons, Inc., New York, 1995), which was consulted frequently while compiling this information.

Editor: Amy Lyons
Project Editor: Heather Santiago
Layout Artist: Kevin Mak
Text Design: Sheryl Kober
Maps: XNR Productions, Inc. © Morris Book Publishing, LLC

ISSN 1529-5893
ISBN 978-0-7627-5670-4

Printed in the United States of America
10 9 8 7 6 5 4 3 2 1

ABOUT THE AUTHOR

Judy Colbert, an award-winning writer and photographer, has lived in this area her entire life, so far. She has written numerous guide books to Maryland, Delaware, Virginia, and Washington, D.C. Her biggest delights come from finding something wonderful and unusual and then hearing someone say, "I've lived here for decades and never knew that."

Oh, a third delight comes from traveling and exploring with her granddaughters, Rockzana and Sabrina, and watching them grow into extraordinary young women.

ACKNOWLEDGMENTS

Many people helped make this book possible. Professionals, real and virtual friends, relatives, and people who heard the *Insiders' Guide to Baltimore* was being updated and wanted to contribute. With the certainty that I will forget someone, I nonetheless will try to acknowledge as many helpers as I can recall. Thanks to (in no particular order): Edith Chase, John J. Davis, Paul Hartgen, Maryland Restaurant Association; Robert Einhorn, M. Silver Associates; Monee Cottman, Visit Baltimore; Brooke Hall, Brooke Hall Creative; Michele Kruchkowski; Hillel Kuttler; Mark Farrell; Nikki and David Goldbeck, food writers; Lisa Harrison, Emanate PR; Nik Mody, Members Hotel Network; Vance Gulliksen and Aly Bello-Cabreriza, Carnival Cruise Lines; Jennifer Sullivan, Gramercy Mansion; Beth Ravery; Susan Q. Amiot; Madeline Wilson, Corks; Peggy Conrad; Mike Evitts, Downtown Baltimore; Jason, Fellspointmainstreet.org; Ed Weisberg; Gail Farrelly; Daniel Shea; Jill Feinberg, Baltimore County Department of Economic Development; Barbara Cromwell, Fell's Point Preservation Society; Hadley Schroll; Kate Hendrickson, CTA, Port Discovery Children's Museum; Caroline Sanfilippo; Connie Yingling and Cathryna Brown, Department of Business and Economic Development; Charmaine Easie-Samuels; Andrew Crosby; Rebecca Dougherty; Rebecca Devine, ARCWheeler; Carey Paytas, Baltimore Orioles; Jeannie Lee, Roy's Restaurants; Robin Jay, Las Vegas Convention Speakers Bureau; Robin Sax, former Los Angeles prosecutor; Bobbie Dickerson; Ruth E. Thaler-Carter; Linda Glinos, Hilton Pikesville; Jeff Donaldson, Elias-Savion; Tom D'Agostino, director of marketing Fairfield Inn and Suites; Jack Gerbes, Maryland Film Office; Jenny Fordham, Baltimore's Tremonts; Kathleen Dombrowski, Springhill Suites; Monica Floyd, Sheraton Inner Harbor; and Sharon Lemon, Zest Communications.

Special appreciation goes to Mary Lou Malzone, Bev Westcott, Liz Griffin, and Frank Francois, who know just when to be there for me and when to stay out of my way.

My thanks go to Drs. Gail Anderson, James Wang, and Eric Finzi, who keep my parts running.

Thanks, hugs, and love to my family whom I adore: Raul, Jazz, Rockzana, Sabrina, and Maritza Flores, and GG and Jumper.

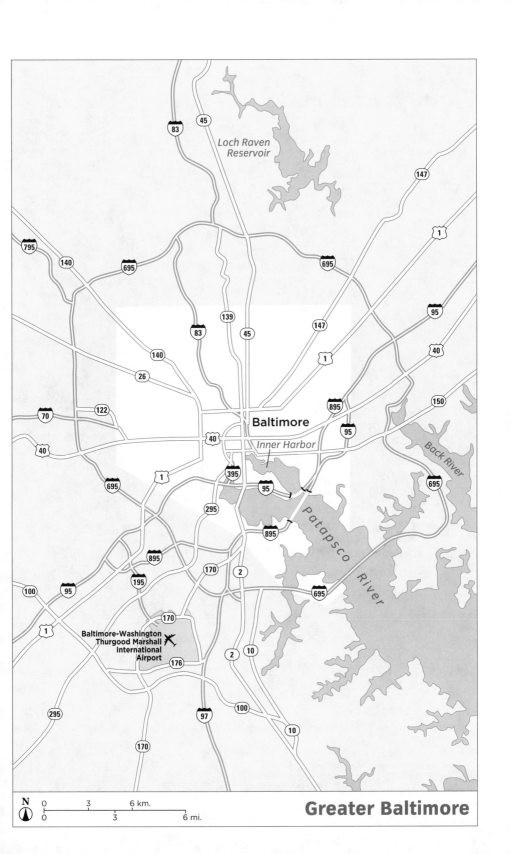

Greater Baltimore

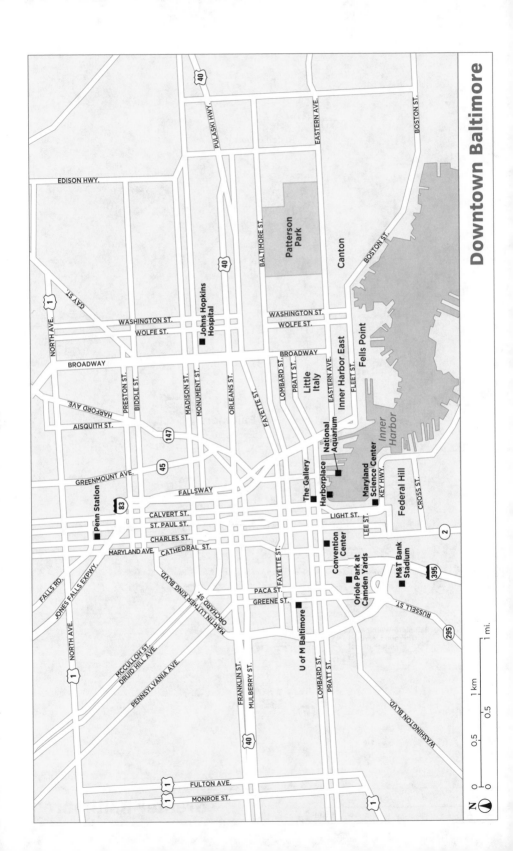

Downtown Baltimore

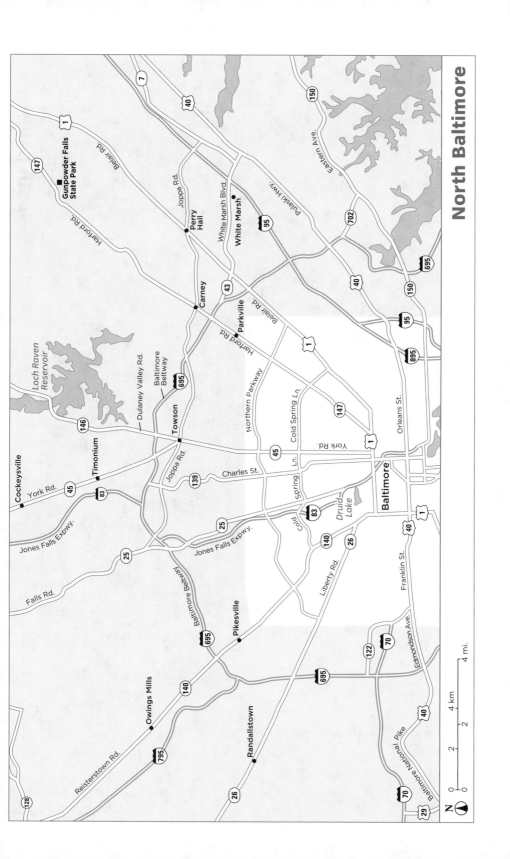

North Baltimore

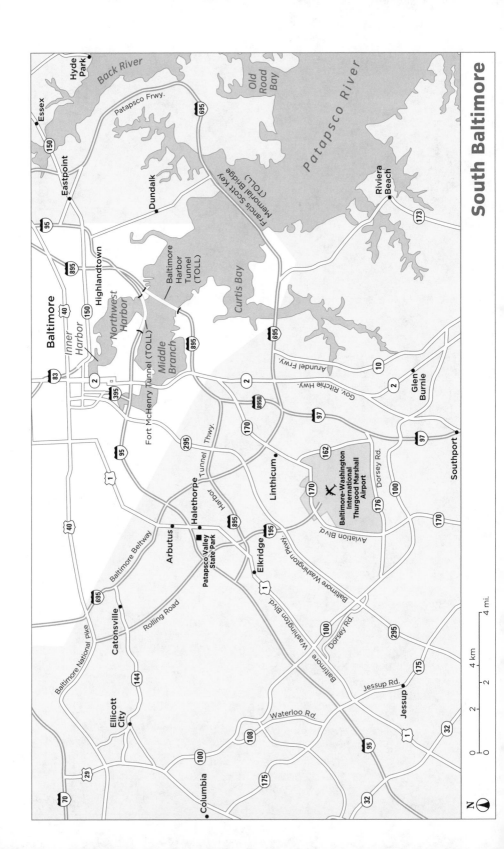

South Baltimore

PREFACE

Baltimore and its residents are passionate. If you learn only one thing from this *Insiders' Guide to Baltimore*, you must realize and appreciate this. They are passionate about football (they bleed purple), baseball, lacrosse, boating, culture, medicine, medical research, intelligence, scientific research, food, history, hiking, and the list continues.

You can almost feel the zeal, enthusiasm, and gusto in the breezes that come off the Inner Harbor or sweep through the parklands. All these pieces come together and meld almost as well as a professional sports team. They aren't quite perfect, but in football you're given four tries to move the ball 10 yards. So, there's a little chink here and a little blemish there. The components all work to produce the City of Baltimore.

Formerly a hard-working, blue-collar city that was focused around industry and the port, it is now a city known for its medical and technical superiority, its smorgasbord of home-style and cuisine dining, and its widely acknowledged reputation as a great city for the arts. Its downtown core is compact and walkable, causing Visit Baltimore to note that the city is "two feet away from everything."

A lot of people have worked to create this metamorphosis.

Politically, Thomas D'Alesandro Jr. (former mayor of Baltimore and U.S. Congressman) and Thomas D'Alessandro III (former mayor of Baltimore), the father and brother of Nancy D'Alessandro Pelosi, Speaker of the United States House of Representatives, were a Maryland influence from the mid-1920s until the early 1970s.

William Donald "Willie Don" (and in some cases "The Donald" long before that young whippersnapper called "The Donald" came along) Schaefer, former mayor of Baltimore (1971-1987) and governor of Maryland during his 50 years of public service, was irascible, stubborn, and any number of other not-so-nice adjectives. Yet, he's responsible for guiding the creation of the Inner Harbor, Oriole Park at Camden Yards, M&T Bank football stadium, and the Light Rail transportation system. Sometimes criticized for pouring a lot of money into Baltimore it is said that his thinking was the improved status had to start with downtown Baltimore or else the hole in the donut would always be an eyesore and blemish on the city. Although politics and other issues changed and entered the 21st century, Schaefer never did.

On Monday, November 2, 2009, on the former governor's 88th birthday, the City of Baltimore officially unveiled a 7' 2" larger-than-life-size sculpture honoring the larger-than-life Schaefer. It stands at the Harbor West Shore Garden, between the Harborplace Light Street Pavilion and the Baltimore Visitor Center at Light and Conway Streets. Rodney Carroll created the sculpture that was a gift of Whiting-Turner President and CEO Willard Hackerman.

Senator Barbara Mikulski, the senior ranking female United States senator, was a citizen activist who led the fight to prevent a 16-lane interstate highway from bisecting the Fell's Point and Canton areas of Baltimore.

And beleaguered former Baltimore Mayor Sheila Dixon seemed to be leading the charge to improve Baltimore even more.

Yes, there have been a few scandals along the way. They just add spice to life, most notably (nationally) former Vice President Spiro T. Agnew who came from Baltimore. In 1973, he pleaded nolo contendere (no contest) to tax evasion and bribery during his days as governor of Maryland.

On the medical front, Dr. Carol W. Greider (with Elizabeth H. Blackburn and Jack W. Szostak), a professor of microbiology at Johns Hopkins University, shared the 2009 Nobel Prize in Medicine for research into cancer and how it grows. Johns Hopkins Hospital is annually acknowledged as the best hospital in the country. Other superb medical facilities include the University of Maryland Medical and Dental Schools, and the Shock Trauma Center. Dr. Ben Carson, the noted director of pediatric neurosurgery at JHS, is considered a Baltimorean even though he was born in Detroit.

Baltimore is a city of firsts with the country's first railroad, shopping center, Ouija board, umbrella, and African American newspaper chain.

John Waters and Barry Levinson started their divergent paths into cinematic history here; ironic, particularly in Waters' case, because it's also the state where Mary Avara ruled over the last movie censor board in the country that wasn't abolished until 1981. If you base your impressions of the city from Waters' films and such TV series as Homicide: Life on the Street and The Wire, then you have a very narrow view. Of course, according to sociology professor William J. Wilson, the series "has done more to enhance our understanding of the challenges of urban life and the problems of urban inequality." The series will be a course of study at Harvard University and that joins similar classes at Duke University and Middlebury College.

Weather geeks love this area for it goes from the suffocating heat, humidity, and haze of a summer day (or week) to the debilitating Nor'easter that dumps 28.2" of snow, as happened on February 15-18, 2003, and the record-breaking snows that fell in the winter of 2009-2010 that took more than a month to clear. Territorial beasts that we are, anyone who slaved and shoveled to free a car from the depths promptly placed a trash can, lawn chair, potted plant or some object defining "this is my cleared spot, don't even think of parking here." Newly installed (February 4, 2010) mayor Stephanie Rawlings-Blake allowed the illegal space-saving tactics for a few days and then issued warnings against the practice.

The first monument dedicated to George Washington is here, as are the first Methodist church in America and the first Catholic cathedral and seminary. The Pride of Baltimore II, a replica of the famous Baltimore clipper ships, is here, as is the Constellation (the U.S. Navy's last all-sail ship).

Old Baltimore does have its own language and pronunciation guide including ways to pronounce the city's name, including "Bawlmer" or "Bawlamar." Affectionately, you should feel flattered when someone calls you "hon" (that's pronounced hun). People are nice, for the most part, and if you're caught in the wrong lane on Pratt Street during rush hour, they'll even let you change lanes, if you signal your intent.

It's time for you to find your passion here and share it with everyone you know, hon.

HOW TO USE THIS BOOK

First, this book tries to tell you what you'd want to know if you had lived here for two or three decades or generations except you just moved here last week. Or, maybe you have lived here and had completely forgotten why something is done the way it is. What's the story behind the clock face on the tower that spells out BRO-MOSELTZER? Why is there such media coverage over a kitschy pink flamingo over the Café Hon restaurant? How do you score a seat on the Light Rail going home after an Os game? What's the weight of each oriole bird weather vane that sits on top of the Os scoreboard? Are the rooms on one side of a hotel quieter than the other? Yes, it's a little trivia, it's a lot of research, and, I hope, it's interesting and a lot of fun, and it makes you feel like an Insider.

For less than a tank of gasoline, there are innumerable interesting things to do, places to see, and restaurants to sample. *Insiders' Guide to Baltimore* pretty much focuses on the downtown Baltimore City and several of its neighborhoods. A few things are mentioned that are beyond the city limits. Most of them are within the Beltway. Then, there are a couple of items that are outside the Beltway (e.g., the airport) yet, they belong to a Baltimore book. For more travel information for areas farther afield, pick up a copy of *Maryland and Delaware Off the Beaten Path, Virginia Off the Beaten Path* (both of which I author), and *Pennsylvania Off the Beaten Path* by Christine O'Toole. All three are from Globe Pequot Press (GPP) and available through Amazon.com, your neighborhood bookstore, or www.globepequot.com.

In each chapter, you'll find **Insiders' Tips,** indicated by **i** as well as sidebars which offer up useful information and tips you might not find elsewhere. Sprinkled throughout the book are Close-Ups, which offer detailed looks at some intriguing aspects of Baltimore.

Moving to Baltimore or already live here? Be sure to check out the back of the book, where you will find the **Living Here** appendix that offers sections on relocation, real estate, education, heath care, and media.

As you consult these pages, keep in mind that this book should merely be used as a starting point. Often, favorite spots are those discovered by accident, so don't be afraid to stray from this book when deciding what to do here. There are so many great restaurants, shops, clubs, bars, and attractions in this city that you just might stumble upon something fantastic. Also bear in mind that some recommendations and information may be out-of-date by the time you read this book. New businesses are constantly cropping up and older ones are often moving or closing their doors. Even long-standing shops, restaurants, clubs, theaters, and attractions often change their hours or days of operation, so it is always a good idea to call ahead before heading out and seeing the city.

With that in mind, go ahead and start getting to know Baltimore—whether in your chair (or airplane seat) as you read this book or as you try to navigate your way around the city. If you catch an error or think a particular restaurant, bar, store, or other spot should have been included in this book, please let us know. *Insiders' Guide to Baltimore* will be updated periodically and your feedback would benefit the next edition. Please write to us at Insiders' Guide to Baltimore, GPP, P.O. Box 480, Guilford, CT 06437-0480 or at editorial@globepequot.com.

WHICH WAY IS NORTH?

Some people zip around Baltimore as though they have GPS chips implanted in their feet. Others get lost looking at their feet. Mostly, Baltimore streets follow a north-south and east-west grid. That should be easy enough, but then a lot of streets have one-way traffic. So, you know you have to go from here to there, but you have to drive six blocks to arrive at your destination five doors away.

Downtown is divided north-south by Baltimore Street. All streets north of it are called North and all streets south are designated South. The east-west divide is along Charles Street. If a street is East Something, then it is east of Charles Street. The official downtown is roughly bounded by Martin Luther King Jr. Boulevard to the west, Mt. Royal Avenue to the north, President Street to the east, and the Inner Harbor area to the south. In practice, there are other dividing lines. Many visitors use Pratt and Light Streets as a starting point. This is where Harborplace is so they use that as a landmark. Others indicate something is east of I-83 (Jones Falls Expressway). Others figure whatever is worthwhile is within the areas of Federal Hill, Little Italy, or Fell's Point. Other than the Downtown Project that promotes the Downtown area, it probably doesn't matter where you divide things as long as you understand where it is.

BALTIMORE TIPS

Telephone Numbers

In Maryland, you must dial the three-digit area code to make any call. When the Maryland population (and the use of cell phones, etc.) increased enough to warrant additional area codes, two new area codes were overlaid on the existing two area codes. That means a 443 area code phone can reside next to a 410 area code and the same for the 301 and 240 area codes. Don't worry about it; just do it. There's no need to dial 1 first, but you have to dial all 10 numbers no matter what. When calling 443 or 410, the call is local. The same goes between numbers that are in the 240 and 301 exchanges.

Highway Numbers vs. Road Names

Some roads are known by their name or route number or both. Where clarity might be an issue, everything is included the first time and then just the most common. The Baltimore Beltway, I-695, is a 51.46 mile concrete loop around the city that connects with the rest of the I-95 northeast corridor between Boston and Atlanta. The "inner" loop (often referred to on TV station crawls as IL) is the one where traffic moves in a clockwise pattern, and the "outer" loop (or OL) has traffic going in a counter-clockwise pattern. Related to the circumferential are the two tunnels under the Baltimore Harbor (technically, the Patapsco River): I-895 is the original Harbor Tunnel and I-95 refers to the newer four-tubed structure, the Fort McHenry Tunnel. The Francis Scott Key Bridge completes the beltway by going over the river instead of under it. The Jones Falls Expressway (JFX) is I-83.

When asking for directions, give the place you are trying to get to and the street address, whenever possible. Based on this information you should be able to find the right way, probably using common road names rather than the highway numbers.

AREA OVERVIEW

Baltimore is a fascinating mixture of old and new. Its buildings, its businesses, its people, and its image run the gamut from progressive to old-fashioned—sometimes all in the same block. This chapter provides a general overview of some of these people and places and directs you to other chapters in which you'll find more information about these subjects.

Baltimoreans are good neighbors. We're the kind of folks who will stop to give you directions or will help you find your lost cat. We might not agree with your politics, but that won't stop us from watching your house while you're away on vacation.

We like to get together. In addition to all the citywide festivals that are held every year, neighborhood bazaars, flea markets, bingo nights, crab feasts, ham and oyster suppers, and dances abound. Even though we're a big city, we gather like small-town folks at our houses of worship and our schools and we love to linger over dinner at our local restaurants.

We get together for group yard sales, block parties, and just talking over the backyard fence (real or virtual). Baltimore is not a place where people walk by with their heads down and their eyes averted, fearing to speak. We are congenial. Philosophical dissertations with a stranger while standing in line at the grocery store are not uncommon. We come in all colors, shapes, and sizes. Overall, we're a good group.

THE PLACE

Perhaps one reason Baltimoreans are such good neighbors is that most of us live in a neighborhood. There are about 225 of them at last count. Few of these neighborhoods were intentionally laid out, so geographic boundaries can be vague. Yet, each neighborhood exudes a distinct character that is often defined by its historic origin and its population.

The general ethnic mix of Baltimore and its neighborhoods continues to change, but many of the neighborhoods retain their original flavor and, in some cases, the descendants of their original resident populations. Just the names of the local places of business will sometimes tell you what the main industry of the original community was or what its ethnic origin is.

Little Italy, Little Lithuania, and Greektown are easy to grasp. Butchers Hill, Brewers Hill, and Pigtown are easy, too. OK, Pigtown is west of the warehouse building and the pigs were brought to market from the warehouse that now houses the Baltimore Orioles offices.

Many of the neighborhoods in Baltimore were culled from the estates of prominent citizens. Homewood, Guilford, Bolton Hill, Mount Clare, Mondawmin, Walbrook, and many others carry the names of their original estates.

Some neighborhoods sprang up because a local industry drew workers. Fell's Point in Downtown was established in 1730 by shipbuilder William Fell and his family and became the hub of shipbuilding (and privateering) in Baltimore during the Revolution (see the History chapter). The streets he named and the area he laid out are still here, populated with local crafters, great little shops, and lovers of old things. Baltimore has many neighborhoods that were once mill towns. Hampden, in Northwest Baltimore, is one of those, as are other neighborhoods that cluster around the Jones Falls Valley. The valley was once lined with mills that were powered by the swiftly running waters of the Jones Falls.

Baltimore does have a few neighborhoods, however, that were specifically designed as residential tracts. Peabody Heights, established in the 1890s and renamed Charles Village in the mid-1970s, is one of these areas. You can see the original tracts in the different housing styles that were constructed by each builder: porch fronts in the 2800 block of Maryland Avenue and bowed fronts in the 2600 block; five-story, 20-foot-wide houses on Charles Street; two-story, 13-foot-wide houses on Howard Street. There were houses for every income and every size family in the original Peabody Heights, and Charles Village continues today as one of Baltimore's most eclectic areas.

Interestingly, Baltimore also boasts the first neighborhood ever designed specifically as a suburb. Walbrook was laid out in 1870 but did not have a long suburban life span—it was annexed by the city in 1888.

Fun on the Web

If you find yourself with some downtime, by all means, go downtown. Three Web sites are devoted to encouraging you to spend time downtown. The Downtown Partnership, a nonprofit organization that promotes the Downtown area for business and pleasure, maintains a good Web site, www.godowntown baltimore.com. Anything going on in the next couple of weeks usually is listed here. Look for concerts, lectures, festivals, and restaurant promotions. The Greater Baltimore Cultural Alliance produces www .baltimorefunguide.com. This is a pretty comprehensive listing to the upcoming events at the museums, stadiums, and other fun places around town. Visit www.KidsLove DowntownBaltimore.com, which has an updated list of events and special offers available at downtown attractions, museums, and restaurants.

BIG BUSINESS

Baltimore's location prompted the growth of Baltimore's business interests. Because we have the best protected harbor in the world and are central to the Eastern seaboard (halfway between New York and Massachusetts to the north and Norfolk and the Carolinas to the south), Baltimore was an obvious choice for businesses that needed to touch North and South and reach West. Because of its location, it's also at least 200 miles closer to the Midwest than other East Coast ports.

The cotton mills that made Baltimore the largest supplier of southern cotton duck canvas in the entire world were a natural. Baltimore, an industrialized city with plenty of water for power, was just a hop, skip, and a short rail commute to the raw cotton suppliers of the South. As for customers, they were right here, as long as most ships that came to port were under sail.

It was this ability to get products to market just about anywhere in the United States that made Baltimore boom, and much of its current economy still revolves around the transportation industry. The port with a 50' channel depth has a huge economic influence, with 33 million tons of cargo coming through the port in 2008. Railroads, warehousing, and distribution are a rapidly growing sector of business in Baltimore, and Baltimore–Washington International Thurgood Marshall Airport has become one of the busiest airports in the country.

i If you're moving to Baltimore (or anywhere in Maryland), you must exchange your valid out-of-state driver's license and your car registration for their Maryland counterparts within 60 days. Call MVA at (800) 950-1682 or go to the Web site, www.mva.maryland.gov to read about the rules and regulations governing motorcycle licenses, minimum age requirements, proof of lawful presence, fees, and other important information.

Selected Baltimore Firsts

In 1800 Alexander Brown opened the first investment banking house in America in Baltimore. The original building, which miraculously survived the Great Baltimore Fire, still stands at the southwest corner of Baltimore and Calvert Streets. Now known as Deutsche Bank Alex. Brown, the company is still going strong.

In 1803 Thomas More invented the first icebox refrigerator.

Samuel Morse inaugurated the first commercial telegram service here in 1844—which was appropriate, since the first telegraph line in America was erected here that same year.

—Excerpted from *Baltimore— America's City of Firsts,* a pamphlet published by Baltimore Bicentennial Celebration, Inc.

Baltimore also has retained a solid manufacturing base. McCormick Spice Company and Under Armour Apparel have facilities in Baltimore. We also claim a growing number of high-tech, defense industry manufacturers, perhaps, in part, due to our proximity to the nation's capital. Being near Washington, D.C., also spurs some of the smaller businesses in Baltimore, particularly those related to real estate and tourism. A great many people who come to visit Washington also make the short trip north to Baltimore, and many residents of the Washington area come here regularly to shop at the Inner Harbor, see the sights, and attend sporting events. Some former residents of D.C. have settled in Baltimore because of the relatively short commute by car or train (about 60 minutes) and because the real estate is less expensive and the quality of life is excellent.

The growing business focus in Baltimore can be found in the service industries. Education, medicine, international banking and investment, international trade, real estate, and tourism are all big business in Baltimore.

Maryland rates as the best-educated workforce in the country due largely to the many hospitals and research universities in town, specifically such world-renowned colleges and research universities as Johns Hopkins and the University of Maryland. Between them, they have 45 top federal research labs. According to 2006 (latest available) data from the National Science Foundation and U.S. Department of Labor, Bureau of Labor Statistics, Maryland houses the highest concentration of employed doctoral scientists and engineers, is first in employed Ph.D. scientists and engineers per 100,000 employed workers, and is first in employment of mathematical sciences, biological sciences, and health; third in physical sciences; and seventh in computer and information sciences.

Once a state known primarily for its blue collars and its blue crabs, Maryland is now home to a burgeoning high-tech and biotech industry. Some of the most exciting research in the areas of genetics and biotechnology is taking place right in Baltimore's backyard. Maryland is home to 300 of the most vital, fastest-growing bioscience firms in the world, including Gene Logic and Human Genome Sciences.

Struever Bros. Eccles & Rouse, Inc., is focusing its mixed-use programs in such places as Brewer's Hill (the Natty Boh building will be the first project to utilize Maryland's Green Tax Credit program), the Jones Falls Valley, Harbor Point, Greater Fell's Point, and, most recently, State Center (where Mount Vernon, Upton, and Marble Hill meet).

Baltimore has a comprehensive banking sector that began with the first mortgage banking house in the United States, Alex. Brown & Sons. Now known as Deutsche Bank Alex. Brown, the company's history includes underwriting the first initial public offering in America: the Baltimore Water Company in 1808 and then the B&O railroad. Baltimore is also home to such financial industry giants as T. Rowe Price and Legg Mason.

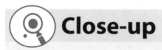

Close-up

How to Speak like a Native

People make entire careers out of trying to eliminate a Baltimore accent. A former radio announcer friend who thought for sure that she had won that battle, was on a lift (elevator) in England, when someone interrupted her by asking where she lived in Baltimore. Part of the Baltimore "accent" is the way we shape our o's and part of it vocabulary, particularly when it comes to edible items. As examples:

Snoball—flavored shaved ice in a paper cone, topped with marshmallow crème or chocolate sauce. You may know of similar desserts called snowcone or snowball, but they're made from crushed ice and probably don't have the topping. Do not confuse Snoballs and anything else.

Arabber—a (disappearing breed) street vendor who sells produce and other goods from a horse-drawn wagon and the various forms as in to arab. This does not begin to suggest that the vendor is an Arab or of any Arabian descent. Only the word is entomologically related.

Front steps—particularly referencing the white marble steps in front of Baltimore row houses. They are not stoops.

Sub—a sandwich that in other parts of the country may be a hoagie, grinder, hero, etc.

Whereas in some areas of the country, all cola drinks are called Cokes or Pepsis even if they're Diet Rite, in Baltimore if you want a Pepsi-Cola, you must order **"Pepsi,"** and a **"Coke"** is a Coca-Cola. And don't ask for a pop, unless you don't care what you get. We call anything that fizzes a "soda." If you ask for an orange pop, you're likely to get frozen orange ice on a stick!

Some generic names have distinctive pronunciation. **"Zinc"** is one such word. "Sinks" were originally made of zinc. So when we put our dishes away at the end of a meal, we put them in the "zinc." (We are not mispronouncing "sink.") If you're used to having your hamburger or sandwich on a bun, ask your waitress for a "roll." If you want a sweet roll with your morning's breakfast, ask what types of "buns" are available.

In the summer, we don't barbecue, we **"cook out."** We live in row houses, or row homes, not town houses.

The o's are broad, unless spoken before a consonant, and the t's often come out as d's, as in "wudder." (Wudder, by the way, is the clear, cool liquid that often rains on us. We spell it water.) Sometimes the t's get lost altogether, or syllables are simply omitted , as in "Bawlmer," the town in which we live.

L's are often swallowed, and words tend to run together as if there were no space between them. "B'lair" is one of those. It is how we locals pronounce Bel Air, a nearby town in Harford County, and also a road in Bawlmer.

Some words become so **Bawlmerized** they are hardly recognizable. On a cold winter night, smoke goes up our "chimbly." When school's out, we like to go "down-e o'shun" to "Ocean

THE COST OF LIVING

As cities go, Baltimore is a relatively inexpensive one. The real estate boom that skyrocketed rents and housing costs in most major cities certainly affected the housing costs locally, but Baltimore still is less expensive than neighboring Washington. The Baltimore cost of living is pegged at $121.9 (with 100 being the average for all urban areas) compared to Washington at $137.4 and New York at $219.8. The average home cost in Baltimore in 2008 was $235,000, down considerably from 2005. Housing runs the gamut from the exorbitant to the modest. A few years ago you could scoop up a fixer-upper in Canton for the low fifties; now those rehabbed beauties are selling for $500,000. Bargains can still be found in

City, Murlin" (that would be Maryland), or "Rehoebet Beach, Delaware." "The shure," on the other hand, is much closer. If someone you know in Baltimore is going "down-e shure" for the weekend, they're probably only going as far as Middle River, about 25 minutes away. All shure places are on the Chesapeake Bay and the rivers that flow into it.

Bawlmerese plays havoc with pronoun references and adjectives and direction. Don't faint if you hear a native say that "Me and him went to see dem Birds last night." **"Dem Birds"** are also known as **"dem Os"** or **"dem Orals"**—our baseball team. In fact, a common greeting from a Baltimorean after a winning baseball game is "How about dem Os?" ("A great game!" would be an appropriate response.)

When you're going to an Orioles game, ask for directions to the Yard or Camden Yards or just follow the traffic. You realize, of course, that this stadium (unlike its neighboring M&T Bank Stadium) is not a sponsored or named facility, so there was a discussion about the new stadium's name. The powers-that-be wanted to call it Oriole Park, the fans wanted to call it Camden Yards. A compromise was reached with Oriole Park at Camden Yards. Baltimoreans, however, don't care what the formal name is. We call it "Camden Yards" or, more simply, **"the Yard."**

We're stubborn like that. Although our airport was long ago renamed Baltimore–Washington International and then Baltimore Washington International Thurgood Marshall Airport, you may still find some old-timers who call it "Friendship," the airport's original name.

You should feel flattered when someone calls you **"hon."** The waitresses do it. Store clerks do it. It's a term of endearment and, yes, part of Baltimore's "charm." William Donald Schaefer, the former mayor and governor, was known to call everyone "hon." While he was governor, the Welcome to Baltimore sign on the northbound lanes of the Baltimore-Washington Parkway (Route 295) frequently had a sign with the word "HON" on it below the Baltimore. It was actually three pieces of cardboard. Yes, police officers or sanitation people or someone would remove the sign only to see the cardboard guy had installed a new one a day or two later.

As you enter or leave a building, someone will hold the door for you. The appropriate response is, "thank you" and if you don't say it, you may hear the door-holder say it for you, sarcastically, of course. A smile is always welcome.

When you signal to change lanes, someone will let you do that. Raise your hand as a thank you as you pass. It's expected.

Thanks are often given to the store clerk who helps you or the antiques dealer who lets you look around the store. We thank our bus drivers and cabbies when they let us out at our stops, and often the response is not "you're welcome" or another "thank you," but "have a good one . . . " "One" is the day, the afternoon, or the evening.

And you will, we hope. Have a good one, that is. Knowing a little bit about the native tongue will help you get settled. Enjoy Bawlmer, hon!

the city, for renting, buying, and investing. (See the Relocation chapter for more information.)

Groceries and eating out are reasonable. Groceries for a family of four will cost about $150 per week if that family buys brand names. Eating out is easy with a laundry list of chains and a high volume of outstanding locally owned cafes and restaurants. Clothing and amenities can also be found at reasonable prices. Although a lot of national chains are in the Baltimore area, great creativity and super personalized service are in the local shops and boutiques. Some of our consignment stores offer designer and vintage clothing for a steal.

When it comes to making a living, Maryland has one of the country's lowest poverty rates and ranks among the top states in median household and per capita personal income. Staying on the job is easier, too, when you have some of the best child care in the country. Maryland was ranked fourth in the nation in the National Association of Child Care Resource and Referral Agencies' 2007 survey of child-care standards.

Baltimore earned a bad reputation for its high number of drug-related homicides in the mid-1990s, but the homicide rate of 305 in 1999 dropped to 261 in 2000 and 254 in 2002. That's still seriously high and, unfortunately, gang and gang-related violence has increased and the homicide rate has started climbing again. Those deadly areas are in fairly specific locations and not citywide. Baltimore is extremely safe and people walk the streets all the time. There are certain areas where you don't want to spend time, particularly at night. Lock your car; remove attractive items (GPS, cell phone) away from view. Every major city has a similar problem.

Baltimore's mayor and police force are dedicated to reducing crime on our city streets. Although Baltimore can feel like a small town, it is a city and it does have its share of muggers and panhandlers. The Downtown Baltimore people have a "Your Change Can Make Change" program where they tell you it's OK to say "No" to panhandlers but "Yes" to giving to homeless outreach programs. Make a Change meters can be found throughout Downtown. Change collected from these meters supports homeless services in Downtown Baltimore. Please consider donating your spare change to one of Downtown's Make a Change meters.

CLIMATE

Name your favorite climate and sooner or later you'll find it in Baltimore. The dominant waterway in the area is the Chesapeake Bay, which is large enough to create its own weather. We're along the Atlantic Ocean, west of the Gulf Stream, and on the downside of the Appalachian Mountains. In other words, our summers can be hot and humid with the occasional hurricane. In the winter, we have been known for some monumental blizzards and a season known for "If this is Friday, it must be snowing" or "If it's snowing, it must be Friday" and suddenly you realize we've had 70" of snow in one season. Normal annual snowfall accumulation is between 16" or 18" and usually comes in very small increments. Of course, the word snow is enough to start a run on the grocery stores for the white things—milk, bread, toilet paper, tooth paste—and schools opening two hours late or closing two hours early.

In plain language, according to www .weather.com, the average highs range from mid-40s to low-90s and the average lows range from the high 20s to the mid 70s. The site says on average, the warmest month is July and the highest recorded temperature was 107 degrees in 1936. May is the average wettest month and the lowest recorded temperature was -70 in 1934. Temperatures will be 10 degrees cooler on the Eastern Shore and as much as 20 or 30 degrees cooler in Garrett County where they receive more snow annually than Anchorage, Alaska.

Baltimore also has what is known as "Indian summer." The term describes periods of warm weather following the first freeze.

To offset hot steamy summers and cold blustery winters, we have the most marvelous spring and fall seasons. A friend from Israel and Los Angeles flew into Baltimore on a mid-June day and in the 48 hours he visited, he must have said he couldn't get over the trees 50 times. The changing leaves can leave you breathless with their hues. The most important thing to remember during those lovely seasons is to wear layers. It may be 50 degrees in the morning, 85 in the afternoon, and drop to 70 by the time the late news is being aired.

Vital Statistics

Mayor: Stephanie Rawlings-Blake

Governor: Martin O'Malley

Surrounding and nearby counties: Baltimore County, Carroll County, Harford County, Howard County, Montgomery County, Anne Arundel County

Populations:
City: 636,919 (2008 estimate)
State: 5.6 million

Nickname: Charm City (most common), Monument City

Average temperatures:
July: High 88° F, Low 72° F
January: High 41° F, Low 28° F

Average rain: 41 inches
snow: 20 inches
sun: 120 days

Major universities: University of Maryland System, Johns Hopkins University, Towson University, Loyola College, Goucher College, Morgan State University

Major area employers: Port of Baltimore; Johns Hopkins Institutions; the University of Maryland, Baltimore; Deutsche Bank Alex. Brown; St. Paul Companies

Major airport: Baltimore–Washington International Thurgood Marshall Airport (BWI)

Maryland military bases: Aberdeen Proving Grounds, Fort Detrick, Fort Meade, Patuxent River Naval Air Station, United States Naval Academy, Andrews Air Force Base, United States Coast Guard Yard at Curtis Bay

Alcohol laws: DUI limit is .07; must be 21 years old to purchase or consume alcohol; bars open until 2 a.m.; liquor stores closed on Sunday, but bars can be open and packaged goods may be bought from bars on Sunday.

Daily newspapers: *Baltimore Sun, Daily Record, Examiner*

Sales tax: 6 percent state sales tax, 11.5 percent tax on car rentals

Major interstates: Interstate routes are I-68, I-95, I-70, I-83, I-795, I-695 and are marked with a blue and red interstate shield-shaped sign.
United States routes are US 1, US 15, US 40, US 113, US 301, and US 219 are marked with a white U.S. shield-shaped sign.
Maryland State highways MD 2, MD 45, MD 140, and MD 404 are marked with a white Maryland rectangular sign.

Public transportation: Maryland Mass Transit Authority (410) 539-5000, (800) 543-9809, www.mta maryland.com)—Light Rail, Baltimore Metro Subway, Maryland Rail Commuter Service (MARC) Train, Maryland Mass Transit Authority Buses, mobility/paratranist (410-764-8181)

Driving traffic safety laws (as provided by the Maryland State Highway Administration):
Maryland law limits the extent to which speed limits may be raised or lowered. The most notable restrictions are those that prohibit any speed limit greater than 65 miles per hour and any limit above 55 miles per hour anywhere except on interstate highways or other expressways.

A new law, effective in 2009, prohibits texting while driving ($500 fine). Unfortunately, it doesn't prohibit reading texts, a legislative measure that may pass in 2010.

Baltimore has started employing speed cameras at intersections near schools and construction. A first notice will be a warning with future citations costing you $40.

Every child younger than four years old, regardless of weight, and every child weighing 40 pounds or less, regardless of age, must be secured in a U.S. DOT–approved child safety seat. Children and young people up to 16 years of age must be secured in seat belts or child safety seats, regardless of their seating positions. It is strongly recommended that all children ride secured in the rear seat. Drivers and front-seat passengers, regardless of their ages, are required to wear seat belts. It is strongly recommended that all occupants wear seat belts.

Maryland has a mandatory adult seat-belt law that covers the driver and the front-seat passenger next to the door, if the passenger is at least 16 years of age. Maryland's law allows primary enforcement, i.e., police may stop a vehicle and issue citations to violators solely for violating the seat-belt law. The driver and an adult passenger may receive tickets for not wearing seat belts.

Motorcycle operators and passengers are required to wear U.S. DOT–approved helmets. Operators must wear eye protection as well.

Stay alert and give driving your full attention.

Show courtesy to other drivers, pedestrians, and cyclists.

Comply with our traffic laws and heed all traffic signs, signals, and markings.

Avoid driving aggressively.

Wet leaves on the ground in fall are very slippery and deserve special caution.

Vehicles must stop for school buses when the bus's red flashers are on (except when the bus is on the opposite side of a highway divided by a barrier or median strip).

After stopping and yielding to pedestrians and other vehicles, a right turn or left turn from a one-way street to another one-way street may be made on a red signal, except where prohibited by a sign.

Chamber of Commerce and Visitors Bureaus:
Maryland Office of Tourism Development, 401 East Pratt St., 14th Floor, Baltimore 21202; (866) 639-3526, (410) 767-3222; www.visitmaryland.org
Annapolis and Anne Arundel County Conference & Visitor Bureau, 26 West St., Annapolis 21401; (410) 280-0445, (888) 302-2852; www.visitannapolis.org
Visit Baltimore, 100 Light St., 12th Floor, Baltimore 21202; (410) 659-7300, (877) BALTIMORE; www.baltimore.org
Baltimore City Chamber of Commerce, 312 Martin Luther King Jr. Blvd., Baltimore 21201-1221; (410) 837-7101; www.baltimorecitychamber.com
Baltimore County Visitor Center, 44 West Chesapeake Ave., Towson 21204; (410) 296-4886 ext. 3, (800) 570-2836; www.visitbacomd.com
Baltimore Office of Promotion and The Arts, 7 East Redwood St., Suite 500, Baltimore 21202; (410) 752-8632; www.bop.org
Calvert County Department of Economic Development, Courthouse, Prince Frederick 20678; (800) 331-9771; www.co.cal.md.us/visitors
Carroll County Visitor Center, 210 East Main St., Westminster 21157; (410) 848-1388, (800) 272-1933; www.carrollcountytourism.org

Dorchester County Tourism, 2 Rose Hill Place, Cambridge 21613; (410) 228-1000, (800) 522-TOUR; www.tourdorchester.org

Garrett County & Deep Creek Lake Chamber of Commerce, 15 Visitors Center Dr., McHenry 21541; (301) 387-4386; www.visitdeepcreek.com

Harford County Office of Tourism, 220 South Main St., Bel Air 21014; (410) 638-3327, (888) 544-4695; www.harfordmd.com

Howard County Tourism Inc., 8267 Main St., P.O. Box 9, Ellicott City 21043; (410) 313-1900, (800) 288-8747; www.visithowardcounty.com

Kent County Office of Tourism, 400 High St., Chestertown 21620; (410) 778-0416; www.kentcounty.com

Ocean City Convention & Visitors Bureau, 4001 Coastal Hwy., Ocean City 21842; (410) 289-8311, (800) OC-OCEAN; www.ococean.com

St Mary's County Division of Tourism, 23115 Leonard Hall Dr., P.O. Box 653, Leonardtown 20650; (800) 327-9023; www.co.saint-marys.md.us

Talbot County Office of Tourism, 11 South Harrison St., Easton 21601; (410) 770-8000; www.tourtalbot.org

Washington County Convention & Visitors Bureau, 16 Public Sq., Hagerstown 21740; (301) 791-3246, (888) 257-2600; www.marylandmemories.org

Time, temperature, and weather phone number: (410) 662-9225

GETTING HERE, GETTING AROUND

Baltimore is served by international, national, and regional air service at Baltimore Washington International Thurgood Marshall Airport (it's a Southwest Airlines hub); Amtrak and MARC trains; Greyhound and other national and regional buses; and major cruise lines (Carnival and Royal Caribbean Cruise Lines offering year-round service) providing about 165,000 people with a great sea-going getaway every year. Several interstate highways weave north/south and west across the state. I-95 travels 1,925 miles connecting and directing traffic from Houlton, Maine and Woodstock New Brunswick, Canada on the North through to Miami, Florida on the South (except for a portion in the Pennsylvania-New Jersey area that is projected to be complete in 1914, maybe). Interstate 70 starts in Baltimore and doesn't stop until or make you stop for a traffic light (except for a small portion in Breezewood, Pennsylvania) for almost 2,200 miles, until it reaches its western terminus in Cove Fort, Utah. All roads in Europe may lead to Rome; lots of roads in the United States lead to Baltimore. Forty million people live within a six-hour drive of the city.

Getting around is relatively easy with Light Rail, subway, and bus service. Most of the tourist attractions are within walking distance of each other and those parts of the city are relatively easy to walk.

So, c'mon people. Baltimore has made visiting about as easy as one could hope and its residents are waiting for you.

GETTING HERE

By Air

BALTIMORE–WASHINGTON INTERNATIONAL THURGOOD MARSHALL AIRPORT
Eastern end of I-195 East, Linthicum
(410) 859-7111, (800) I-FLY-BWI
www.bwiairport.com

Baltimore–Washington International Thurgood Marshall Airport (referred to by locals as BWI or BWI Marshall, and sometimes Friendship by the longtime locals) honors the first African-American Supreme Court justice and a Baltimore native. Four domestic concourses (essentially, concourse A and B connect and together serve Southwest Airlines) and one international concourse have 70 gates, including 12 for commuter aircraft. Thirty-three commercial airlines carry more than 56,000 passengers daily with 650 flights, with Southwest Airlines carrying more than half of the passengers. A total of 20,488,881 passengers used the airport in 2008, making BWI the country's 24th busiest airport.

Hourly parking is available, immediately inside the arrivals/departures travel ramp. The garage has a green and red lighting system that lets you see exactly where the open parking spaces are.

A "cell phone" lot lets you park for free while your incoming passengers clear the plane and pick up their luggage. A call to you, and the arriving visitors and you can be curbside at the same time. Voila!

BWI Marshall is one airport that's treated as part of a solution to an area problem with great connections to street and rail traffic. Ten minutes from the airport, via free shuttle service, is the BWI Airport Amtrak station with MARC (Maryland Rail Commuter) and Amtrak service to Baltimore and points north and to Washington, D.C., and points south.

In July 2009, the first airline just for pets began service to BWI Marshall Airport. Pet Airways will initially cater to dogs and cats. Birds, reptiles, pigs, and other animals are being considered for future expansion. Pet attendants individually load the animals onto Beechcraft 1900 turboprops, whose seats and overhead bins have been removed. The animals are then placed into secured kennels. Attendants accompany the flights. Owners may drop off their pets up to 72 hours before flight time or leave them overnight at the arrival city at the airline's Paws Lodges. Pet Airways offers flights between BWI and regional airports in New York, Chicago, Denver, and Los Angeles areas. For more information visit www .petairways.com.

Getting to the Airport

Access to the airport is convenient from the Baltimore and Washington Parkway (BW Parkway) and I-95 using I-195, a feeder road built to connect those major north-south highways and the airport.

The Light Rail system offers transportation to and from the airport, Concourse E, for a fee of $1.60 one way. The Light Rail will take you to Downtown Baltimore or as far north as Hunt Valley. Tickets are available at the Light Rail ticket box. Call (410) 539-5000 or check the Web site (www.mtamaryland.com/services/lightrail) for more details.

You can take MARC or Amtrak to the BWI Airport railroad station and then take the free shuttle that runs about every 10 minutes to the departures level of the airport.

No downtown Baltimore hotel offers complimentary shuttle service to/from the airport. Check with Super Shuttle (www.supershuttle .com or 410-859-0803), the Airport Shuttle (www .theairportshuttle.com or 410-381-2772), or other taxi or shuttle service.

i When driving within a 5-mile radius of BWI Marshall, tune into 1040 AM on your radio for current conditions. Or look for variable message boards.

Once at the Airport

BWI Marshall is a two-story terminal, with check-ins (departures) on the second (upper) level and luggage carousels and pickups (arrivals) on the lower level. The loading and unloading locations directly in front of each airline's check-in area are convenient spots for departing passengers. Don't even think of parking or having others park in the loop near the terminals. This is a security issue, a fuel-saving issue, and it eliminates (to some extent) the traffic issue of having to drive around cars stopped and double or triple parked while waiting for someone. The airport has stopped its paging services as a consequence of state budget deficiencies and the reality that almost everyone has a cell phone.

Duty-free shops (Concourse E), gift counters, fast and quick food eateries, bars, magazine stands, and candy stores are open during the day and early evening in the central terminal area, between gates B and C, and between gates C and D. Arcade machines, fax phones, and a courtesy phone to contact taxicabs and hotel shuttles are in these corridors or in the luggage pickup or lower level. Large bathroom facilities with baby changing stations are available.

i If you have children, the Observation Gallery between Concourses B and C, has a playground with miniature plane, luggage cart, and fuel truck. The upper deck has control panels and a 147-foot-long window overlooking the runways and concourses. The rocking chairs offer a special charm, regardless of your age.

Rental Cars at BWI Marshall

The airport has a separate off-site rental car facility at Stoney Run and New Ridge Roads, about a 10-minute ride from the airport. Free shuttle services take customers to and from the airport. Arriving passengers should take the shuttle from the lower-level terminal. Those returning rental cars should follow the signs on the way to the airport. Some of the rental car providers include Avis, (410) 859-1680; Alamo, (410) 859-

8092; Budget, (410) 859-0850; Dollar, (800) 800-4000; Enterprise, (800) 325-8007; Hertz, (410) 850-7400; National, (410) 859-1136; and Thrifty, (410) 850-7139. Avis, Enterprise, Hertz, and Thrifty have hand-controlled cars available. Rates range from $30 to $80 a day, depending on the size and make of the car, the options you choose, and how long you are planning to rent.

Airport Security

Security has tightened at all U.S. airports, and BWI Marshall is no exception. The U.S. Transportation Security Administration passenger screening at security checkpoints are prior to the departure gates. This can translate into long lines and delays, so plan to arrive at least two hours before your scheduled departure. You are required to have your ticket and a government-issued photo identification before going through the security screening areas.

GETTING TO BALTIMORE

By Roadway

Interstates and Highways

I-695, known locally as the Beltway (if there's any chance your driving directions head toward Washington, D.C., you should specify whether you're talking about the Baltimore Beltway or the Washington Beltway), forms a circle outside the city limits. No matter where you get on, you will end up in the same place in about an hour's driving time. (We don't recommend this, unless you are really, really bored or curious.) Unless, of course, you're driving during "rush" hour when a 5-mile trip can take an hour all by itself. Traffic alternates between zippy traffic and a parking lot—somewhat similar to an accordion. If you'll be commuting along this route on a daily basis, you may want to map out some alternative surface road routes for bad traffic days. As with some other circumferential constructions, the Baltimore Beltway became a heavily used commuter roadway instead of the city bypass that was intended. Whether you travel through one of the Baltimore Harbor tunnels or use the Francis

Scott Key Bridge, you will pay a $2 toll for a four-wheel passenger vehicle. EZ Pass is accepted. To avoid the toll, you must travel the western arc of the Beltway.

I-83, the Jones Falls Expressway (aka JFX), heads south into the city from Pennsylvania, with a slight zig and then a zag. From the Pennsylvania line to I-695 (the Baltimore Beltway), about 30 miles, is a straight shot, but at the Beltway southbound traffic has to get onto the Beltway for one exit before veering right, then left (south) onto I-83 again. Once back on I-83, southbound traffic will find itself dropped right near Little Italy leaving a convenient trip of about 4 blocks west to reach the Inner Harbor.

> **i** The JFX is a commuter road, so expect heavy traffic during rush hours.

I-95 runs north to Maine and south to Florida, passing on the southwest and east side of Baltimore. During rush hour, traffic backs up at the entrances to the Baltimore Beltway, near White Marsh in the northeast and in the southwest corner. The highway goes through the Fort McHenry Tunnel, one of two tunnels beneath the Patapsco River toward the Inner Harbor area.

MD 295, the Baltimore–Washington Parkway, connects Baltimore and Washington, D.C., in a planned parkway setting, with acres of trees, and some deer, lining the Parkway. No trucks are allowed. Heading north, the highway passes the Capital (Washington) Beltway (I-495 around Washington), I-195 (which takes you to BWI Marshall Airport), and I-695 (the Baltimore Beltway) before suddenly stopping as traffic is dumped onto Russell Street near Oriole Park at Camden Yards and M&T Bank Stadium. Turn right at Pratt and within a few blocks you're driving past the Convention Center and then you're at the Inner Harbor.

Heading south into Washington, the highway merges into New York Avenue (Route 50), that takes you into the city. Or, you can take Route 295 (Kenilworth Avenue) off the B-W Parkway that takes you toward the D.C. Beltway, the Woodrow Wilson Bridge, and Richmond, Virginia, and other points south.

I-395 becomes Martin Luther King Jr. Boulevard after carrying motorists from I-95 into Downtown Baltimore and during morning rush hour the road into the city is bottlenecked; in the afternoon, the lanes carrying motorists out of the city are filled. Also, if heading out of the city on this road, keep right to head north, following signs for northbound I-95 and New York. Heading south toward Washington requires motorists to stay to the left to feed into southbound I-95.

I-795 heads from Reisterstown in northwest Baltimore County to the Baltimore Beltway (I-695). It serves as a major feeder route to and from bedroom communities in Owings Mills and Reisterstown and connects, via Highway 140, to Westminster, a community about 40 miles northwest of Baltimore.

I-895, the Harbor Tunnel Thruway, is a bypass for I-95's Fort McHenry Tunnel offering motorists a second way under the Patapsco River near the Inner Harbor. The older of the two sets of tunnels beneath the river costs $2 to go through and connects to the Baltimore Beltway. It also provides access to I-97, which leads to Annapolis, the state capital, about 25 miles southeast of the city.

US 40 is a major east-west highway running through Baltimore. As the highway runs through the city, at times it takes on the names Pulaski Highway on the east side and Orleans Street downtown. It's the Baltimore National Pike in Catonsville and Ellicott City. However, the US 40 signs are clearly marked. It's a good alternate route to I-95 and I-895 that doesn't require a toll—you don't have to cross the Patapsco River. Instead, you'll catch lots and lots of traffic lights. Still, it's a good route for seeing different parts of the city.

I-70 comes into the Baltimore Beltway as the major route for traffic coming in from Pittsburgh or other points west. It does not reach the city limits.

By Bus

BALTIMORE TRAVEL PLAZA
6523 O'Donnell St.
(410) 633-6389
www.greyhound.com

EZ Pass

If you are likely to use the Chesapeake Bay Bridge, one of the harbor tunnels, or head north on I-95 on a regular basis, you should consider getting an EZ Pass. A $1.50 monthly service fee has been initiated, so this is one of those math things that include time vs. cost. The pass may not save money, but it could save time.

You can pick up the EZ Pass transponder at any Motor Vehicle Administration office and keep your account full by check or via electronic fund transfer.

Once you see all the traffic you're not sitting in, you'll be glad you got the pass. For details, visit www.ezpassmd.com.

Lots of free parking and bright, clean, inviting facilities are the lure of the Baltimore Travel Plaza, conveniently located off I-895 and I-95 in Northeast Baltimore. If you are planning to take a Trailways or Peter Pan bus heading to New York City, Atlantic City, or a variety of other locations up and down the East Coast and beyond, then this is the place to catch it in the Baltimore area.

Like the Greyhound terminal on Haines Street near Baltimore's Inner Harbor, the Baltimore Travel Plaza also offers access to Greyhound buses, traveling to New York City more than 10 times a day and to points farther north, south, and west. In addition, a number of tour buses heading to points all over the mid–Atlantic, especially Atlantic City, Pennsylvania Dutch Country, and western Maryland, also offer pickups and drop-offs at the Travel Plaza.

The plaza offers clean and open counters for purchasing tickets, plenty of wood tables and chairs for waiting for the bus, and a variety of time-killing ideas.

It's about a 15-minute taxicab ride from the Travel Plaza to the Inner Harbor area. The plaza is also accessible by city bus.

"CHINATOWN" BUSES
5625 O'Donnell St.
Baltimore Travel Plaza

APEX BUS
(202) 449-9758 (9 a.m. to 7 p.m.)
www.apexbus.com

NYDC EXPRESS
(212) 244-6132
www.nydcexpress.com
Several companies run frequent and inexpensive bus service between Boston, New York, Philadelphia, Baltimore, Washington, D.C., and other stops. As they used to originate and travel to New York's Chinatown, they are known generically as "Chinatown" buses. Fares may start at $1 each way if you reserve far enough in advance. Otherwise, they may be $20 up to $30 or maybe more. Generally, the buses are clean, have a clean restroom on board, have electrical outlets so your device batteries don't run dry, Wi-Fi Internet connection, and sometimes a TV/DVD for your entertainment. Sometimes they take a vote among the passengers about whether or not they want a movie shown during the 3.5-hour trip. They may or may not make a stop at one of the service plazas along the New Jersey Turnpike. Apex and NYDC Express are two lines that are running from the Travel Plaza to New York and other cities as of this writing. If they don't fit your schedule or you're interested in another company, do a Google or Bing search for Chinatown buses.

GREYHOUND LINES
2110 Haines St.
(410) 752-1393

Best Western Hotel
5625 O'Donnell St.

Baltimore Travel Plaza
(410) 633-6389
www.greyhound.com

The downtown (Haines Street) station has baggage and package express services and the station is open 24 hours a day. The Travel Plaza stop does not handle luggage although they do offer package express and 24-hour service.

By Train

AMTRAK
Penn Station, 1525 North Charles St.
(410) 291-4261, (800) USA-RAIL
www.amtrak.com
Penn Station is a marvel, with beautiful lightwood benches with high backs waiting for weary travelers to sit on for a minute or a day. A major terminal between New York and Washington, Penn Station is served by the Acela Express trains that travel the Northeast corner, and Acela Regional trains that have a few more stops along the way. Located conveniently on Charles Street and just off I-83 (the Jones Falls Expressway), a parking garage is available for dropping off and picking up passengers. During normal business hours, you can find a store selling juices, candy, and magazines, and it has a small sandwich counter.

Amtrak also has a station at the BWI Marshall airport, about 11 miles south of Baltimore. It offers free bus transfers to the airport terminal. It's a small station that is open from about 5 a.m. to 10 p.m., with a ticketing office, a snack stand open during the usual business hours, restrooms, and a small waiting area. There's plenty of parking, too. The MARC trains stop here, too.

i MARC and weekday AMTRAK trains usually have a quiet car where you are not allowed to use cell phones or even hold a normal-voice conversation. It's wonderful.

By Ship

PORT OF BALTIMORE
2001 East McComas St.
(800) 638-7519, (866) 427-8963
www.cruisemaryland.com
www.marylandports.com

Because Baltimore serves two-thirds of the country's population and because the Port facilities have been updated and expanded, Baltimore is becoming a busy cruise departure city. In cruise-speak, this is home porting where ships now depart from many smaller markets instead of just Florida or Los Angeles. Carnival Cruise Lines started year-round departures in 2009 and Celebrity Cruises has 10 sailings from Baltimore in 2010. Leaving from Baltimore saves the two to four hours or more of driving time to get to Philadelphia and New York and cuts almost a day off your at-sea time leaving New York or Philly, which can be particularly nasty during the winter. You don't have to worry about missing your flight or having your suitcases go someplace else. Another way of putting it, your five-day getaway could cost you seven days if you depart from a port farther away. The parking charge is $15 per day and you don't need advance reservations to park in the secure lot. When you return, you're home in an hour or two. How convenient.

If you don't have a car (you've flown into BWI Marshall), taxis are available and you may find a Cruise Maryland package at a number of hotels. Eighty-one departures are scheduled for 2010, going to the Caribbean, Chesapeake Bay, and fall foliage in New England and Canada.

Check the port's Web site for current information at www.marylandports.com or call (866) 427-8963.

The following cruise lines are scheduled to sail from the Port of Baltimore in 2010:

Aida, www.Aida.de, (1.49.381.4440)
American Cruise Lines, www.AmericanCruise lines.com, (800) 814-6880
Carnival Cruise Lines, www.Carnival.com, (888) Carnival, (888) 227-6482
Celebrity Cruises, www.celebritycruises.com, (800) 647-2251
Costa Cruises, www.costacruise.com, (877) 88-COSTA
Hapag-Lloyd Cruises, www.hl-cruises.com, 1-49 (40) 3001-4600
Royal Caribbean International, www.Royal Caribbean.com, (866) 562-7625

The World, www.residensea.com, 1-954-538-8400
Watermark Cruises, www.watermarkcruises .com, (410) 268-7601

i When the 960-foot-long Carnival *Pride* cruise ship made her maiden voyage out of Baltimore in September 2009, she was presented by a look-a-like cake created by Ben and Katie Rose of Duff Goodman's Ace of Cakes shop. The cake, at two feet in length, took three days to make and came complete with a Baltimore skyline in the background. The cake was presented to *Pride* Captain Allessandro Galotto and shown on a Food Network program. The *Pride* sails every week on seven-day cruises to the Caribbean, Bahamas, and Florida and is expected to carry 115,000 passengers annually.

GETTING AROUND

On Foot

When you're Downtown and feeling confused, look for **Downtown Baltimore Guides** (formerly Public Safety Guides) who can help you whether you're a local employee, resident, or visitor. Guides carry hospitality kits with discount coupons and promotional items to area attractions and periodically conduct a random act of street intercept to give you a free item from the kit. It could be a coupon for a cool drink on a hot day, a discount museum admission, or even a present.

Michael Evitts (410) 244-1030 is the Downtown Baltimore coordinator for this program. The Guides provide Hospitality Escorts for anyone who would like extra peace of mind while walking to his or her car or bus or waiting for a taxi after dark. Safety escorts are available within the Downtown district from 10 a.m. to 10:30 p.m. seven days a week. Call (410) 244-8778 during business hours or (410) 802-9631 after hours.

Most of Downtown Baltimore is an easily walkable city as promoted by the convention and visitors people by saying that everything in Baltimore is only two feet away.

Selected Baltimore Firsts

Edward Warren, reported to have been only 13 years old at the time, made the first American hot-air balloon ascension in 1784.

The first horse-drawn streetcar line opened in Fell's Point in 1859.

The Baltimore Union Passenger Railway Company, the first commercial electric streetcar line in the Western Hemisphere, began service in Baltimore in 1885.

Baltimore ushered in the modern era when the first drive-in gas station opened for business in 1917. Baltimore got a treat in 1920 when Hubert Latham made the first nonstop airplane flight over a city. He circled Baltimore's skyline 22 times.

The first coal-burning, steam locomotive, the Tom Thumb—a stagecoach on wheels—was built here in 1830 by B&O, and the first electric locomotive was built in 1894. The elevated electric railway to run it on was erected in 1893.

The first commercial carrier and the first passenger train left from Baltimore in 1827 and 1830, respectively.

The first train to operate at 30 miles per hour got on the B&O tracks in 1830.

The first train to have a center aisle boarded passengers in 1831, and the first air-conditioned train in the world, B&O's Columbian, left Baltimore in 1931.

We also lay claim to the first city railroad station, the President Street Station, which opened in 1853.

—Excerpted from *Baltimore— America's City of Firsts,* a pamphlet published by Baltimore Bicentennial Celebration, Inc.

By Public Transportation

The Maryland Transit Administration runs the city's Light Rail, bus system, the Metro Subway, MARC trains, and mobility transportation for people who need assistance. You can find almost everything you need to know at their Web site, www.MTAMaryland.com; although it's a little weak still, you can try to find the best method and route to get from point A to point B.

Scheduled to start in fall 2009, then delayed until at least January 2010, is the downtown Charm City Circulator, and that date was wishful thinking as of this writing. The free shuttle system of 21 hybrid-electric EcoSave IV clean-energy buses should loop every 10 minutes, will connect people and destinations along three routes that will connect Penn Station, Harbor East, the Science + Technology Park at Johns Hopkins, and the Baltimore BioPark. Look to their Web site, http://yournameyourride.com for information.

i If you are planning to use public transportation frequently on any given day or month, you can buy an all-day pass allowing unlimited travel on the buses, Light Rail, and Metro subway for $3.50 or a Transit Link Card (TLC) by adding $50 to your MARCH monthly pass and get a month of unlimited travel on the MARC, Baltimore Metro, buses, and Light Rail.

By Bus

The MTA operates local and express bus lines throughout the Baltimore area, covering most of the city and much of Baltimore County.

You pay when you board the bus, and exact change is mandatory. You're going to be putting your money into a machine that gobbles up extra change without a thought for returning the extra coins. Plan ahead. Really. Fares are $1.60 for a one-way pass or $3.50 for an all-day pass. A weekly pass costs $16.50.

Keep your eye out for your stop and press the yellow strip running above the windows of the bus to notify the operator of your stop. Drivers don't call out stops unless you request it, so either ask someone to remind you when your stop is coming or stay alert. Smoking, eating, drinking, and playing radios without earphones are all prohibited on MTA buses.

Bus routes are marked with small signs (white with blue trim) on the right side of roadways. Route numbers are on the signs. Schedules are available at most hotels, tourist attractions, and visitor centers. The MTA will also mail one to you. Schedules are also on the MTA Web site, www .mtamaryland.com/services.

By Rail

It's only fitting that the city that was home to the first railroad places a major emphasis on rail travel. In the last decade, Baltimore's old rails have been put to significant use by the area's growing Light Rail and MARC (Maryland Rail Commuter) systems. Baltimore also is a stopping point for Amtrak trains.

MARC
(800) 325-RAIL
www.mtamaryland.com/services/marc
Maryland Rail Commuter trains operate on three lines running throughout the Baltimore–Washington corridor, eight Maryland counties, and northeastern West Virginia. In all, MARC serves some 31,000 commuters Monday through Friday.

For Baltimore, the Camden Line runs between Baltimore and Washington's Union Station (a major hub for transportation in all directions). The Camden Line terminal is at the Camden Yards Transportation Station at Oriole Park.

MARC's Penn Line starts about 50 miles north of the Inner Harbor in Perryville, off I-95 near the Susquehanna River in Cecil County, and continues south to Penn Station and on to Washington.

The Brunswick Line services between Martinsburg, West Virginia, and Frederick County, Maryland, to Washington, D.C.

LIGHT RAIL LINE
(410) 539-5000, (866) RIDE-MTA, ext. 2
www.mtamaryland.com/services/lightrail
Baltimore's Light Rail Line operates from Hunt Valley, about 25 miles north of the Inner Harbor,

through the Downtown area near Oriole Park at Camden Yards and on to Cromwell Station/Glen Burnie, about 10 miles south of the Inner Harbor in Anne Arundel County. Light Rail also goes to BWI Marshall Airport with most trains heading south toward Cromwell. You can take a Cromwell train as long as you remember to transfer to an airport train at any station along the way but definitely by the time you reach the Linthicum station. This is not necessarily a speedy way to get there, but it does avoid traffic jams. A stop at Penn Station, where passengers can pick up Amtrak service, is also operated as a spur. Light Rail runs about every 17 minutes during normal hours and every 8 minutes during rush hour.

Hours of operation are from 6 a.m. to 11 p.m. Monday through Saturday, and 11 a.m. to 7 p.m. Saturday. The line also operates special service for baseball and football games. Tickets cost $1.60 for one-way trips with an all-day option (good if you'll be using Light Rail more than once a day) and passage on regular bus and Metro Subway, and senior fares are $1.10.

Buy your ticket from the machines at the stations. You MUST have your ticket with you. They aren't always checked, but often enough that you don't want to be caught trying to ride for free.

> **i** The front/first doors on the Light Rail car, behind the driver, do not open from the outside. They are used by people in wheelchairs, using crutches, or who for some reason need a level access from the platform into the train.

METRO SUBWAY
(410) 539-5000, (866) RIDE-MTA, ext. 2
www.mtamaryland.com/services/subway
Baltimore's Metro provides service between Johns Hopkins Medical Campus to the east and Owings Mills in southwestern Baltimore County. The 15.5-mile subway system has 14 stations scattered east to west across the city. It takes about 25 minutes to reach the Downtown area from Owings Mills. Parking at most stops is free, and the parking at Owings Mills is close to a large mall, Owings Mills Town Center. If you want to

head to the city for a day of sightseeing, the subway from Owings Mills is a fun, clean, and affordable way to go. It's also a great way to get to Johns Hopkins Hospital, which can be a tough place to find parking.

Ride passes are available (exact change only) at machines at each stop, and the cost is $1.60 for a one-way fare, or $3.50 for an all-day pass. Subway cars run about every 8 minutes during rush hour, every 10 minutes during the day, and every 15 minutes in the evening and on Saturday. The subway operates from 5 a.m. to 12:30 a.m. Monday through Friday and from 6 a.m. to midnight on Saturday and Sunday. Lexington Market East and Charles Center East entrances close at 8 p.m. Bicyclists are welcome to bring bikes except when trains are crowded.

By Car

As mentioned, Baltimore's downtown street system, for the most part, is a grid on a north/south and east/west layout. Many streets are alternately one-way. Of course, it's going to seem that whatever street you want is going to have traffic going the other way even if you know that it's not true.

A GPS is a really good friend, particularly if you pay for the service that is up-to-date on construction and accidents. Short of that, a *Baltimore Metro Area Thomas Guide* is a good friend. To give you an idea of how rapidly the area is changing, the 8th edition updated and added 1,900 new streets. The book covers Aberdeen, Annapolis, Bel Air, Bowie, Ellicott City, Havre De Grace, Laurel, Manchester, Mount Airy, Sykesville, Taneytown, Westminster, and neighboring communities.

As in most big cities, rush hours and lunch hours can make traffic devilish, to say the least. When you want to be somewhere, the best route often varies with the time of day and the weather conditions.

Major north-south roadways include Belair Road, Harford Road, and Charles Street, and east-west roadways include Northern Parkway, North Avenue, and Frederick Road. Watch out for Hillen Road, which seems to pop up everywhere you

look. It, along with many of the city's less traveled roads, comes and goes, as if someone erased a few blocks then drew it back in. It's confusing, but it gives you a feeling of pride when you overcome it.

Ice, sleet, and snow, any and all of which can occur on winter nights, can be a problem on Baltimore roadways. Even though schools and businesses close at the first sign of snow, those of us who have to or want to drive in inclement weather can often make a mess of things. This isn't the territory where chains are needed, but you do need common sense.

By Taxi

Baltimore boasts an array of options for people without wheels. For $1.80, plus $2 a mile, you can get just about anywhere with local cabbies who speak the language, know their way around, and are willing to share some personality and sightseeing suggestions with you. Many cab companies charge an extra dollar for radio-dispatched calls. If you find yourself needing to get somewhere in the Downtown area, it's probably more cost-effective and more efficient simply to hail a cab. Most major hotels, shopping areas, and the train station have cabbies waiting nearby.

The following companies provide cab service:

Baltimore City

Arrow Cab	(410) 327-0330
Baltimore Taxi Company	(410) 327-7777
Diamond Cab	(410) 947-3333
Raven Cab	(410) 945-2212
Taxi Dispatch	(410) 727-6237

Baltimore County

Arrow Cab	(410) 338-0000,
	(410) 284-3330
Atwater Cab	
(based in White Marsh)	(410) 682-2100
Jimmy's Cab (based in Towson)	(410) 296-7200
Valley Cab (based in Pikesville)	(410) 486-4000

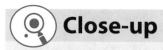

Close-up

Baltimore's Horsepower

Mounted police (www.baltimorepolice.org) are a magnificent sight. The larger-than-average-horses with helmeted officers astride thunder through the city, through lines of unmoving cars, down narrow alleys or sidewalks, their on-the-hoof raw power is awe inspiring. As the police department says, "It's a proven fact that one police officer on a horse is just as effective as 10 police officers on foot."

Their value in a pursuit is in the terror they can engender when riding full-tilt and in their versatility. Rubber horseshoes allow for a comfortable run on city streets, and horses can leave the streets if necessary to gallop across and through places where motorized vehicles can't go.

Baltimore's mounted police unit was formed in 1888, making it the oldest in the United States. The horses are housed at 411 North Holliday St., under the Jones Falls Expressway. Call the barn at (410) 396-2343 to arrange a tour. There is no charge although a group, rather than a single person, is preferred, and a weekday is much better than a weekend.

The officers of the Mounted Police Unit volunteer for this duty and come from all areas of the city's police department. They must have at least three years of patrol experience before they can be considered. Once trained for the unit, each officer becomes responsible for his or her assigned mount, which is considered a fellow officer, right down to being assigned a badge number. The horses work an eight-hour day and get a 30-minute lunch break and a 15-minute break every hour.

In 1888 there were 10 officers in the unit. Since then, the mounted police unit has grown and diminished over the years, depending on the city's needs and its budget. In the 1990s the unit consisted of 23 men and horses.

In 2008-09, city budget cuts threatened the $150,000 annual cost for the six four-footed critters that includes feed, medical care, etc. A public fund-raising effort was established in late summer with about half the year's budget received within a few months. The Baltimore Police Foundation Fund runs the program and you can contribute at www.bcf.org/police.

Baltimore–Washington International Thurgood Marshall Airport/Anne Arundel County

Airline Limousines and Sedan Services	(410) 768-4444
The Airport Shuttle	(410) 381-2772
www.theairportshuttle.com	
Associated Cabs (Glen Burnie)	(410) 766-1234
BWI Marshall Airport Taxi	(410) 859-1103

Hotel Shuttles

Many downtown hotels provide a free shuttle service to the Inner Harbor, local hospitals, businesses, and downtown train and bus stations, usually within a five-mile radius. Downtown Baltimore hotels do not provide shuttle service to the airport.

By Water

Seeing Baltimore's harbor area from the water provides insights into its industries and history.

Depending on the weather, the season, and advanced reservations, you can have a great visit and learn a lot about the Harbor by boat. Yes, the Harbor has been known to freeze. The Chesapeake Bay also has frozen over. The last time was in the winter of 1976 and 1977, known as the "Big Freeze," when nighttime temperatures would go below zero and daytime temperatures barely reached the 20s. Whether it's global warming or more efficient use of ice breakers, the Bay hasn't frozen over since then.

CANTON KAYAK CLUB
9817 Finsbury Rd., Rosedale
www.cantonkayakclub.com
About 400 people belong to the Canton Kayak Club that has 40 kayaks and access to four docks throughout the city, including Dundalk, Locust Point, and Harbor East. New member club dues for May through October are $150. You receive training and have unlimited use of the kayaks for the entire season. No reservations are necessary, making this exercise probably the most stress-free one in town.

ED KANE'S WATER TAXI
(410) 563-3901
www.thewatertaxi.com
Pick a water service and the Water Taxi probably provides it. They run between 3 and 14 blue and white boats ranging in size from 26 to 84 passengers. You can do an inside route (Aquarium, Harbor Place, Science Center, Rusty Scupper, and Harbor East). You can do an Express Route (back and forth between Harbor East and Fell's Point and at the Maritime Park during museum hours). Or, whatever floats your boat, so to speak. An all day unlimited ticket is $9 for adults (cash, check onboard, or charge at the Visitor Center) and $4 for children 10 and under. You can buy tickets online. You can buy a Frequent Floater Annual Pass that is $80 for 12 months or $75 each for two or more.

In addition, the water taxi offers a "Letter of Marque," which combines the all-day ticket with discounts at dozens of restaurants, pubs, shops, and attractions near the water taxi stops.

i Cammie Kane, widow of the late Ed Kane who started the Water Taxi service in the late 1970s or early 1980s, has expanded the service probably more than even Ed thought possible, and that's a tough order. She figures they've served more than 16 million passengers over the years.

WATER TAXI HARBOR CONNECTOR
www.thewatertaxi.com
The city started a free water shuttle in May 2009 that provides transportation every 15 minutes from Frederick Douglass-Isaac Myers Maritime Museum in Fell's Point to the Tide Point business park in Locust Point. A second route, running every 25 minutes, from Canton to Tide Point started on November 1, 2009. Both services run from 7 a.m. to 7 p.m. weekdays unless there is nasty weather. Check the Web site or the radio/TV newscasts for updates. The first boats held 24 passengers and the boats on order will hold 45 passengers. They are climate controlled.

i A particular third-grade class trip took the Baltimore Harbor cruise and after seeing ships being unloaded and loaded and all manner of port-related activities, they decided the most interesting part of the trip was the exhaust vents from the tunnel.

SPIRIT CRUISES
(410) 727-3113, (866) 312-2469
www.spiritcruisesbaltimore.com
The *Spirit* offers a 75-minute cruise that chugs past Ft. McHenry while you hear about the USS *Constellation*, Fell's Point, the National Aquarium, *John W. Brown* Liberty Ship and much more. The cruises depart several times daily from April through October with boarding time set at 15 minutes before departure. Other cruises may be available, so check the ticket booth for a current schedule.

Lunch, brunch, and other cruises are also available, some with themes that might be a pre-Halloween moonlight cruise or a gospel lunch cruise.

Cruises start at about $20.

HISTORY

Although Baltimore is removed from the Atlantic Ocean by about 150 miles, the Patapsco River that dumps into the Baltimore Harbor before going on to the Chesapeake Bay is a tidal river. Thus, this city has been an important seaport since before its formal founding in 1729. One reason it's so popular and busy is that it is closer, by about 200 miles, to commercial markets in the middle of the country than any other seaport on the East Coast. The plentiful natural elements and navigable waterways provided an excellent place for manufacturing and for transporting goods between the United States and foreign countries. While New York was the largest port of entry for immigrants, Baltimore was the second largest. The city served as the capital of the country when Congress met here for a few months in 1776 and 1777.

Perhaps the best known historical event was the Battle of Baltimore during the War of 1812 when the British attacked Baltimore on September 13, 1814, at Fort McHenry. The British were defeated, Francis Scott Key wrote the lyrics to what became our National Anthem. The British went elsewhere. Railroading, so instrumental in the country's growth, was started with the Baltimore and Ohio Railroad which added to the city's shipping and transportation. It's important to note that Baltimore and Maryland did not secede from the Union during the American Civil War. Although plenty of people sympathized with the South, the Union government realized they could not let Washington be surrounded, north and south, by Virginia and Maryland by southern governance. The next major newsworthy event was the Great Baltimore Fire of 1904. It destroyed 1500 buildings in short time and buildings today still can be identified as "surviving the fire" and "built after the fire." Baltimore became the center of interest again with the development of the Inner Harbor, a geopolitical and financial conglomerate that has been the inspiration for 100 other cities and communities.

DISCOVERING "FROTH"

Captain John Smith probably had only a small sense of the bounty he discovered in 1608 while exploring the Chesapeake Bay. He described in his journal the area he had found: "Thirtie leagues Northward is a river not inhabited, yet navigable." The river, one of four major waterways that flow into the Chesapeake Bay, was given its Indian name, Patapsco, which many believe meant "backwater" or "tidewater covered with froth."

What Smith found was vast, relatively flat, open land that the Susquehannock tribe had used for hunting. The Susquehannocks would venture down from northern Maryland on what would become Charles Street in Baltimore. As impossible as it seems now, bears were abundant

then. Over time, the bear proved to be less of an opponent to the Susquehannocks than smallpox and tuberculosis, new diseases brought to America by early colonists at the end of the 17th century. By 1700 only a few hundred Indians lived in any part of Maryland.

DAVID (NOT DAVY) JONES SETTLES

In 1632 George Calvert, an advisor to King James I, was granted a charter to what is now the state of Maryland. Though he did not live to see his colony founded, his son Cecilius sent his son Leonard on the *Ark* and the *Dove* in November 1633 to establish Maryland. They arrived in their new capital, St. Mary's City, on March 25, 1634, to found a colony notable for its progressive policy of liberty of conscience and its decision not to have an established religion. The state, though founded by Catholics, became home to Protestants and Quakers as well. This tolerant stance—although it took a beating throughout the state's early years—became law when the Toleration Act was passed in 1649. By then colonists had sailed north on the Chesapeake Bay to settle what would soon become Maryland's state capital, Annapolis.

In 1659, the first settlers of the Baltimore region established Baltimore County. The county provided settlers with what they and their ancestors had come from England for—economic opportunity in a place where they could freely practice their chosen religion. Settlers soon began taking sites along the water. In the mid-1600s, they settled near where Fort McHenry now stands and along Harford Road in the northeastern section of Baltimore, near Harford Run.

In 1661 one of Baltimore's first settlers, David Jones, moved onto 380 acres along a stream that would later be named Jones Falls in his honor. Today the Jones Falls Expressway, a six-lane highway running parallel to (and sometimes over) that stream, also refers to Jones, when it is not being called by its nickname, "the JFX."

WATER AND WHEELS

Activity on and around the waterfront began to grow. One of the first settlements, Whetstone Point, where Fort McHenry now stands, was named a port of entry by act of legislature in 1706. Five years later, the first mill for the area was built along the Jones Falls by Jonathan Hanson.

Transportation was primarily by water, though some roads had been cut in the woods. In 1704 a new law required trees to be cut down so the main road could be widened to 20 feet and, probably more important, marked. Slash marks charted the course. There was one vertical slash on trees beside the road leading to the church; there were three horizontal lines (one higher than two others close together) on roads heading to the county courthouse.

i Fort McHenry, the five bastioned, pentagonal shaped fort, takes its name from Dr. James McHenry (1753–1816), who served as a medical officer with Gen. George Washington during the Revolutionary War. He later served on the Continental Congress and as secretary of war for presidents Washington and Adams between 1796 and 1801.

Soon settlers began making iron for England and growing wheat for the British colonies in the West Indies. The Jones Falls and two other rivers, Herring Run and Gwynns Falls, provided the water power for the iron furnaces and the mills that turned wheat into flour.

LOTS FOR SALE

With an economy in place, workers needed housing. In 1729, 60 acres of land in what is now Downtown Baltimore were approved for division into one-acre lots. Buyers would have to pay the owners, Daniel and Charles Carroll, either 40 shillings an acre or tobacco at the rate of one penny per pound. Philip Jones, a county surveyor, laid out the land. Three roadways, Calvert, Forest (now Charles), and Long (later Market and now Baltimore) Streets, were created. Nine narrow alleys ran between the three streets, and the lots were numbered and divided.

Land buyers agreed to either build a house of at least 400 square feet within 18 months or forfeit the land. The first 18 buyers, all of whom made purchases on the first day the land was available, bought land close to the Patapsco; Charles Carroll selected a lot at the corner of Calvert Street and the harbor basin on January 14, 1730. The surveyor Philip Jones, who selected second, picked land at the foot of Charles Street near the waterfront.

The growing port on the Patapsco became the outlet for sending wheat from fields in western Maryland and Pennsylvania to England and the Caribbean islands. But economic success bred frustration. Merchants chafed at British taxes and commercial policies. As intolerance for British interference continued to grow, Baltimore found its place in the political world of the colonies.

After representatives of the 13 colonies signed the Declaration of Independence in Philadelphia on July 4, 1776, Baltimore soon became a temporary national capital. Leaders feared a possible attack by British troops, so they fled from Philadelphia to Baltimore, where they convened in a newly built tavern named Congress Hall. For 68 days, from December 20, 1776, through February 27, 1777, the delegates handled big and small matters of state in Congress Hall. Delegates granted George Washington powers to pursue war, and they ordered that pigs and geese stay off Baltimore's unpaved streets.

HOME FOR PESKY PRIVATEERS

Baltimore's economy boomed during the Revolutionary War. Shipyards in Fell's Point, named after the wharf's creator, William Fell, produced warships. Privateers from Baltimore, eager to make a buck by sinking British ships or seizing their assets, filled the waters of the Patapsco River and Chesapeake Bay. Between 1776 and the end of the Revolution, about 250 private ship owners armed themselves and were granted government commissions (called "letters of marque and reprisal") that empowered them to seize enemy vessels—and their assets—on planned attacks or in pursuit of trade. Everyone tied to these seizing ships—the sailors, owners, and financial backers—took their share of the booty from these missions.

During and after the war, Baltimore continued to be a commercial hotspot, benefiting greatly from the on-again, off-again trade wars between England and France. Local leaders decided to pursue status as a city. The commissioner who had been appointed to rule Baltimore County was picked in Annapolis, and merchants and businessmen wanted greater control of their own destinies.

On December 31, 1796, the city of Baltimore was born. As the 19th century began, Baltimore's population swelled. Doubling by 1810 to 27,000 people, Baltimore passed Boston to become America's third-largest city, trailing only Philadelphia and New York.

"A NEST OF PIRATES"

In 1812 Baltimore again would find itself in the middle of a war with England, and again it would prove to be a financial boon. President James Madison's declaration of war on Great Britain was a problem for the U.S. fleet, which numbered 17 ships. Privateers, whose success in the Revolutionary War had provided good training and income more than 30 years earlier, helped increase the U.S. fleet's numbers. Still, at about 1,000 ships, the British fleet significantly outnumbered America's. During the war, the 126 privateers led the water attack, either seizing or sinking more than 550 British ships. Frustrated by this successful tactic, the British war leaders called Baltimore "a nest of pirates" and "the great depository of the hostile spirit of the United States against England."

As successful as the privateers were, British troops, led by Admiral Sir George Cockburn, ruled the Chesapeake Bay in the summer of 1814. By the dog days of August, British forces sailed up the Patuxent River on their way to Washington. On August 24, 1814, Baltimoreans could see the smoke on the horizon as the British burned Washington's Capitol, the White House, and other public buildings 40 miles away. In Baltimore residents took the smoke as a signal that they would be next. Under the leadership of Mayor General Samuel Smith, a veteran of the Revolution and a popular politician, the city quickly prepared for an attack.

With Smith's guidance, the newly created militia fortified Fort McHenry, a strategic location guarding the city and its harbor from invasion up the Patapsco River. The 16,000 men, 90 percent of whom were untrained citizens, were ready for battle, though they had practically no realistic chance of winning. On September 12, about 4,700 British troops took the shore on the west side of North Point, a section of the Patapsco River about 8 miles southeast of the fort, as they prepared to take over the city. The Battle of North Point lasted for more than two hours, as the

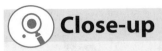

Close-up

Important Dates in Maryland History

10,000 B.C.—First humans arrived by this date in the land that would become Maryland.

1498—John Cabot sailed along Eastern Shore off present-day Worcester County.

1608—Capt. John Smith explored Chesapeake Bay.

1620—Earliest appearance in Maryland of European objects in archaeological context.

1632—June 20, Maryland Charter granted to Cecilius Calvert, Second Lord Baltimore, by Charles I, King of Great Britain and Ireland. The colony was named Maryland for Queen Henrietta Maria (1609-1669), wife of Charles I (1600-1649).

1633—Nov. 22, English settlers on *Ark and Dove* set sail from Cowes, England, for Maryland.

1634-1644—Leonard Calvert, governor.

1659-1660—Jan. 12, Baltimore County known to have been established by this date, when a writ was issued to county sheriff.

1663—Augustine Herrman, first naturalized citizen of Maryland.

1689-1690—Maryland Revolution of 1689. Protestant Associators overthrow proprietary officers.

1727—Sept., *Maryland Gazette,* first newspaper in the Chesapeake, published by William Parks at Annapolis (until 1734).

1729—Baltimore Town established by charter.

1744—June 30, Native American chiefs of the Six Nations relinquished by treaty all claims to land in colony. Assembly purchased last Indian land claims in Maryland.

1766—Sons of Liberty organized in Baltimore County.

1769—Maryland merchants adopted policy of nonimportation of British goods.

1772—March 28, Cornerstone laid for new State House in Annapolis.

1776—July 4, Declaration of Independence adopted in Philadelphia. Engrossed copy signed by Marylanders William Paca, Charles Carroll of Carrollton, Thomas Stone, and Samuel Chase.

1776—July 6, Maryland Convention declared independence from Great Britain.

1777—Feb. 5, First General Assembly elected under State Constitution of 1776 met at Annapolis.

1777—March 21, Inauguration of Thomas Johnson, first governor elected by General Assembly.

1781—March 1, Maryland ratified the Articles of Confederation.

1784—Dec. 30, St. John's College established at Annapolis. General Assembly designated it, with Washington College, as University of Maryland.

1787—Sept. 17, U.S. Constitution signed by Marylanders Daniel Carroll, James McHenry, and Daniel of St. Thomas Jenifer, at Philadelphia.

1788—April 28, Maryland Convention ratified U.S. Constitution, making Maryland the seventh state to do so. Convention adjourned without recommending amendments.

1789—Dec. 19, Maryland ratified federal Bill of Rights, first 10 amendments to U.S. Constitution.

1791—Dec. 19, Maryland ceded land for federal District of Columbia.

1799—Construction began on Fort McHenry, Baltimore.

1814—Sept. 12, British repelled by local militia at Battle of North Point.

1814—Sept. 13, Bombardment of Fort McHenry inspired Francis Scott Key to write "The Star-Spangled Banner."

1827—Feb. 28, Baltimore and Ohio Railroad chartered.

1829—Oblate Sisters of Providence opened school for black children, Baltimore.

1830—Baltimore & Ohio Railroad Station at Mount Clare, first in United States.

1832—In aftermath of Nat Turner rebellion in Virginia, Maryland laws enacted to restrict free blacks.

1837—May 17, *Baltimore Sun* began publication under Arunah S. Abell.

1838—Frederick Douglass escaped from slavery in Baltimore.

1845—Lloyd Street Synagogue constructed in Baltimore, first Maryland synagogue, a Robert Cary Long Jr. design.

1845—Frederick Douglass published narrative of his life in slavery.

1845—Oct. 10, U.S. Naval Academy founded at Annapolis, when Department of the Navy established officers' training school at Fort Severn, Annapolis.

1849—Harriet Tubman escaped slavery in Dorchester County.

1859—Oct. 16, John Brown launched raid from Maryland on federal arsenal in Harper's Ferry, West Virginia.

1861—April, James Ryder Randall wrote "Maryland, My Maryland."

1861—April 19, Sixth Massachusetts Union Regiment attacked by Baltimore mob.

1861—April 22, Federal troops occupied Annapolis.

1861—June 13, Congressional elections returned Unionist delegation.

1862—May 23, Marylanders opposed one another at Battle of Front Royal.

1862—Sept. 17, Battle of Antietam (or Sharpsburg), 4,800 dead, 18,000 wounded.

1863—late June through early July, Lee's army passed through Washington County en route to Gettysburg and in retreat.

1864—Nov. 1, Maryland slaves emancipated by State Constitution of 1864.

1865—Chesapeake Marine Railway and Dry Dock Company, first black-owned business in state, established by Isaac Myers.

1865—April, John Wilkes Booth assassinated President Lincoln, escaped through Prince George's and Charles Counties.

1870—Maryland Jockey Club sponsored racing at Pimlico track.

1872—General Assembly mandated separate but equal white and black schools.

1876—Oct. 3, The Johns Hopkins University opened in Baltimore.

1885—Baltimore-Union Passenger Railway Company, first commercial electric street railway in country.

1887—Pennsylvania Steel (Maryland Steel, 1891) built blast furnace at Sparrows Point.

1888—Oct., Maryland flag of Calvert and Crossland colors flown at monument dedication ceremonies, Gettysburg.

1892—*The Afro-American* founded by John H. Murphy Sr.

1894—Baltimore Orioles won their first professional baseball championship.

1899—Building program began at Naval Academy, Ernest Flagg architect.

1904—Maryland Woman Suffrage Association led by Emma J. Maddox Funck.

1904—Feb. 7-8, Baltimore fire, 70 blocks in heart of business district devastated.

continued. . .

1910—Aug. 30, First statewide primary election in Maryland.

1913—Baltimore Chapter, National Association for the Advancement of Colored People (NAACP), formed, second oldest in country.

1914—Babe Ruth pitched for International League Orioles.

1916—Feb., Baltimore Symphony Orchestra organized under Gustav Strube.

1917—Aberdeen Proving Ground, first testing center of U.S. Army, established.

1920—Nov. 2, women voted for first time in Maryland.

1931—March 3, "The Star-Spangled Banner" adopted as national anthem.

1935—University of Maryland School of Law opened to blacks after NAACP lawyer Thurgood Marshall brought suit.

1941—April–Sept., Bethlehem-Fairfield Shipyard produced first Liberty Ship, *Patrick Henry*.

1941—Dec. 7, USS *Maryland* among naval ships attacked at Pearl Harbor.

1944—Drs. Helen Taussig and Alfred Blalock of Johns Hopkins Hospital performed first heart surgery to save "blue babies," babies born with heart defects.

1946—First photograph of Earth from space is produced at Johns Hopkins Applied Physics Laboratory.

1950—June 24, Friendship International Airport (now BWI Marshall), began operation.

1952—July 31, Chesapeake Bay Bridge opened.

1954—University of Maryland integrated, first state university below Mason-Dixon Line to do so.

1954—First black elected to House of Delegates, from Baltimore.

1954—May, Thurgood Marshall and NAACP won Brown v. Board decision.

1962—First phase of the Baltimore Beltway opened.

1967—Baltimore's Thurgood Marshall was named the first African American to serve on the United States Supreme Court.

1968—Riots followed the assassination of Martin Luther King Jr.

1970—Colts won third Super Bowl.

1977—The 27-story World Trade Center opened on the Inner Harbor and is the world's tallest equilaterally sided pentagonal building.

1982—Cal Ripken's Oriole career began.

1983—Orioles won third World Series in five games against the Philadelphia Phillies.

1984—Robert Irsay moved Colts to Indianapolis in the middle of the night.

1987—Dr. Ben Carson, director of pediatric neurosurgery at Johns Hopkins Medical Institutions in Baltimore, led a medical team that separated West German conjoined twins.

1992—Oriole Park at Camden Yards opens.

1996—Former Cleveland Browns became Baltimore Ravens.

2001—Ravens won the Super Bowl XXXV against the New York Giants.

2007—Sheila Dixon became Baltimore's first woman mayor.

2010—Sheila Dixon resigns as mayor because of criminal case.

hometown militia held off the British by land. The next day the city shook as British troops bombarded Fort McHenry for many hours.

Francis Scott Key, a lawyer who grew up in Baltimore, watched the bombardment from 8 miles away, on the deck of a boat where truce negotiations were in progress. Fearing the worst, with dawn emerging through fog and rain, Key trained a small spyglass on the fort and saw the tattered, 30-foot-by-42-foot American flag. The emotion of the moment stirred him to write a poem, "The Star-Spangled Banner," on the back of a sheet of letter paper. This original document is now housed at the Maryland Historical Society. (See the Attractions chapter for more information on the Maryland Historical Society.) It was Key's brother-in-law who suggested it be set to music. It was played first in Baltimore. The song later became the national anthem, but at the time served as a reminder of the militia's unlikely success in defeating a far superior British force. Baltimore's successful defense, coupled with British losses in battles in upstate New York, helped to force the British to accept the Treaty of Ghent, signed on Christmas Eve in 1814.

BUILDING THE B&O

Baltimore's leaders set out to make the city every bit as historical and cultural as the European cities of their ancestry. Some of the results of this effort remain today. Among them are the Roman Catholic Basilica of the Assumption on Cathedral Street, the first cathedral of American Catholicism; and the Battle Monument. The city also erected the first monument to honor George Washington, known—simply enough—as the Washington Monument. Baltimore soon became known as "Monument City."

In the late 1820s, word of construction of the Chesapeake & Ohio Canal—the first of its kind—running through Georgetown, west of Washington, D.C., challenged Baltimoreans. Fearing a devastating effect on commerce, Baltimorean Charles Carroll began building the Baltimore & Ohio Railroad. He was the grandson of the Charles Carroll who obtained the 60 acres of land in Baltimore in 1729 and who, at that time was 91 years old, was the last surviving signer of the Declaration of Independence. In 1853 the railroad finally reached its goal: the Ohio River at Wheeling, West Virginia. Besides speeding the movement of goods to the port in Baltimore for shipping, the railroad was responsible for bringing thousands of immigrants to the city, where they hoped to reestablish communities for their ethnic groups in a historically tolerant area. The rapidly growing area afforded them the opportunity to work on railroad and construction projects so they could earn a living.

Driven by economic hardships and political upheaval, immigrants streamed to the United States in increasing numbers in the 1830s, '40s, and '50s, and Baltimore received a large number of them, mostly German and Irish.

NORTH VS. SOUTH

South of the Mason-Dixon Line, the surveyed line between Pennsylvania and Maryland, Baltimore found itself in a difficult position as the rumblings of Civil War became a reality. The city's commercial ties were increasingly to the North—ties that could significantly affect its commerce; its emotional ties were to the South, where many relatives of Baltimore and Maryland residents had moved to seek greater prosperity on land that was more open. Slavery had been part of Maryland's agricultural history, especially with its major cash crop—the highly labor intensive tobacco. Opposition to slavery grew as more merchants became successful in endeavors not requiring slaves for labor. By 1860, Baltimore would be home to more freed blacks than any other city in the state; of the 84,000 freed slaves, more than 25,000 stayed in Baltimore.

Regardless of how the locals felt, the federal government knew it could not let Baltimore and the state of Maryland become officially part of the south or Washington, D.C., would be surrounded by southern sympathizers.

Despite efforts to ensure balance, in early 1861 Baltimore was the focus of the war as the first bloodshed of the Civil War occurred in the city. When 1,200 members of the Sixth Massachusetts Infantry passed through the city on their way to Washington to answer Lincoln's call for troops on April 19, 1861, a large group of Southern sympathizers attacked them. After a hail of insults, cobblestones, and pistol shots, the infantry returned fire, creating a riot and ending the lives of four soldiers and 12 Baltimoreans. After the incident, James Ryder Randall, a Marylander living in Louisiana, wrote a poem, "My Maryland," describing his outrage at the "gore that fleck'd the streets of Baltimore" during the riots. Set to the German tune "O Christmas Tree," it soon became Maryland's state song.

By May 13, federal troops occupied Federal Hill, aiming their weapons at Baltimore's downtown. Other federal troops brought weapons and barricades, and fear soon followed, making Baltimore an occupied city. Troops on both sides of the war came from Baltimore, and monuments and other reminders of the war reflect that dual role for the city.

RANDOM ACTS OF KINDNESS

After the Civil War, long before the phrase "random acts of kindness" became popular; several successful Baltimore businessmen demonstrated a new, private type of philanthropy. George Peabody, who came to Baltimore from Massachusetts in 1814, amassed his first million during the next 20 years, and then moved to London to further his fortune. He gave $1.5 million to the city to establish the Peabody Conservatory of Music and Library, built on Mount Vernon Place between 1866 and 1878.

Peabody's donation impressed Johns Hopkins, a friend who had earned his money first as a wholesale commodities dealer, then as a financier and an early investor in the B&O Railroad. In 1867 Hopkins gave most of his $7 million estate for the creation of a university and hospital bearing his name—a fitting gift for a man who never married and whose own formal education ended when he was 12 years old.

Enoch Pratt, a merchant and banker who would become one of the nation's leading hardware dealers, donated $833,000 in city bonds toward construction of an enormous free library bearing his name. He sensed that the Peabody Library, though impressive, was not large enough for the growing city and its increasingly affluent population. In 1886 Enoch Pratt Free Library opened with its shelves stacked with 28,000 books. Today it holds one of the best collections of books, music, periodicals, and other printed materials in the country.

During this era the magnificent Victorian City Hall was built, topped with a giant cast-iron dome, visible today (as then) from miles away. The building, designed by George Frederick, did something practically unheard of today—it came in 10 percent under its $2.27 million budget.

Coinciding with the enhancement of appearances was an incredible population increase. More than 60,000 immigrants arrived at Baltimore Harbor from the 1870s to 1900, creating new enclaves in the city. To the east was a Polish enclave, and to the west near the harbor sprouted up an Italian enclave, appropriately named Little Italy. It remains today as one of the best areas to go for an authentic Italian meal. Jews from Russia also found their way to Baltimore, where established Jewish communities helped them overcome the fear of persecution. Baltimore became a true community of neighborhoods, each having a distinctive style, flavor, and feel that carries over through today.

> **i** On the way to his inauguration in Washington, Abraham Lincoln had to be smuggled through Baltimore in the middle of the night for fear of assassination attempts by Southern sympathizers.

THE GREAT FIRE OF 1904

Just before 11 a.m. on Sunday, February 7, 1904, an automatic alarm signaled a fire at a six-story brick building containing dry goods at Hopkins Place and German (now Redwood) Street. Soon, other alarms were howling, flames were billowing, and strong winds in the cold, blustery day were carrying flames to the northwest. The fire quickly spread, and during the ensuing 30 hours it destroyed 1,545 buildings on 70 blocks, covering about 140 acres.

An earlier fire in 1858 had proven the value of the Alpha, a steam fire engine the city owned and, according to an article in the *Sun*, it was said that "with a few more steam engines properly managed, no fear of an extensive fire need be entertained." That was perhaps a little optimistic, for a fire in 1873 destroyed 113 buildings.

Then, there was the Great Baltimore Fire. More than 1,200 firefighters responded, from Philadelphia, Atlantic City, Washington, D.C., and elsewhere to the calls for help. Unfortunately, the hose couplings on much of the equipment from those jurisdictions didn't match the hydrants used in Baltimore so the trucks were of little help. Other officials came from the Maryland National Guard, Naval Brigade, and police officers from Philadelphia and New York came to assist the Baltimore Police Department. It did start the movement to unified specifications for national standards, including hose couplings, although, reportedly, only 18 of the 48 most populated cities comply. The fire was the impetus for a new building code that emphasized fireproof materials. More than $150 million worth of damage was done. According to lore, no lives were lost during this conflagration, although four men died within days due to pneumonia and exposure to the weather.

YET ANOTHER WAR

The city would again play a crucial role when World War I loomed and became reality. Protected from the open seas, Baltimore provided a safe harbor, impenetrable by the feared enemy submarines that lurked out in the Atlantic Ocean. It also provided a critical link between rail lines to and from the west and water access to Europe.

When the United States entered World War I in 1917, many Baltimoreans enlisted in the Navy, while others were enlisted in 24-hour-a-day operations to manufacture military uniforms, a task the city had performed effectively during the Spanish-American War. By the end of World War I, more than 55,000 Baltimoreans had enlisted to help with the war effort.

By the time peace came in 1918, Baltimore had undergone a major transformation into an industrial center. Leaders also had seen the need for the city to become larger—in 1918 they annexed 62 square miles of largely undeveloped land, some in Anne Arundel County and Baltimore County. The city had grown to 92 square miles. The new suburbs would see new homes popping up everywhere in the 1920s. More than 6,000 homes a year were being built, doubling the previous record. To the north of established row house communities in Mount Vernon Place and Bolton Hill would come the new developments of Guilford, Homeland, Roland Park, and Peabody Heights (now Charles Village). Farther north, into Baltimore County, came the estates of Greenspring, Worthington, and Dulaney Valleys, areas that, today as then, remain as residential areas.

SWEET TIMES

During the advent of air travel during the 1920s and 1930s, Baltimore housed one of the major airplane manufacturers, Glenn L. Martin Company, based in Cleveland. The factory, which was situated on Middle River just outside the city, built thousands of major aircraft and brought the need for new homes to house workers. Shoreline communities, many of which remain today, sprouted everywhere around the facility, and the factory's runways still serve as an airport for small aircraft and the Maryland Air National Guard.

On many of those new residents' doorsteps was the *Baltimore Evening Sun*, featuring the work of H. L. Mencken, a curmudgeon born in 1880 in a row house on Hollins Street in Southwest Baltimore. Arguably the most important journalist of his era, Mencken made sport of most everything he saw wrong with the world. One thing he liked was his hometown: "If the true purpose of living is to be born in comfort, to live happily and to die at peace, the average Baltimorean is infinitely better off than the average New Yorker."

THE CRASH HITS BALTIMORE

In New York the stock market crashed in October 1929, sending the country into the long and painful Great Depression. The toll on Baltimore would be great, but it was lessened slightly by the work of the Public Works Administration in Maryland. The organization spearheaded efforts to expand and improve the city's water supply through such construction projects as Prettyboy Reservoir in Baltimore County. The city continues to get most of its water from county reservoirs (Prettyboy and Loch Raven) along with the Big Inch, a water line created in the early 1960s running from the Susquehanna River, 40 miles north of the city, parallel to I-95. Even with the Public Works Administration projects, about 100,000 Baltimoreans—about one in seven people—had no income during the Depression era.

Fortunately, many of the people who had purchased new homes in the Baltimore area prior to the crash had taken five-year mortgages, so even though they had no income, they were not forced onto the streets. A sign of the times came in September 1931, when the $85 million, 32-story Baltimore Trust Company building was closed. Still, in the face of growing concern, the Baltimore Association of Commerce said in the early 1930s, "Industry as a whole is in good shape." The city's diverse economy kept it better off than most cities, but by Christmas 1933, one in six families in the city was on relief.

Love would soon take Baltimore's thoughts away from the Depression and put the city at the center of the world's attention. On December 10, 1936, England's King Edward VIII renounced his throne so he could marry Bessie Wallis Warfield Simpson, a twice-divorced Baltimore woman the king had fallen in love with. She became the Duchess of Windsor and a spectacle of public attention whenever she and the duke visited her hometown.

SUPPLYING WW II

In September 1939, when World War II began in Europe, Baltimore was providing much of the materials for battle. Overseas orders for Japanese ships were coming in to Bethlehem Steel, and Glenn L. Martin Co. was busy building airplanes. Another $5.5 billion in federal war contracts were soon heading to the city by the bay.

Before long, the Great Depression was forgotten. The 47,000 workers at Bethlehem Steel built 500 Victory and Liberty ships and, along the way, cut the assembly time from 110 to 52 days using automobile assembly line techniques. By 1943 Glenn L. Martin Co. was employing 37,000 people, and another 77,000 people were involved in shipbuilding in the city.

The growing workforce increased the city's population by an estimated 134,000, with another 28,000 families moving into new homes on the outskirts of the city. Baltimore's population eclipsed 1.5 million.

PEACETIME PURSUITS

In the 1950s the state spent $10 million on new schools and devoted $3 million to the construction of Friendship International Airport (now Baltimore–Washington International Thurgood Marshall Airport). Mass transportation and cars enabled suburbanites to get to their jobs in the city—moving to the more open county and beyond became feasible. Brick homes were being built by the hundreds.

With the flight to the outskirts, city housing was left to decay, and business leaders had to do something. They created the first housing court, a body empowered to crack down on the numerous housing violations that were ruining the city's appearance. Under Mayor Thomas J. D'Alesandro Jr., the new "Baltimore Plan" received praise and acclaim for its forward-looking approach. Beyond housing, the plan led to the improvement of bus routes and the construction of a new convention center in the city (now the Baltimore Arena), where entertainment, sporting events, and other activities could be held. A new plan for 33 acres in the center of the city called for the creation of Charles Center, a commercial and retail center on Charles Street, 3 blocks north of the Inner Harbor.

In 1954 the Baltimore Orioles appeared on

the scene, having moved from St. Louis, where they had been called the Browns. (Oddly enough, more than 40 years later the Cleveland Browns football team would move to Baltimore and become the Baltimore Ravens, succeeding the Colts, who left Baltimore for Indianapolis in 1984.) The Orioles played their home games at Memorial Stadium, a ballpark built in the northeastern part of the city as a large memorial to lost wartime soldiers. The Colts, with Johnny Unitas at the helm, also used the field for their incredible brand of play.

After expansion that saw the stadium grow from a starting capacity of 31,000 to 53,371 by 1991, the facility was closed in 1997. The Baltimore Orioles (minor and major league teams), the Bowie Baysox, Baltimore Colts, Baltimore Stallions, Baltimore Ravens, and Baltimore Bays had all played there. At times, the stadium also was called Babe Ruth Stadium and The Old Gray Lady of 33rd Street. There were some who referred to it as the "World's Largest Outdoor Insane Asylum" when discussing the Colts occupancy there.

Now it is the home for low- to moderate-income seniors at Stadium Place apartments with community rooms, a ThanksGiving Place meditative park with a labyrinth, a full-service Y, community-built playground, computer labs, a mini-movie theater, convenience store, and a beauty salon. Residents participate in an Eating Together Program at lunch time and a weekly shopping shuttle, and monthly trips are scheduled. The first building opened in 2004 and the fourth apartment building was completed in September 2008.

Although the Baltimore Colts were secreted away in 1984, the Marching Band stayed put. This band of 150 played on without a football team and without pay, marching at civic events, Thanksgiving Day parades, and at halftime shows for other NFL teams. Barry Levinson, a die-hard Baltimore Colts fan, directed a film *The Band That Wouldn't Die* that has shown on ESPN stations and probably can be found on the Internet. "Just because the team left doesn't mean the marching band has to leave."

> **i** Memorial Stadium has one memory not easily forgotten. On December 19, 1976, a plane crashed into the upper deck overlooking the south end zone shortly after the game between the Baltimore Colts and the Pittsburgh Steelers (Steelers won 40-14) had concluded and almost everyone had vacated the stadium. Pilot Donald Kroner is said to have been arrested for violating plane safety policies.

AN URBAN RENAISSANCE

In September 1970 the first City Fair was held at Charles Center and the Inner Harbor in an effort to heal the city's wounds and bring people back together. Just two years after rioting, representatives of almost all of Baltimore's neighborhoods gathered under tents to share their heritages; more than 300,000 people attended. For many of these people, a trip to the city for something other than work was rare. In the following years the city played host to summers filled with ethnic festivals.

In 1971 Baltimoreans elected William Donald Schaefer mayor. Although the movement had started with several leaders before him, Schaefer quickly became the embodiment of Baltimore's urban renaissance. In 1973 a homesteading program began, allowing people to buy city-owned houses for $1 if they agreed to refurbish them. (There were some who still thought they were overpriced.) The program was an immediate success, leading to the restoration and renovation of more than 500 old homes. Some of the best examples are the 100-year-old homes in the Otterbein, Ridgely's Delight, and Reservoir Hill neighborhoods.

Commercial improvements were also in the works. In time for the nation's bicentennial, the Maryland Science Center opened in a $10 million, four-story building on the Inner Harbor. In July 1976 the city held a giant fireworks display, where the rockets' red glare fell on eight beautiful "tall ships" visiting from faraway ports. In February 1977 the city launched its own goodwill ambassador vessel, the $467,000, 90-foot *Pride of*

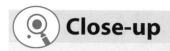 **Close-up**

Getting to Know Baltimore Architecture

In a way, Baltimore is a working museum. Down every street where people live and work are architectural examples from almost every historical period that harmonize across Baltimore's landscape. Yet, even those of us who are used to the give and take of old and new are sometimes astounded by the contrasts. Baltimore's original cityscape was created by architectural names like Latrobe, Cassell, and Pope. The people who hired them were the Peabodys, the Pratts, and the Hopkinses—city benefactors, philanthropists, businessmen.

The Colonial Style and Georgian Revival

Anyone who has ever been to or seen pictures of restored buildings at Williamsburg, Virginia, has a good idea of what the Colonial period wrought architecturally. Also known as English Georgian, the Colonial style is characterized by white columned porticos, peaked roofs, red brick, and multipaned dormer windows. Good examples of Colonial-style in Baltimore include Mount Clare Mansion, Old Otterbein Church, and Captain John Steele House.

The Federal and Jeffersonian Styles

The Federal style has much of the Colonial in it, but scaled back. Columns are narrower, their caps simpler with no more than one level of decoration. The Jeffersonian style, which was a simplification externally even on the Federal, often does not have any decoration at all. Rooflines are dotted with hound's-tooth molding or are without adornment. Dormers may be curved instead of peaked, and if it peaked the pitch is not steep. Windows have fewer panes. Overall, lines are simpler, coming as they do from a time when function was prized above form.

An example of a Federal building in Baltimore is Homewood House, the restoration of which was completed by Johns Hopkins University on whose campus it sits.

Classical Revival

At the turn of the 19th century, there was a return to the classical styles of Greece and Rome. Whereas a Federal-style portico might have, at most, four columns, the classically styled portico might have eight, and in place of a simple column cap, there might be swirls or copious foliage. The thinner one-story columns of the Federal style gave way to two-story-high, giant fluted columns. Rooflines include domed towers and central rotundas.

One of the most famous examples of Classical Revival architecture in Baltimore is the Basilica of the Assumption, which was designed by Benjamin Henry Latrobe, who also designed the U.S. Capitol in Washington, D.C. Later examples that adhere to this style are also visible in Baltimore, however. The War Memorial across from Baltimore's City Hall is noted as one of them, although it has some Art Deco elements as well.

Gothic Revival

To think of Gothic is to think of times when myth held the reins of terror in Europe. The original Gothic style was heavy, almost cumbersome, in its uses of tower and gargoyle, gray stone and ironwork. Gothic Revival of the late 18th and early 19th centuries uses these elements but to a much lesser degree. Rooflines are punctuated with steep, peaked caps over doorways and windows. This was the beginning of bay and oriel windows with pointed caps or crenellated stone tops, which reflected the corner watchtowers of a castle.

A straightforward example of such style is the main gate at Greenmount Cemetery, which was designed by Robert Cary Long Jr., who also designed five Gothic churches in Baltimore and buildings reflecting other architectural styles.

Antebellum

Antebellum architecture in Baltimore was driven by one main economic engine, the railroad. By the time the B&O Railroad reached the fertile Ohio Valley in 1652, Baltimore was finding many uses for such products as iron ore dug from the Appalachians and returned to the city by rail. Iron was already a big industry in Baltimore before the Civil War, and one of the forward-thinking items it produced was prefabricated ironworks. Facades for buildings, circular staircases, railings, window grills, balconies, and the like became part and parcel of the buildings of that time. It has been said that 90 percent of the famed wrought iron work in New Orleans was manufactured in Baltimore.

One of the most astounding interior uses of iron prefabrication in Baltimore is the five-tiered interior of the George Peabody Library, built in 1857 and designed by Edmund George Lind. The facade of the main gallery of the City Life Museums on President Street is also all iron, as is the City Hall dome, which was designed and built here in Baltimore by Wendel Bollman.

Victorian Styles

After the Civil War and through the turn of the 20th century, Baltimore was in its heyday. The railroad and the industries that had blossomed from it ruled the cityscape. Money was being made hand over fist in a time when there were no income taxes, no zoning laws, and still plenty of land to go around. The 1850s Gothic and Classical styles gave way to French and Italian Renaissance stylings. The features include broad verandas, formal gardens, and mansard roofs. Houses from this period are often made of wood, with shingle. The mansard roofs are decorated with gingerbread trim that looks like rows of thick lace. Towers, bowed walls, and bay windows add to the look, although the Italian Renaissance styles tend to be squarer, with roofs pitched lower.

Examples of Victorian architecture are found in Roland Park, Lutherville, and other country neighborhoods of the time. More formal examples are easily seen at Mount Vernon Place and the Belvedere at Chase and Charles Streets.

Art Deco

As the 1920s roared into town, Baltimore, like most big East Coast cities, was ready to become thoroughly modern. Victorian evolved into what is called Nouveau. Nouveau was really an interior and fashion style more than a building style, but buildings that were rendered during this period tend toward smoother lines overall, with larger visuals and more glass, while still reflecting the gingerbread and visual clutter of the Victorian era.

By 1925, builders were ready for the cleaner, less cluttered appearance. The style is called modern decorative, Art Deco, or simply Deco. Deco style cuts off all corners . . . literally. A typical Deco building has rounded edges. If design was rendered in brick, designers tended to use yellow instead of red, and the bricks were larger. Other building choices included smooth stone or stucco. There was a lot of chrome and a lot of glass, including glass block, and interiors tended to be rendered in lighter woods including oak and ash rather than cherry or mahogany.

Whereas Victorian and nouveau glass renderings tended to be intricate and three-dimensional like a Tiffany lampshade, Deco was rendered boldly and often two-dimensionally—three petals above a single stem etched into a blue glass mirror. You can, in fact, see that actual item over the water fountain inside of the decidedly Deco Senator Theater.

A Word About Formstone . . .

As you move through Baltimore, you will see a great many buildings—particularly marble-stepped, two-story, 19th-century row houses—covered with a substance that you may not be able to identify. It looks like multicolored stone from far away, but when you get up close it seems to be some kind of formed stucco. The substance is called formstone, and it is not original to any of the buildings to which it adheres. It can be removed, blasted, and chipped away to uncover the original brick, and we are seeing more and more of this today.

We believe that formstone was originally sold as a way to waterproof and insulate homes. This supposition makes sense, for without formstone, an old brick house that was having leakage problems would have to repoint all the brick, an expensive process, and to insulate would require losing floor space by adding depth to interior walls, which, when your living room is only 10 feet by 13 feet, hardly seems practical.

Baltimore, a replica of the clipper ships that had been popular on the area's waters more than a century earlier. Several years later, the ship sank during an Atlantic storm, taking with it several sailors. But the *Pride of Baltimore II* followed—a clipper ship replica with modern safety features that has sailed to all parts of the world.

In 1978 Baltimore voters approved the construction of Harborplace, a 3.1-acre complex of shops, restaurants, and food stalls to be constructed at the center of the Inner Harbor. This wasn't an easy battle because many had become comfortable with the wide greenways along the harbor bulkhead and weren't sure they wanted commercial entities in the green space. Built for $10 million by the Rouse Company, Harborplace's opening in July 1980 was the crowning glory of the urban revitalization effort: a tourist attraction that would bring locals and visitors to the city's downtown area in droves for years to come.

Propelled by the city's newfound $625-million-a-year tourist industry, a new convention center opened just ahead of Harborplace in August 1979, and the 500-room, 13-story Hyatt Regency opened in 1980. With the Hyatt boasting that company's second-highest occupancy rate (92.3 percent) in its first year, other hotels soon followed. The Stouffer, Sheraton, and Harbor Courts were soon taking reservations from people hungry to visit a city that had been profiled in *National Geographic, Time, Newsweek,* and a host of travel articles in national and international newspapers. An enduring image of Mayor Schaefer, wearing an old-style striped bathing suit and sporting a yellow rubber duck, jumping into a tank at the National Aquarium, brought the city even more positive publicity.

BUILDING ON SUCCESS

Schaefer's own success led him to the State House, where he served as governor from 1986 to 1994. During his tenure as governor, he further fortified the city, leading trade missions to the Far East and other areas to woo businesses. His administration pushed for the construction of Oriole Park at Camden Yards, a new stadium for the Baltimore Orioles that was within walking distance of the Inner Harbor. Camden Yards, as it is now referred to by most people, opened to sellout crowds in 1992 and played host to baseball's All-Star Game in 1993 and the American League Championship in 1997. A companion football stadium, now called M&T Bank Stadium, was built for the Baltimore Ravens and opened in the fall of 1998 across the parking lot from the baseball-only park.

Baltimore found great success and visibility in the film industry. Such movies as *Diner, Bedroom Window, Tin Men,* and *The Accidental Tourist* were shot in Baltimore, many made by local filmmaker Barry Levinson. In 1992 Levinson used his hometown as the setting for a television project—the dramatic series *Homicide: Life on the Streets.* The show garnered critical acclaim for its gritty portrayal of Baltimore's finest, using location shoots throughout the city and especially in Fell's Point.

With Schaefer's departure for the governorship in Annapolis, the reins for Baltimore's municipal leadership were taken by mayors from the city's minority population. Clarence "Du" Burns became mayor when Schaefer was elected to the governor's seat and served the last 11 months of Schaefer's term. Burns was succeeded by fellow African American Kurt L. Schmoke, a Rhodes Scholar from Yale and former prosecutor for the city, who served as Baltimore's mayor for 12 years.

THE FACE OF THE FUTURE

In 2000 Baltimore welcomed a young (46 years old) energetic mayor, Martin O'Malley, who asked us to "Believe." With bumper stickers and banners and signs all over the city, he launched a program to renew the city and boost morale. He was so dynamic he caught the attention of the national media. *Esquire* magazine named him "The Best Young Mayor in the Country" in 2002, and he appeared in *Time* magazine as one of America's "Top 5 Big City Mayors" in 2005. That same year, *Business Week* called him one of "Five Fresh Faces" to lead the Democratic Party. So it was no surprise when he won the gubernatorial seat in 2006.

As O'Malley left office in 2007, Sheila Dixon, the City Council president, stepped up to take the mayor's office and become the first African-American woman to lead Baltimore. She was elected to serve in her own right in the November 2007 elections. Dixon got to work, setting as her goals cleaner streets, opportunities for the city's youth, and smoke-free restaurants and bars, effective in January 2008. She resigned in February 2010, as part of a plea deal reached that ended a years-long corruption investigation and prosecution.

Development in general is bustling throughout the city. Our West Side is seeing a massive overhaul, while the Inner Harbor continues to spread east along the water with new hotels, businesses, and housing. The national trend of young professionals and empty nesters moving back into cities can definitely be seen in Baltimore. The city has seen an influx of luxury high-rises, and empty office and corporate buildings are finding new life as residential buildings, bringing a whole new life to the heart of the city.

ACCOMMODATIONS

Baltimore has had, and continues to have, a thriving hospitality business since the port city was established. Whether you're looking for a bed-and-breakfast, posh or merely functional, unique or cookie-cutter, you're pretty sure to find it here. Some properties are old, some are new, and some are new that have been crafted from old. As an example, the Springhill Suites on Redwood Street occupies the old Manufacturer's Building and Trust bank building (that survived the 1904 fire). Rather than trying to remove the huge vault from the basement, it's been furnished to provide what should be one of the most secure board meeting facilities anywhere. The Monaco hotel sits in the old B&O Railroad building and proudly shows and uses the two large marble staircases.

Baltimore has at least 85 hotels, motels, and other accommodations with about 10,000 rooms within comfortable distance of the convention center.

You may assume that any property mentioned allows service animals, is ADA compliant, and does not allow smoking in most, if not all, public and private areas. Unless otherwise noted, parking includes all in-and-out privileges, but the fees cited are before tax. Wi-Fi or Internet access should be available in all hotel chain properties and most individual hotels.

When available, each listing includes the local and toll-free phone number, an Internet address (URL), a price estimate, and anything that make it special.

Baseball fans may want to try to find where the visiting team is staying to catch sight of your favorite player and possibly ask for a photo and autograph. For years, most of the teams stayed at the Marriott Inner Harbor and the Cross Keys before that. They seem to have moved to the InterContinental these days. You'll find that there are always one or two teams that stay elsewhere. Don't be obnoxious when you approach the players and please realize the players may not be too friendly after the game if the Os won.

The hotels are listed alphabetically inside the downtown area (including Fell's Point, Federal Hill, etc.) and then alphabetically outside. There is a separate listing of hotels in the BWI Marshall Airport hotel zone and nearby Arundel Mills.

Following hotels are listing of Bed and Breakfasts found in Baltimore's neighborhoods. Staying at a B&B is one of the best ways to feel like an instant Baltimore Insider!

HOTELS

Price Code

The basic room rate is the Rack Rate. That's the hotel room rate if you don't belong to any organization, don't ask for a discount, and don't have a friend in the business. As you probably know, hotels have special rates if you're a 50-upper, member of AAA, attending a convention, visiting on a week day or weekend when nothing is happening in town, or celebrating a birthday or anniversary or the last child off to college. If you have access to the Internet, you should be able to find a less expensive price or a value-added package that gives you free parking, access to museums or theatrical productions, free breakfast, or all of those things. When you consider booking through an Internet site, be sure to include any fees they may charge into your calculations. Many hotels' Web sites now guarantee that they will have the lowest price available online.

Remember to ask about jurisdictional room taxes. In Baltimore County, that's 8 percent and 13.5 percent in Baltimore City. Therefore, you might want to compare room rates and taxes where you can walk to where you're going versus renting a car, taking a cab, or using public transportation.

Check various hotel and local convention and visitors' bureau Web sites for upcoming special events.

$	Less than $80
$$	$80 to $125
$$$	$126 to $150
$$$$	$151 to $199
$$$$$	$200 and more

ADMIRAL FELL INN $$$$
888 South Broadway, Fell's Point
(410) 522-7377, (866) 583-4162
www.harbormagic.com
In the heart of historic Fell's Point at the foot of Broadway is the historic (natch) Admiral Fell Inn. Eighty rooms are spread through eight buildings, some of which date from the 1770s. Specialty rooms may have a canopy bed, a hot tub, or a balcony. The corner suite rooms have a king bed and a separate sitting room. There is even a bi-level suite with a sitting room downstairs and bed and hot tub upstairs. Wireless Internet access is available in all public areas and each guest room. The room price includes a light continental breakfast. You may request exercise equipment be brought to your room, or you can enjoy the MAC Wellness health club that has a 25-yard, four-lane lap pool, four salt-water pools, and exercise classes. Valet parking is $29 per day. The hotel is pet friendly with a $90 value travel kit for $49 per stay (not per day).

i Guests are invited to the Admiral's Welcome, Monday through Thursday from 5 to 6 p.m., for a complimentary signature cocktail and meeting your Experience Specialist who will help implement your perfect stay. The Admiral's Tea is held every Saturday from 4 to 5 p.m.

BALTIMORE MARRIOTT INNER HARBOR AT CAMDEN YARDS $$$$–$$$$$
110 South Eutaw St.
(410) 962-0202, (800) 228-9290
www.marriott.com
Two downtown Marriott hotels can cause confusion. This one, the Marriott Inner Harbor, is at Pratt and Eutaw Streets across from Camden Yards and a block from the Convention Center. The other one, the Marriott Waterfront, is the 32-story building on the water and a long stone's throw from Little Italy and Fell's Point. Make sure you know which one you want when you register.

Built in 1984, this 10-story hotel has 490 traditional rooms and 34 suites. A gift and sundry shop in the lobby, full business center, secretarial services, and safe deposit box at the front desk are among the services available. Each guest room has a Marriott Revive bed and high-speed Internet access (fee). A fitness center with cardiovascular equipment, free weights, treadmills, stationary bikes, and Nautilus machine are available for those who like to work out while they're away from home. The indoor pool no longer exists. Dine at the Café Promenade and or enjoy light bites at The Yard.

The Marriot has seasonal rates, particularly around the baseball season. Packages are available that include breakfast. Another package includes two tickets to the Baltimore Aquarium. The attached garage, which is independently operated, costs $24 per day.

BALTIMORE MARRIOTT WATERFRONT $$$$–$$$$$
700 Aliceanna St.
(410) 385-3000, (800) 228-9290
www.marriott.com
The Marriott Waterfront is the second largest hotel (after the Hilton Baltimore, which opened in August 2008 and has 757 rooms) in the city. The hotel, 32 floors of it, overlooks the harbor and is within walking distance to various shops and

popular restaurants including the ESPN Zone, Hard Rock Cafe, and Little Italy. There are three restaurants, a deli, and a lounge, either in the hotel or attached. This huge hotel offers 733 guest rooms and 21 suites, each with a harbor view. When you're stuck in meetings and just have to have a break, you can use the heated indoor pool and fitness center. The hotel is located at a water taxi stop—a great way to get around the harbor (see the Getting Here, Getting Around chapter for information on the water taxi). Self-parking is $25 and valet parking is $38 daily. Oversize vehicles cannot be accommodated. With nothing between the hotel and the sky and harbor, this is a terrific location whenever the city has a fireworks display. You can request rooms ending in 01, 03, 07, 34, and 43 and watch them from your room. The windows aren't huge, however, and you only hear the muffled boom, boom, boom of the shells, so an even better way is to head toward the observation deck on the fifth floor, by the pool. That's where you can enjoy the panoramic sky experience, see the fireworks, and feel the full compression of each explosion.

As mentioned in the description for the Marriott Inner Harbor, make sure you know which of the two hotels has your reservation.

i Concierge Gene Fedeli, a native Baltimorean, has been with the Marriott since 2001 and knows just about everything a concierge needs to know including friendships he's been cultivating all this time. Need a last-minute reservation? Ask Gene. He's trimmed a guest's hair so he'd look top-notch for an important meeting, and he'll even shine your shoes for you.

BROOKSHIRE SUITES
INNER HARBOR $$$$–$$$$$
120 East Lombard St.
(410) 625-1300
www.harbormagic.com
In a city filled with historic architecture, the Brookshire Suites goes beyond modern in design and color scheme. Whether you're staying a day or the rest of the year, the Brookshire Suites provides a spacious living room, separate bedroom, bathrobe, and an oversized work space. They tell you up front that "every room is on the concierge level" because you have access to the Cloud Club with gorgeous views of the Inner Harbor. Within the Cloud is a business center with two computers and copying, printing, and faxing services. There are other benefits including breakfast (pancakes, eggs, bacon, and daily chef specials) from 6 to 10 a.m. Monday through Friday and 7 to 11 a.m. on weekends. An open bar and hors d'oeuvres and more are available weeknights from 5:30 to 7:30 p.m. A guest coin-operator laundry is available 24 hours a day. A marketplace off the lobby carries quick meals, snacks, magazines, sundries, and more. The rooms are pet-friendly.

Some suites have a view of the harbor. Valet parking is $29 a day. The hotel has an exercise room or you can receive a pass to a nearby health club. The Brookshire Suites has two sister properties, the Admiral Fell Inn and Pier 5 Hotel. When you're a guest at one, you can use the facilities at the other two.

COURTYARD BY MARRIOTT,
BALTIMORE INNER HARBOR $$$–$$$$
1000 Aliceanna St.
(443) 923-4000
www.marriott.com
Situated in a new development of buildings and hotels known as Inner Harbor East, this Courtyard is across the parking lot from the towering Baltimore Marriott Waterfront and a few blocks from the Inner Harbor and Fell's Point. Ten guest-room floors provide 205 rooms and suites. There is an indoor pool and exercise room on-site. Daily parking is $22. A Whole Foods natural food market with a great salad bar, deli, and sushi stand; a CVS; and a Starbucks are right around the corner.

DAYS INN, INNER HARBOR $$$
100 Hopkins Place
(410) 576-1000
www.daysinnerharbor.com
The Days Inn is the closest hotel to the convention center (as in across the street) and only 3 blocks west of the Inner Harbor. It has 250 rooms

and each has complimentary high-speed Internet (and in public rooms, too), microwave, and a refrigerator. Because the hotel is so close to Camden Yards, its busiest season is baseball season. Overnight parking service is $20 a day. The hotel has a free-form heated outside swimming pool, open May through September (no lifeguard), and a fitness center. There is also a restaurant, Hopkin's Bar and Grill, and a Java Café for a cup of coffee or a specialty drink (coffee style, not alcoholic) and snacks. Sign up on the Web site for discount coupons and sale announcements.

i Check with Gerald Salgado, the night manager, for suggestions about dining and activities. The native New Yorker started in Baltimore in 2000, spent a while at a property in Coral Gables, and returned in 2003.

1840S CARROLLTON INN $$$–$$$$$
50 Albemarle St.
(410) 385-1840
www.1840scarrolltoninn.com
1840s Carrollton Inn, a boutique bed-and-breakfast in Baltimore's historic Jonestown neighborhood, is just a block from Little Italy and a short walk from the Inner Harbor, up-and-coming Harbor East, and Fell's Point. Comprised of several interconnecting rowhomes (some from the early 19th-century) that surround a courtyard. Thirteen elegantly furnished guest rooms and suites are available. Eventually, they anticipate 25 rooms and suites. Overnight accommodations include complimentary full gourmet breakfast served from a menu, high-speed wireless Internet, concierge service, and discounted parking. All rooms feature a fireplace, whirlpool tub, and luxury bath amenities.

FAIRFIELD INN & SUITES DOWNTOWN
INNER HARBOR $$–$$$
101 President St.
(410) 837-9900
www.greenfairfieldinn.com
Once the site of the Baltimore Brewing Company, the Fairfield Inn opened July 2009 with the knowledge that it is the first LEED Certified Silver Marriott Hotel in the city. Tavern 101 features an American menu including Maryland (tomato-based) crab soup and local organic beers. It is one of the few Fairfield Inn properties that has a tavern on-site. Public areas and guest rooms have wired and wireless high-speed Internet access. Valet parking fee is $27 a day. The green roof prevents heat from seeping into the hypoallergenic and fragrance-free facility. No artificial air freshener or carpet freshener is used. The building is 25 percent more energy efficient than a similar building, so they can pass the energy savings on to you in the form of a lower rate.

HAMPTON INN AND SUITES
BALTIMORE INNER HARBOR $$–$$$$
131 East Redwood St.
(410) 539-7888
www.baltimoreinnerharborsuites
.hamptoninn.com
The staff at the Hampton Inn and Suites say they're always trying to make things better. They started with a restored historic building—the old USF&G and Baker Watts office. Guests in each of the 116 rooms can use the indoor lap pool and exercise room. Although the Web site indicates otherwise, pets are not welcomed. A complimentary On The House hot breakfast is served daily or take advantage of their Hampton's on the Run breakfast bag with a quick bite and bottle of water (available Monday through Friday).

i The circular dining/meeting room on top of the hotel, now used for events, is said to have been the first revolving restaurant installed in a hotel in the country.

HILTON BALTIMORE CONVENTION
CENTER HOTEL $$–$$$$
401 West Pratt St.
(443) 573-8700
www.baltimore.hilton.com
This Hilton is the Texas of Baltimore. With 767 rooms and suites, it has more rooms than any other hotel. The 25,000-square-foot grand ballroom is the city's largest. It is directly across the

street from the Convention Center and is linked by a skybridge. It has a 32,000-square-foot (that's a little larger than the Ravens' football field) green roof, the largest in the city. It's also probably caused more of a stir (among people who think this stuff is important) because it blocks the view of the Bromo Seltzer Tower from Camden Yards, and the architectural design leaves a lot of people shaking their combined heads. Many of us have come to love the Brutalist architecture of the Morris Mechanic Theatre and we may come to love the design of the Hilton Hotel. Maybe.

Enjoy the indoor pool on the fourth floor. Hook up with the Wi-Fi (fee). Self-parking is $26 a day; valet is $36 Despite the fact that the hotel opened in fall 2008, lots of people still don't know it exists. Maybe they should offer a "say the magic word and. . ."

i More than 60,000 one-inch plugs of six different species of plants were used just on the East building of the Hilton Baltimore. The benefits of a green roof include reducing storm water runoff, the HVAC cooling loads, heat islands (because there isn't a blacktop roof), and creating natural habitats for birds and other wildlife. Hensel Phelps, Ralph J. Meyer Co. roofers, Ridge Roofing of Baltimore, Furbish Company, and Emory Knoll Farms were all involved in the project.

HOLIDAY INN EXPRESS AT
THE STADIUMS $–$$
1701 Russell St.
(410) 727-1818
www.holidayinn.com

This motel is 8 blocks south of Camden Yards, even closer to M&T Bank Stadium, and almost in the shadow of the onramp to I-95. So, although it's not a garden-setting location, it is terrific for getting out of town after the game. The motel is a clean place to call home for a time, particularly if you're traveling on a budget. It offers cable TV, complimentary Express Start Breakfast Bar with hot entrees and their exclusive cinnamon rolls

and Smart Roast coffee. Parking is $10 a day. There is a swimming pool in summer (no lifeguard). A free shuttle service is available to local offices and attractions, including the Aquarium, Johns Hopkins, University of Maryland, and elsewhere within a 7-mile radius.

HOLIDAY INN EXPRESS $$–$$$$
221 North Gay St.
(410) 400-8045
www.hiexpress.com

This original 20th-century building served as the headquarters of the Old Town National Bank of Baltimore. Designed in a Classic Revival style by Frederick Fletcher, the Gay Street building has a stately exterior with Corinthian pilasters flanking bronze doors at the main entrance and an ornate lobby with a mezzanine. It was a bank until the 1960s, which was converted to office space, and had been sitting empty for the three years before it was converted to a hotel. The fitness center is open 24 hours. Your pet is welcomed. A $50 deposit is required. The Holiday Inn Express is the closest hotel to the Johns Hopkins Medical Campus. Complimentary shuttle service is available to Johns Hopkins and Mercy Hospitals, Baltimore Convention Center, and Baltimore Penn Station.

HOLIDAY INN INNER HARBOR $$
301 West Lombard St.
(410) 685-3500
www.innerharborhi.com

The downtown Holiday Inn is two buildings, an east wing and a west wing. The lobby, restaurant, meeting rooms, and pool (lower level) are in the east wing. Therefore, the rooms in the west wing probably are quieter, but they are farther away from the action. A two-level parking garage is in between. Management has implemented a good start to a green program in the 375-room hotel with compact fluorescent light bulbs in each guest room and hallways, a linen reuse program, and recycling bins in every guest room and in public spaces. Suites also have whirlpools. There is a $21 daily parking fee.

HOTEL MONACO BALTIMORE $$$$–$$$$$
2 North Charles St.
(443) 692-6170, (866) 973-1904
www.monaco-baltimore.com

Built into 10 floors or so of the 13-story Beaux Arts B&O Building (other floors are occupied by office space), the Monaco is the city's first Kimpton luxury boutique hotel. The building was the tallest in the city when it opened in 1906. Priced at $65 million, the 202-room hotel represents the stability, grace, and quirkiness of Baltimore to a tee. Architecture lovers may just want to park out overnight in the three-story lobby because it is spectacular with its original marble floor and Tiffany stained-glass windows that just seem to want to take you to the golden age of something. Maybe the golden age of today. Valet parking is $36 a day.

The two-story B&O American Brasserie (443-692-6172, www.bandorestaurant.com) is located immediately off the lobby and is open for breakfast, lunch, and dinner. The upper level is not wheelchair accessible other than employees who will carry the chair and passenger upstairs if desired. Chef E. Michael Reidt (yes, the same one who's been written about in national food and travel publications) is at the helm. He says his experience has shown him that a "traditional" Maryland crab cake does not have to be lump meat and that most locals do not like Old Bay seasoning.

In 2001, the building was listed as one of the "Ten Enduring Landmarks of Baltimore's Central Business District" by the National Parks Service's Historic Buildings Survey.

Your pet is welcomed (no additional charge) and if you don't have a chance to bring your Fifi or Jumpers with you, the Monaco will supply you with their own brand of guppy love. It's really a goldfish swimming around in a little bowl, but guppy love sounds better than goldfish love. Because they know some people have allergies, the pets are restricted to rooms on the 10th floor. Following the pet's check-out the room is super cleaned. Of course, pets do have to come into and out of the hotel, up the elevators, etc., so you might have some exposure to them.

HYATT REGENCY $$$$–$$$$$
300 Light St.
(410) 528-1234, (800) 233-1234
http://baltimore.hyatt.com

The glass-clad Hyatt sits on an Inner Harbor prime spot for convenience and spectacular views. Each of the 488 rooms and suites has a harbor, water, or city view and each has a Hyatt Grand Bed. Try the menu at Bistro 300; and during good weather you can play tennis, shoot hoops, hit the jogging track, or enjoy the pool on the skyline deck. When you want that special event to have a skytop view, then check out Pisces. The hotel's location is still one of the city's best for visitors because of its proximity to the Inner Harbor and convention center, both accessible by skywalk. Valet parking is available for $36 per day; self-parking is $27 per day.

INN AT HENDERSON'S WHARF $$–$$$
1000 Fell St.
(410) 522-7777, (800) 522-2088
www.hendersonswharf.com

Henderson's Wharf was built on the "point" of Fell's Point. Built in 1894 for the B&O Railroad, the site is a registered National Historic Landmark. The 38-room inn takes up only the first floor of the building, with the second through sixth floors serving as private apartments and condominiums. After a near-disastrous visit from Hurricane Isabel in September 2003, the property did the lemons-into-lemonade thing. From merely classic beauty, it became even more amazing. The inn presents such gifts as a bottle of wine upon arrival, and provides 24-hour fitness center access and continental breakfast daily. Come by car or by boat and there's a parking space or slip for you.

Or, just rely on the nearby water taxi. Half of the rooms have a view of the water; the others overlook the inner courtyard, with its cobblestone patio and wooden tables sheltered by white umbrellas.

INTERCONTINENTAL HARBOR COURT HOTEL $$$$$
550 Light St.
(410) 234-0550
www.harborcourt.com

Architecturally, the Harbor Court, with its huge, twin, redbrick towers, is one of the most striking hotels in Baltimore. The English country interior is just as phenomenal. The grand staircase is reminiscent of ball gowns and footmen. The pickled oak paneling in the lobby was imported from England. The Harbor Court has 195 rooms and 22 suites of varying size, and two restaurants. Guests may take advantage of 24-hour room service and a full-service health club, including tennis and racquetball courts, tanning salons, and massage. There's a concierge staff of three.

To view the Fourth of July fireworks over the Baltimore Harbor, request a king harbor view room. There are about 100 of them, including suites, with absolutely unobstructed views. Special packages are available. Depending on the market, booking a year ahead of time is not unreasonable, but you also might be able to book a great room two or three weeks ahead of time.

MOUNT VERNON HOTEL $$-$$$
24 West Franklin St.
(410) 727-2000, (800) 245-5256
www.mountvernonbaltimore.com

For more than 50 years, the downtown YMCA was housed at this address. When the Comfort Inn bought it and renovated it for a hotel, it traded the swimming pools for underground parking. A little later on, the Baltimore International College took over the site in 1994 and completely renovated the building, and redecorated the lobby and in-house Bay Atlantic Café in 2008. It offers 135 rooms on nine floors, including single, double, and wheelchair-accessible rooms and bi-level lofts and Jacuzzi suites. Parking is available on-site for an extra $14 a night. Pets are not allowed.

PEABODY COURT HOTEL $$$$$
612 Cathedral St.
(410) 727-7101, (877) 424-6423
www.choicehotels.com

Formerly the Latham, this boutique Clarion Collection a Peabody Court Hotel has 104 rooms and is set in the heart of the Mount Vernon Cultural District. It's 1 block from the Washington Monument and walking distance to all the galleries, restaurants, and shops along Charles Street. Each room features a heated towel warmer, pillow-top mattresses, full marble bathrooms, and imported French marble-topped furniture. You'll drool over (and be thankful you don't have to clean) the 6' Baccarat chandelier in the main lobby. The in-house restaurant, aptly named George's On Mount Vernon Square, is in honor of the "Three George's" of Baltimore—George Washington, George Peabody, and George Herman ("Babe") Ruth. The hotel also offers a fitness room, and a business center with high-speed Internet access. Wireless Internet service is free. Valet parking is available for $29 a night, and pets are welcomed with a $50 non-refundable cleaning fee.

PIER 5 HOTEL $$$$-$$$$$
711 Eastern Ave.
(410) 539-2000
www.harbormagic.com

When visiting the Pier 5 Hotel, you pull into Harbor Magic Drive, past the Power Plant entertainment complex and the National Aquarium, and when you look to the Inner Harbor, everyone will understand if your jaw just drops. This is the only hotel with an Inner Harbor location that sits right on the water. And it's right in the thick of things. Pier 6 Concert Pavilion is out the door to your right. Look one way and you'll find Ruth's Chris-Pier 5, and then there's McCormick & Schmick's off the hotel lobby. The convenience isn't the only wow factor—you can enjoy a hotel full of fun. From 5:30 to 6:30 p.m. Monday through Friday, you can whip up a savory batch of Pier 5 Maryland Crab Dip or Crabby Crepes. You can win trivia prizes and wear wacky crab hats. The hotel offers 65 rooms on three floors, including seven suites. Guests can self-park for $21 a day on two lots, next to and across the street from the hotel. Valet parking is $28 a day. Twenty-four-hour concierge service and room service are available. Even with all this, however, the Art Deco ambience and the sound of the water lapping up against the dock are probably the best features of the Pier 5 Hotel.

ℹ The Pier 5 Hotel has two sister properties, Brookshire Suites and the Admiral Fell Inn. When you're a guest at one you can use the facilities at the other two. A shuttle connects the three properties.

QUALITY INN $$–$$$
110 St. Paul St.
(410) 637-3600
This Quality Inn is in the downtown area and has 96 guest rooms. Self-parking is available for $13. Some rooms have a DVD player for guests who bring movies or games for their children.

RADISSON PLAZA LORD BALTIMORE $$–$$$$
20 West Baltimore St.
(410) 539-8400, (888) 201-1718
www.radisson.com/hotels/mdbalhar
Built in 1928, the Art Deco Radisson Plaza Lord Baltimore is the city's only National Historic Landmark hotel. It's located right in the heart of the city, within walking distance from many attractions. Plush carpet, warm wood, brass, and a three-story lobby complement the 439 deluxe guest rooms, including suites with a full kitchen, living room, and whirlpool tub. Some rooms have a "Sleep Number" bed by Select Comfort and some have Serta Beautyrest. You can upgrade to a Plaza Level room and be lavished by private concierge attention, silver service continental breakfast, and evening cocktails and hors d'oeuvres. The Lord Baltimore Grill is open for breakfast, lunch, and dinner with a themed weekday lunch buffet and a three-for-$20 dinner menu. The Lobby Bar serves cocktails and a light fare menu. The Bistro 20 West has a daily happy hour from 5 to 7 p.m. with $3 house wine and $4.95 crab dip as two of the options.

Modern amenities abound, including a gym (elliptical, free weights, LifeCycle, Stair Master, Nautilus unit, treadmill, and a sauna), in-room fax and e-mail service, free Wi-Fi, and personalized concierge attention. Rooms can range drastically in price depending on the time of year. Self-parking at the Edison garage is $18 (request

voucher) and valet parking is $31 per night. Shuttle service is available to Johns Hopkins.

RENAISSANCE HARBORPLACE BALTIMORE HOTEL $$$$–$$$$$
202 East Pratt St.
(410) 547-1200, (800) HOTELS-1
www.marriott.com
The Renaissance Harborplace Hotel is directly opposite the Pratt Street Pavilion at Harborplace, the World Trade Center, and the National Aquarium. Built in 1988 and renovated in 1996 and 1998, its 586 guest rooms and 34 suites on 12 floors were completely renovated, along with the restaurant and public spaces, in 2007. The hotel says they are the largest rooms of any hotel in the city. Club Level rooms include a continental breakfast and hors d'oeuvres and dessert in the evening. A daily fee covers in-room high-speed Internet access and unlimited local phone calls. An indoor pool is designed for lap swimming (no lane lines and no lifeguard) and family frolicking. At the pool lounge, you can order room service while the children swim and you work on your laptop. There is an adjacent exercise facility. It doesn't take much imagination to conjure a view of swimming indoors while it's snowing outside. There is also the Watertable Restaurant, and a lounge that overlooks the harbor (see the Restaurants chapter). There is a $26 daily self-parking fee and a $36 per day valet parking fee. Call (410) 599-4597 if you have an oversized vehicle. The Deluxe Harbor View guest rooms (numbers 36 through 106) afford a great view of the harbor, particularly for fireworks.

RESIDENCE INN BY MARRIOTT BALTIMORE DOWNTOWN/ INNER HARBOR $$$–$$$$$
17 Light St.
(410) 962-1220
www.marriott.com
Each of the 188 studio and one- and two-bedroom suites has a fully equipped kitchen with refrigerator, microwave, and coffee maker. It's Baltimore's only upscale, all suite extended-stay hotel and is just one block from a Metro station with

direct access to Johns Hopkins University. Pets are allowed with a $100 non-refundable sanitation fee. Contact the hotel directly when you're planning to take your pet. Guests receive a complimentary buffet breakfast, coffee in the lobby, and an evening manager's reception. The on-site fitness center, open 24 hours, has cardio equipment and free weights. The hotel has the "new bed" that's supposed to be fluffier and nicer and friendlier than other beds, except maybe yours at home. The on-site restaurant, 17 Light Restaurant and Lounge, is open for lunch, dinner, and room service. Valet parking is $29 a day (garage clearance is 6 feet).

SHERATON BALTIMORE
CITY CENTER $$–$$$
101 West Fayette St.
(410) 752-1100, (800) 325-3535
www.starwoodhotels.com
Two Sheraton hotels, about five blocks apart, offer lodging in Baltimore. This one was a Wyndham and has 706 rooms on 27 floors. It is not on the Inner Harbor but 3 blocks north and 2 blocks west of it. It's situated directly across Liberty Street from the Baltimore Arena. A subway stop is just beyond the cab stand, and the hotel is only a few blocks east of the Light Rail. The Sheraton offers singles, doubles, triples, quads, junior suites, and suites. There's an exercise room on-site. The hotel includes two award-winning steak houses, Shula's Steak House and Shula's Steak 2. Weekday self-parking is $24 and valet is $34; weekends $19 and $29. When booking a king room, ask for higher floors with rooms ending in 2, 7, 10, and 15. They are the corner rooms with a great view. Similarly, double rooms ending in 21, 26, 29, and 34 are corners with a view.

SHERATON INNER HARBOR HOTEL $$$$
300 South Charles St.
(410) 962-8300, (866) 226-9330
www.starwoodhotels.com
The Sheraton Inner Harbor, the Orioles official hotel, has 337 rooms of which 20 are suites. It is,

essentially, across the street from Camden Yards and celebrates its team connection at the Orioles Grill. When you're coming to town for a baseball game, check with the hotel for their "Take me out to the ballgame" package that includes tickets. A Morton's of Chicago provides serious beef-centric meals. A new gathering place has been established where you can bring your laptop and order something to drink and eat. An indoor pool and health club with sauna are on the third floor to help you maintain your home-away-from-home exercise routine. Parking in the Sheraton garage is $24 for self-parking and $32 for valet per day.

i The Sheraton is very popular whenever fireworks are scheduled over the Harbor because rooms ending in 01 through 08 have great harbor views, particularly from the seventh floor and up. When the economy is going gangbusters, you may have to reserve a room as much as a year in advance. When it isn't, you might even find an opening for New Year's Eve the week or two beforehand. On the other hand, when you want a view of Camden Yards, ask for one of the rooms ending in 27 through 33.

SPRINGHILL SUITES MARRIOTT $$$
120 East Redwood St.
(410) 685-1095, (888) 245-1965
www.marriott.com
When is a bank not a bank? When the building's exterior notes that it's the former Manufacturer's Building and Trust. And, who could deny the stability of this bank by the impression of this edifice? The interior was converted into an all-suite hotel. Each of the 99 suites has a pantry area with a small refrigerator, wet bar, and microwave; free high-speed Internet and local calls (all public areas have wireless access); and complimentary continental breakfast. A 24-hour exercise room has cardiovascular equipment, elliptical machine, and treadmills. Valet parking is $28.

i A secret cool aspect of the Springhill Suites Marriott is the bank vault room downstairs that can hold 10 or so people for a board meeting, and you don't even have to be a guest at the hotel. You don't even have to have a board meeting. One enterprising CPA proposed marriage to his girlfriend amid roses and other romantic touches in this room.

TREMONT PLAZA HOTEL
222 St. Paul Place
(410) 244-7300
www.tremontssuitehotels.com
Referred to collectively as The Tremonts, the Tremont Plaza, the Tremont Grand (225 North Charles St.) and the Tremont Park Hotel (8 East Pleasant St.) offer mini-suites and larger accommodations. An outdoor splash pool is adjacent to the 24-hour health club and a lifeguard is on duty daily from noon to 8 p.m. from about Memorial Day through Labor Day, weather permitting. A shuttle is available to take you where you're going within a 2-mile radius. Various dining options are available and it seems that something is always being promoted here, whether it's a complimentary wine and cheese tasting or half-price menu items on Mondays in May.

Kevin Scheuing is the Tremont's pastry chef and he's responsible for all the desserts and breads made daily and served at Tug's Bar & Grille, Grand Café (443-573-8423), and Plaza Deli (443-528-8800). Considered one of the best (or the best) place for live local jazz while you dine, Tug's Bar & Grille has a $12 food or drink minimum per person; Friday from 7 to 10 p.m. and Saturday from 9 p.m. to midnight.

Also on Friday and Saturday evenings you can hear smooth live jazz at the Celebrities Lounge of the Tremont Park Hotel. Performances run from 6 to 9 p.m. on Friday and 7 to 10 p.m. on Saturday. Admission is free and they have door prizes and drink specials. They promise "Great music, great food, great fun in an intimate setting."

Outside of Downtown

BEST WESTERN HOTEL &
CONFERENCE CENTER　　　　$$–$$$
5625 O'Donnell St. and I-95
(410) 633-9500, (800) 633-9511
www.bestwestern.com/Baltimore
When travelers were looking for a place with easy I-95 access, this travel plaza was a great choice. Then, a couple of years ago Toby Orenstein opened a satellite station of her famed Toby's Dinner Theatre out here (www.tobysdinner theatre.com). What a concept! Tour group operators love it because the driver takes the group to the hotel, they check in, they eat, they enjoy the evening's entertainment, and the bus doesn't move one bit. The convenience is great, but the secret also lies with Toby and her energy and talent. Another joy to staying here is an indoor pool, a free local shuttle, and a Greyhound bus station on the premises.

BURKSHIRE MARRIOTT GUEST SUITES &
CONFERENCE CENTER　　　　$$
10 West Burke Ave., Towson
(410) 324-8100, (800) 435-5986
www.marriott.com
Situated on the campus of Towson University, the Burkshire Marriott's 137 guest apartments were built as retirement condominiums. They're great for a family visit, particularly if you have a student who is visiting Towson. In 2009, they completed renovations on 85 units with new carpeting, kitchens, bathrooms, and high-tech amenities, so you should request one of them. Should you not care to mess up their kitchen, local restaurants will deliver. Each apartment comes with its own washer and dryer. There are one-, two-, and three-bedroom units available. There is an on-site fitness room, but all guests of the Burkshire Marriott have access at no additional charge to the sports facilities at Towson University, which includes racquetball, tennis, and wallyball courts. Long-term parking is hard to find in Towson, so the hotel's free underground parking lot is an added bonus. Discounts off already low prices are available for people who have business with the university.

CHASE SUITE HOTEL BY WOODFIN   **$$$**
10710 Beaver Dam Rd., Hunt Valley
(410) 584-7370, (800) 433-6141
www.chasehotelhuntvalley.com
The Chase Suite Hotel has one- and two-bedroom suites and single and double studios. Each room comes with a full kitchen. Although this property is technically outside the scope of *Insiders Guide to Baltimore*, it is convenient to the Light Rail and Maryland State Fairgrounds. The Chase Suite Hotel allows pets for an additional $10 charge per night. A complimentary hot breakfast buffet is served daily and a complimentary manager's social is held Monday through Thursday night from 5:30 to 7 p.m. An outdoor pool is open seasonally. A scheduled shuttle service is available for destinations within a 5-mile radius.

COMFORT INN BALTIMORE EAST   **$**
8801 Loch Raven Blvd., Towson
(410) 882-0900, (800) 4CHOICE
www.choicehotels.com
This five-story, 185-room hotel offers free parking, an on-site restaurant and lounge, complimentary breakfast, and free HBO. They apply a $1.50 per night (plus tax) charge for the in-room safe. About 20 minutes from downtown Baltimore and minutes from Towson Town Center, the hotel is close to shopping, movies, golf, and bowling. Also within a short distance are Towson University, Morgan State University, Goucher College, Loyola College, the College of Notre Dame, and the Johns Hopkins University.

HILTON PIKESVILLE   **$$-$$$$$**
1726 Reisterstown Rd., Pikesville
(410) 653-1100, (800) 774-1500
www.pikesville.hilton.com
The Hilton Pikesville has never been your ordinary Hilton. It opened in 1975 almost before anything else had moved out to that the Pikesville area. When the old Painters Mill Music Fair was the suburban stage for such entertainers at Victor Borge and Liberace, chances were good that they stayed at this Hilton. Fast forward to today, years after Painters Mill burned to the ground, and

new interstate roads and rapid transit have been constructed, and the Hilton is still the beacon on the top of the hill that it always was. More than 80 percent of the hotel has enjoyed a total renovation including all 169 guest rooms and a new lobby design.

The Baltimore Health & Tennis facility attached to the hotel has a full selection of exercise equipment, free weights, aerobic machines, and, oh, yes, six indoor tennis courts. The facility is free although there is a charge and reservation request for the tennis courts.

The FountainSide restaurant and lounge has been refreshed and serves American cuisine. Pets, up to 75 pounds, are allowed with a $75 non-refundable fee. An outdoor pool is open seasonally and is frequently the venue for events. To the best of her knowledge, Linda Glinos (sales department) says that they have never had a wedding at the pool or the tennis courts.

INN AND SPA AT THE COLONNADE   **$$-$$$**
A Doubletree Hotel
4 West University Parkway
(410) 235-5400
www.colonnadebaltimore.com
The Colonnade is a high-rise condominium building, across from the playing fields of the Johns Hopkins University's Homewood Campus, on the southern edge of the community known as Tuscany-Canterbury. The Doubletree takes up the first three floors of the building, with 125 rooms and suites on the second and third floors. Rates are based on availability. Valet parking is $24 with unlimited in-and-out privileges; self-parking is based on an overnight rate of $20 plus hourly rate (you do not have free unlimited in-and-out privileges). Your pet is welcomed and is provided with a Doubletree Sweet Dream Dog Bedding and a gourmet pet cookie upon arrival. There is a $50 service fee and a $100 refundable deposit. An indoor pool is available. Contemporary French and Asian cuisine is available at Alizee, under the stewardship of executive chef Christian deLutis, whose credits include a stint at the Harbor Court Hotel, Corks, and the Wine Market.

NORTHWEST BALTIMORE DAYS INN
WEST—SECURITY BOULEVARD $-$$$
1660 Whitehead Court
(410) 944-7400, (800) DAYS-INN
www.the.daysinn.com
Built in 1958 the hotel and its 100 rooms were totally renovated in 2009 and celebrated with a grand re-opening on November 2, 2009. Right in the thick of west Baltimore's suburban business centers, the hotel is near the Social Security Administration headquarters, shopping, fitness centers, and tennis courts. The two-story building has exterior hallways, an outdoor seasonal pool (with lifeguard and you must provide a pass from the front desk), restaurant, and lounge on-site. Parking is free. Pets are welcomed with a $15 fee.

QUALITY INN HARBOR SOUTH $$
1401 Bloomfield Ave.
(410) 646-1700
www.qualityinn.com
This Quality Inn is located inside the Beltway, off South Caton Avenue, a stone's throw from the I-95 and I-695 interchange, or about equidistant from BWI Marshall and downtown Baltimore. It has exterior corridors, an exercise room, and an outdoor pool that's open seasonally. The hotel offers a stay and fly program for passengers going to BWI Marshall. The rate ($69 as of this writing) is modest as is the $5 per day rate to leave your car. However, they don't offer a shuttle service to the airport, so you have to add the price of a taxi or shuttle to and from BWI Marshall.

With two Quality Inn hotels (this one and the Harbor South near the Beltway) within a few miles of each other, make sure you know which one has your reservation.

RADISSON HOTEL AT CROSS KEYS $$-$$$
Village of Cross Keys
100 Village Square
(410) 532-6900, (800) 333-3333
www.radisson.com
You'll hear people refer to the hotel as the Inn at Cross Keys, the Cross Keys Inn, and the Radisson. It's all the same.

The Radisson is located in the Village of Cross Keys, within the bounds of one of the oldest developed neighborhoods in Baltimore, Roland Park. The inn has 147 rooms and junior suites on four floors. Screened windows allow you to open your room windows. On the fourth floor, rooms have a cathedral ceiling and you'll find birdhouses, weathered benches, and Eddie BauerTM furnishings. It sits at the west end of the community shopping center, which boasts some of the more exclusive shops in the area. The inn serves mainly business travelers and neighborhood guests. A complimentary scheduled shuttle service is offered to the Inner Harbor area and nearby medical facilities. When you want a balcony room, request even room numbers between 302 and 326. Even people who have never thought of jogging or walking fast enough to break a sweat can enjoy the countryside. Ask the front desk for a jogging and walking trails map that leads through the 72 wooded acres

i Yes, the Radisson is the hotel where, on September 21 and 22, 1985, Billy Martin—during his fourth term as manager of the New York Yankees—scuffled with someone at the hotel bar and then had his right arm broken by Yankee pitcher Ed Whitson in a late-night set-to in the same bar.

SHERATON BALTIMORE
NORTH HOTEL $$$-$$$$
903 Dulaney Valley Rd., Towson
(410) 321-7400, (800) 433-7619
www.sheratonbaltimorenorth.com
Right in the heart of the Towson business district and at the edge of the Goucher College campus is the Sheraton Baltimore North with 282 guest rooms. Unlike all other Towson area hotels, this one provides complimentary valet parking and a skywalk connecting you directly to the Towson Town Center. With plenty of walking options (care for a mall walk?) you can still use the heated indoor pool for exercise if you want to stay indoors. Pets are allowed with a security deposit. The Sheraton prices according to

demand, so rates can fall precipitously depending on whether or not it's busy. For quieter rooms (away from the traffic below), request a room that ends in 25 to 31 (toward the end of the hallway).

BWI Marshall Area Hotels

More than two dozen hotels service the BWI Marshall Airport—in the airport hotel zone in and around Linthicum and a little farther away in Hanover near Arundel Mills Mall. They generally provide free shuttle service to and from the airport (and the BWI Amtrak train station and the nearby Light Rail station). The Four Points Sheraton is basically on airport property. They are listed here, alphabetically, regardless of whether they're in Linthicum or Hanover because when there are two or more hotels with the same or similar names from the same brand, it's easy to confuse which one has your reservations. Please, make sure you remember which one has your reservation.

However, several hotels share the shuttle service so the "promised" shuttle may be late or may not arrive because it was filled up at the prior hotels. Every hotel has been checked for its current shuttle policy and that status is included in the listing.

Several hotels offer a stay and fly program where you spend your pre-departure night (and sometimes your return night) at the airport and you may leave your car parked there for the length of your trip at no additional charge. One hotel lets you park your car for less than the airport and private parking lots charge. Otherwise, no hotel in the airport area charges for nightly parking for hotel guests.

When you arrive at BWI Marshall, the hotels request that you pick up your luggage before you call for the shuttle because there is no place on the airport driveway loop for them to stop to wait for you.

ALOFT BALTIMORE–WASHINGTON INTERNATIONAL AIRPORT $$–$$$
1741 West Nursery Rd., Linthicum
(410) 691-6969, (877) GO-ALOFT
www.aloftbwi.com

The Aloft (Starwood) opened in August 2009 with 155 loft-like rooms; a slightly hip, urban attitude; and free Wi-Fi throughout the property. Re:mix is a public space for shooting pool, watching the big game on the four-panel LCD TV screening wall, or just relaxing. The Re:fuel shop is open 24 hours and has grab-and-go savory and healthy foods. A splash indoor pool and re:charge fitness center (including a yoga space) add to your ability to stay and meet here or use as a sightseeing base. Natural cork and sustainable wood veneers were integrated into the hotel's design. Parking is complimentary. The airport shuttle service is shared with another hotel, but it does run 24 hours a day. Pets, up to 40 pounds, are welcomed with a bed, bowl, and a bag of woof-alicious treats and toys.

BEST WESTERN BALTIMORE–WASHINGTON AIRPORT $–$$
6755 Dorsey Rd., Elkridge
(410) 796-3300, (800) WESTERN
www.bestwestern.com

For those who can't break the 24-hour news cycle, the Best Western has a 5" TV with radio in the bathroom where you can receive HBO, CNN, ESPN, Comedy Channel, and more. The indoor swimming pool has window walls so you can watch the weather while you do your laps. When your BWI Marshall flight departs before the sun rises, you can stay here in their Sleep and Fly program that provides free parking for up to 14 days when you stay one, two, or three nights. Free shuttle service to and from the airport and the nearby Light Rail station. The Best Western has its own airport shuttle.

CANDLEWOOD SUITES BALTIMORE–LINTHICUM $$–$$$
1247 Winterson Rd., Linthicum
(410) 850-9214
www.ichotelsgroup.com

Pets are allowed with a $75 non-refundable deposit. An on-site guest self-laundry lets you pack less so you can avoid luggage charges and waiting at the luggage carousel. Each suite has a fully equipped kitchen with full-size refrigerator/

ice maker and a microwave. You can purchase food items at the hotel's on-site convenience store or opt into their room with breakfast package. Candlewood Suites has its own airport shuttle; note, however, that the service does not start until 7 a.m. and ends at 11 p.m.

COMFORT INN–BWI $$–$$$
6921 Baltimore Annapolis Blvd., Linthicum
(410) 789-9100
www.comfortinn.com
Comfort Inn offers comfortable (of course) accommodations near the airport with the Rose restaurant and Rose Pub on the premises. There is a large exercise area, which includes Jacuzzi and sauna, and a video game room. Wireless Internet service is free. Guests are treated to a full buffet breakfast. Up to two pets are allowed with a $50 one-time fee. There's a restaurant on-site. Shuttles take guests to the airport or train station. The Light Rail station is adjacent to the hotel. "Stay and Fly" package ranges from $79 to $99 (at this writing) for one night with free parking for up to 14 nights. The Comfort Inn and the Sleep Inn are on the same lot and share the airport shuttle service.

COUNTRY INN & SUITES BY CARLSON BWI $$$–$$$$
1717 West Nursery Rd., Linthicum Heights
(443) 577-1036
www.countryinns.com
Whether you're spending an extended amount of time near BWI Marshall, the VIP Extended Stay Suites provide separate sleeping and sitting rooms, a six-person dining table, and two bathrooms. One-bedroom and studio suites are also available. For that romantic touch, try the whirlpool suite with a whirlpool tub fit for two, a wet bar area, and mini kitchen. A heated indoor lap pool (limited hours for lifeguard protection) and fitness center let you maintain (or start) your fitness program. When you've finished reading the book you brought along, stop by the hotel's lending library for a new read. The Country Inn has its own airport shuttle service.

COURTYARD BY MARRIOTT BALTIMORE– WASHINGTON AIRPORT $$–$$$$
1671 West Nursery Rd., Linthicum
(410) 859-8855, (800) 321-2211
www.courtyard.com
This Marriott Courtyard is a low-rise building with 137 guest rooms and caters to the business traveler, as many of the airport hotels do. Look for the GoBoard in the lobby that provides an interactive information display so you can access information about driving directions, view local weather, catch up on headline news, and find a local restaurant. The business library has free high-speed Internet access and printing capabilities. You can grab a bite to eat for breakfast and dinner at the Bistro while you check your e-mails in the privacy of a media pod, located in the lobby. Pets are not allowed. An indoor pool is open from 10 a.m. to 10 p.m. on weekends and 5 to10 p.m. on weekdays, with a lifeguard on duty during pool hours. The shuttle service for this Courtyard by Marriott is shared with the four other Marriott airport properties. The van is supposed to seat up to 20 people. It starts at 5 a.m. and runs every 15 minutes, and stops at midnight.

EMBASSY SUITES HOTEL BALTIMORE AT BWI AIRPORT $$$$–$$$$$
1300 Concourse Dr., Linthicum
(410) 850-0747, (800) 362-2779
www.baltimorebwiairport.embassysuites.com
The Embassy Suites information says each of its 251 suites "oozes comfort and relaxation" as each overlooks the multi-level garden atrium. The hotel provides a complimentary cooked-to-order breakfast, complimentary manager's reception, and a Precor fitness center (with a window wall) that's available 24 hours a day. The in-house International Pier Lounge, open late afternoon and evening, and Chophouse 13, open for lunch and dinner, provide other food and beverage options. Each suite has a full-size refrigerator, microwave oven, and coffeemaker. The presidential suite includes two full baths and a jetted bathroom tub that should easily let those aches and pains ooze from your body. An on-site laundry room has washers, dryers, and supplies. The Embassy Suites has its own shuttle that operates 24 hours a day.

FOUR POINTS BY SHERATON BWI AIRPORT $$–$$$$
7032 Elm Rd., Linthicum
(410) 859-3300
www.fourpoints.com

The Four Points Sheraton at BWI Marshall offers 201 rooms, each with the Four Points by Sheraton Four Comfort Bed and a 32" flat screen TV, and is on the grounds of the airport. Other than convenience (you could walk to the airport if you really had to), amenities include an outdoor pool, exercise room, and jogging area. Michener's, a full-service restaurant known for its jumbo lump crab cake and filet mignon, is on-site; and room service is available 24 hours, which is good in case your flight is super late. Connecting rooms are available, but not guaranteed. Call the hotel directly if you want this convenience. Pets up to 60 pounds are allowed with a $25 non-refundable rate per pet per night and only a limited number of rooms are available. Call the hotel directly if you are bringing a pet. On-site parking is free. The Four Points has its own shuttle. Smoking is not permitted in public spaces or guest rooms and a $200 cleaning fee will be charged to any guest who violates this policy.

HAMPTON INN BALTIMORE/WASHINGTON INTERNATIONAL AIRPORT $$$–$$$$$
829 Elkridge Landing Rd., Linthicum
(410) 850-0600
www.hamptoninnbwiairport.com

The Hampton Inn has Cloud Nine bedding by Hampton that has a covered duvet (in other words, no potentially seriously yucky bedspread because the duvet cover is laundered), a choice of foam or down pillows, a lumbar pillow for when you want to read or watch TV, and a lap desk. Your room rate includes a complimentary continental breakfast buffet, free local phone calls, and free parking. Weekday valet laundry service is available. The Hampton Inn has its own shuttle.

HILTON GARDEN INN—BWI $$–$$$$
7491-A New Ridge Rd., Hanover
(410) 878-7200
www.hiltongardeninn.hilton.com

HOMEWOOD SUITES BY HILTON $$–$$$$
7491-B New Ridge Rd., Hanover
(410) 878-7201
www.hiltongardeninn.hilton.com

The Hilton Garden Inn and the Homewood Suites by Hilton are an interesting concept where two Hilton properties share the same building and footprint. Enter on one side for Hilton Garden Inn rooms that occupy floors 3 through 6. Enter from the other side for the Homewood Suites with rooms on floors 7 through 11. No, you don't really have to drive to the specific entrance—they are connected on the ground floor. The hotel shuttle will take you to Arundel Mills Mall where you can join the morning walk when the weather is too inclement to walk outdoors. An indoor swimming pool and fitness center are available. Each room has a 32" HD LCD TV and complimentary high-speed wireless Internet access. The Homewood Suites operation is geared toward the traveler who plans to stay five or more nights, and each of the 99 suites has a fully equipped kitchen with full-size refrigerator, microwave, dishwasher, and dining table (aka workspace). At the Garden Inn you can partake of the breakfast buffet for $9.95; the Homewood Suites price includes your breakfast. The two properties in one building share the shuttle to the airport.

HILTON GARDEN INN BWI AIRPORT $$$–$$$$
1516 Aero Dr., Linthicum
(410) 691-0500
www.hiltongardeninn.hilton.com

This Hilton Garden Inn has 158 rooms with the Hilton Garden Sleep System, Herman Miller ergonomic chairs, refrigerators, and microwaves. The complimentary business center is available 24 hours a day. Breakfast and dinner can be had at the Great American Grill, and the Lobby Bar is open for beverages. An indoor pool and Precor fitness center help you keep your exercise routine. The hotel has joined the EarthPact program toward environmentally responsible lodging. The Garden Inn shuttle services just the Garden Inn.

HOLIDAY INN EXPRESS—BWI $$-$$$
7481 Ridge Rd., Hanover
(410) 684-3388, (888) 465-4329
www.hiexpress.com

Head to bed with the HI Express Simply Smart bedding and bath initiative and awaken to the complimentary Express Start Breakfast Bar with their signature cinnamon rolls. The hotel fitness center is open 24 hours for guests only. An outdoor pool is open seasonally. An on-site self-laundry is available. The 159 guest rooms, with interior corridors, were renovated in 2008. Holiday Inn Express shuttle provides rides 24 hours to the airport, MARC Commuter train, Light Rail, Amtrak station, and local attractions within 5 miles. Pets (other than service animals) are not permitted. The hotel has a list of nearby kennels.

MARRIOTT BWI AIRPORT $$-$$$
1743 West Nursery Rd., Linthicum
(410) 859-8300, (800) 228-9290
www.marriott.com

This high-rise hotel has 302 rooms and 7 suites and, are you ready for this, the First Ultra Adaptable Room. Among other things, the adaptability lets you plug in your pluggables, regardless of how they connect or talk to each other, watch two things on the split screen on the 37" LCD HDTV (your laptop work and the news—the imagination is unlimited at this point). You can recharge things, and, well, why bother traveling? Monikers Grille, with a continental menu, is open for breakfast, lunch, and dinner. Champions Sports Bar and Restaurant is open for lunch and dinner. For $12.95 a day, you receive high-speed Internet access and unlimited local and within-the-country long distance calls. The shuttle holds up to 20 people (with luggage) and is shared with the Marriott Courtyard. Service starts at 4 a.m.

MARRIOTT RESIDENCE INN $$$-$$$$
1160 Winterson Rd., Linthicum
(410) 691-0255, (800) 331-3131
www.marriott.com

The 120 one- and two-bedroom suites at the three-story Marriott Residence Inn are designed for comfort over the long term. Each suite features a fully equipped kitchen. A complimentary continental breakfast is served each morning; and regular (not necessarily every evening) socials feature a complimentary light dinner, which might be anything from a sandwich to the weekly guest barbecue. An outdoor pool is open seasonally. Relocation and temporary housing discounts are available. Pets are allowed for a $75 non-refundable sanitation fee. Contact the hotel directly for details. The Residence Inn shuttle is shared by two other Marriott properties; however, they do have two shuttles.

RAMADA $-$$$$$
7253 Parkway Dr., Hanover
(410) 712-4300
www.bwiramada.com

Early to bed, etc., means Ramada guests can enjoy a free continental breakfast from as early as 4 a.m. Executive guest rooms have a microwave and a refrigerator. Each room has a 27" cable TV. An outdoor pool is available seasonally. An on-site restaurant and lounge, Parkstone Grille, is open Monday through Saturday, with after-dinner entertainment (open-mic, karaoke, DJ) on select evenings. Park, Stay and Fly programs allow up to 14 days parking with one night stay and $5 per night parking for more than that. A fee is applied to extra BWI shuttle trips. The Ramada shuttle serves only their hotel and operates 24 hours.

RED ROOF INN WASHINGTON, DC-BWI AIRPORT $$-$$$
827 Elkridge Landing Rd.
(410) 850-7600
http://redroof.com

The inn offers complimentary shuttle service to and from BWI Marshall Airport, the Amtrak Station, and the Light Rail station daily. One "well-behaved family pet per room" is welcomed. A daily fee applies for Internet access via TV. Children under 17 stay free when staying with an adult family member. The Red Roof Inn has its own shuttle.

RESIDENCE INN ARUNDEL MILLS
BWI AIRPORT   **$$$$–$$$$$**
7035 Arundel Mills Circle
(410) 799-7332
www.marriott.com
No need for a shuttle to the Arundel Mills Mall, unless perhaps it's to help you schlep all your purchases back to your room. Within the hotel, there's an outdoor pool open seasonally, a multi-purpose SportCourt, and a billiard room and library. A complimentary hot breakfast buffet is served daily and frequent evening social events are scheduled. Each of the 131 suites has a fully equipped kitchen with refrigerator, stove, microwave, and coffeemaker. Choose from a studio, one- or two-bedroom suite. Some have a fireplace. Pets are allowed with a $100 non-refundable sanitation fee. Contact the hotel directly for details. Two shuttles run 24 hours a day for four hotels and will take you wherever you need to go within a 5-mile radius.

SHERATON BALTIMORE WASHINGTON
AIRPORT HOTEL   **$$$–$$$$**
1100 Old Elkridge Landing Rd., Linthicum
(443) 577-2100
www.starwoodhotels.com
The Sheraton boasts that it uses soundproof glass and they're outside the BWI Marshall Airport flight path so life is serene within their walls and in their 203 guest rooms and suites. Each room has the plush Sheraton SweetSleeper bed and duvet. An indoor pool invites you to swim or relax, and the Olde Line Grill and Lounge is available on property. The Club Lounge, accessible to Sheraton Club guests, has complimentary breakfast, evening hors d'oeuvres, and a variety of beverages. Pets, up to 40 pounds, are allowed with a daily fee of $25 per pet. Dogs are not permitted in the food and beverage areas. The Sheraton has two airport shuttles. One is dedicated to Sheraton guests and the other is shared with the Westin.

SLEEP INN & SUITES AIRPORT   **$–$$**
6055 Belle Grove Rd., Linthicum
(410) 789-7223
www.sleepinn.com

Next to the hotel is The Rose Restaurant and Pub with live music on Friday and Saturday nights. Guests in the 145 rooms receive a hot breakfast daily and have use of a 24-hour business center and a large fitness center. The Stay and Fly package allows for 14 nights of free parking and airport transportation after spending a night at the hotel. Pets are accommodated with a $50 one-time fee per room with a maximum of two pets per room. The Sleep Inn and the Comfort Inn are on the same lot and share the airport shuttle service.

SPRINGHILL SUITES BALTIMORE
BWI AIRPORT   **$$$$**
899 Elkridge Landing Rd., Linthicum
(410) 694-0555
www.marriott.com
The SpringHill Suites is set up for long-term guests and also welcomes short-term and families with packages that include shopping, museums, and zoos. They claim their 133 suites/rooms are 25 percent more spacious than traditional hotel rooms, with separate eating, working, and sleeping areas. There is an on-site, coin-operated laundry and valet dry cleaning. They offer an indoor pool (open Monday through Friday from 5 to 10 p.m. and on weekends from 10 a.m. to 10 p.m.) and a state-of-the-art exercise room. A free breakfast buffet is available for guests. Pets are not allowed. The SpringHill Suites shuttle runs 24 hours and is just for this hotel.

STAYBRIDGE SUITES BWI
AIRPORT   **$$–$$$$**
1301 Winterson Rd., Linthicum
(410) 850-5666, (877) 238-8889
www.staybridge.com
Staying at the Staybridge includes a complimentary breakfast buffet. You can take advantage of their on-site guest self-laundry, full kitchen, and the on-site health/fitness center. You can end the day with a cocktail at the Sundowner Managers' reception. Pets, up to 80 pounds, are allowed with a fee of $75 for up to six nights and up to $150 for up to 14 nights. You must have a record of current vaccinations and sign the pet

agreement upon registration. An outdoor pool is open seasonally. The Staybridge airport shuttle operates 24 hours and is used only for the Staybridge. Because the hotel is pretty close to the Baltimore-Washington Parkway, you might want to ask for the odd numbered rooms that are on the back side of the building.

TOWNEPLACE SUITES $$–$$$
1171 Winterson Rd., Linthicum
(410) 694-0060
www.marriott.com
Each of the 136 studio, one- and two-bedroom suites has a 32" LCD flat-panel HDTV, a kitchen, signature Home Office, and includes a complimentary breakfast and a nightly reception. There is a 24-hour fitness center and on-site market. Pets are welcome with a $100 non-refundable sanitation fee. There is a barbecue/picnic area outdoors. Two shuttles provide service for the TownePlace suites and three other Marriott hotels, with departures from this property set for 15 and 45 minutes after the hour, from 4:45 a.m. (first hotel departure) to 11:45 p.m. (last airport departure).

TOWNEPLACE SUITES ARUNDEL
MILLS BWI AIRPORT $$$–$$$$
7021 Arundel Mills Circle, Hanover
(410) 379-9000
www.marriott.com
Each suite in the Arundel Mills TownePlace Suites has an in-room safe, fully equipped kitchen with microwave and refrigerator, 32" flat-panel TV, and separate living and sleeping area. A heated outdoor pool is available seasonally. A 24-hour exercise room and food market are available. The complimentary shuttle runs 24 hours and serves two hotels in addition to the TownePlace. Pets are welcomed with a $100 non-refundable service fee.

WESTIN BALTIMORE WASHINGTON
AIRPORT $$$$–$$$$$
1110 Old Elkridge Landing Rd.
(443) 577-2300
www.starwoodhotels.com

The Westin opened in late 2007 with 260 rooms that feature the Westin Heavenly Bed, Heavenly Bath, and a flat-screen TV (all of which Westin assumes are essential to your comfortable stay). The WestinWORKOUT Gym, with cardio and free weight equipment, and a glass-enclosed lap pool are available to maintain your daily regimen. Luminous, a Pan-Asian restaurant with an indoor bar and an outdoor lounge, is on property. Pets, up to 40 pounds, are allowed with a $25 pet fee per room, per night. Shoeshine and dry cleaning services are available. The Westin has its own shuttle and shares a shuttle with the Sheraton.

WINGATE BY WYNDHAM $$$$
1510 Aero Dr., Linthicum Heights
(410) 859-0003
www.wingatehotels.com
Each of the 129 guest rooms has free local calls, high-speed and wireless Internet access, and Neutrogena bathroom amenities. Guests are invited to enjoy the complimentary hot breakfast buffet, including make-your-own waffles. The business center is available 24 hours, and the indoor lap pool is heated. No pets allowed. The airport shuttle, which services just the Wingate, runs every 30 minutes (on the hour and half-hour) from the hotel and on demand from the airport.

WESTERN BALTIMORE TURF VALLEY RESORT
& CONFERENCE CENTER $$$–$$$$$
2700 Turf Valley Rd., Ellicott City
(410) 465-1500, (888) 833-8873
www.turfvalley.com
Turf Valley may be the only "resort" in the Baltimore area. It's about 30 miles from downtown and has two 18-hole golf courses, Har-Tru tennis courts, fitness center, spa, two restaurants, a lounge, indoor and outdoor pools, 171 hotel rooms and suites, 40,000 square feet of meeting space, and a bunch of one-, two-, and three-bedroom villas for extended visits. Turf Valley offers a wide range of special events from a night of entertainment by the Fabulous Hubcaps to hot air balloons to a bridal extravaganza for those contemplating a wedding.

BED-AND-BREAKFASTS

The owners and operators of the bed-and-breakfast establishments listed here are part of their communities; therefore, they can provide insights into where to eat, what to do, how to get around—things that might not be available to you in any other way. If you really seriously want a quiet getaway, talk with the owner to see how close the bed-and-breakfast is to Saturday night revelers or if the room with the balcony overlooks a secluded garden where even the sunrise barely makes a noise. Just as with the rest of Baltimore, you just might find a surprise or two. You'll definitely feel the passion.

Price Code

Prices can range from $125 to more than $175, depending on whether it's a weekday or weekend, the size of the room, the location, and the time of the year.

A safe average would be about $150 a night, which includes a full breakfast in the morning. Most rooms are not open to children or pets. Because many bed-and-breakfasts are often in older buildings, they usually offer poor wheelchair accessibility. Don't even think about smoking.

The price codes shown reflect the weekend rates. Rates do not include city and state taxes, which usually add about 15 percent to the bill.

$.................... $125 or less
$$ .... $126 to $175
$$$ .... $176 and more

Just as with hotels, these places enjoy the influx of guests on special days, during the baseball or football season, the boat show, etc. The earlier you book, usually, the better.

A sizable portion of the bed-and-breakfast trade in the Baltimore area is geared toward businesspeople who visit the area, often with a spouse or other family members. A number of people staying at bed-and-breakfasts are friends or relatives of people living nearby. There's always the appeal to area residents who just want to get away and not be too far away.

ANN STREET B&B $
804 South Ann St.
(410) 342-5883

In 1988 Baltimore's innkeeping veterans, Joanne and Andrew Mazurek, opened Ann Street B&B in the house where Andrew had grown up. Restored to an earlier era when Andrew's ancestors lived there, the inn features double poster beds, original hardwood floors, and a country colonial charm. Each room has a private bathroom and two have a fireplace. The inn also features central air-conditioning. Twelve fireplaces help to keep the place warm in the winter as guests talk, snack, visit, and read. Another favorite feature of the house is the private garden, which from spring to fall is the ideal location to relax, away from the hustle and bustle of modern life.

Located in the heart of Fell's Point, there's no limit to the dining, dancing, and imbibing possibilities near the inn. The Mazureks are active participants in the Fell's Point business community, offering guests insights into special-interest restaurants and stores in the area. According to Joanne Mazurek, their goal is to provide guests "not a real formal place to relax for a while."

CELIE'S WATERFRONT INN
BED AND BREAKFAST $$–$$$
1714 Thames St.
(410) 522-2323, (800) 432-0184
www.baltimore-bed-breakfast.com

In the heart of the Fell's Point waterfront, Celie's Waterfront Inn Bed and Breakfast features open rooms, many with skylights, and lots of modern conveniences for a bed-and-breakfast. All seven rooms offer a private bath, air-conditioning, and a choice of king-, queen-, or single-size beds. Rooms vary in their offerings, some with fireplaces, whirlpool tub, private balcony, and harbor views. Everyone can spy the city skyline from the rooftop deck and visit the private gardens maintained by innkeepers Kevin and Nancy Kupec. The Courtyard Room is wheelchair accessible and has its own courtyard.

Guests will find many antiques and collectibles, fresh-cut flowers, down comforters, flannel sheets, thick terry robes, and bath sheets in all of the rooms. They'll also find a TV; refrigerator; stocked with soft drinks, juices, and mineral water; and even VCR and coffeemaker are available. The most popular rooms are the Harbor Front rooms, where guests can have a king-size bed, wood-burning fireplace, wicker seating, a whirlpool tub, and three windows facing the harbor.

Although it's not close to the university, Celie's offers discounts to Johns Hopkins Hospital patients and "family members" during weekdays. Children older than age 10 are welcome; and smoking is prohibited. Private telephone lines are in all rooms, and breakfast is a combination of fresh fruits, juices, baked breads, and cereals. Celie's is a Maryland Bed and Breakfast Association member.

1870 GUEST HOUSE   **$**
21 South Stricker St.
(410) 947-4622
www.bbonline.com
Located in a restored Italianate-style row home in Union Square, the 1870 Guest House offers accommodations complete with a fully equipped private kitchen and bath. Set in Southwest Baltimore, sometimes referred to as SoWeBo, the house faces the 1.3-acre Union Square Park that was established in 1847. The 1870 Guest House is a close walk to the B&O Railroad Museum, H. L. Mencken House Museum, and Hollins Market, which was built in 1836 and is Baltimore's oldest market still in use. The third-floor suite features a queen-size bed, bath with tub and shower, AC, TV/VCR, and private phone. The kitchen is stocked with a substantial breakfast and guests may serve themselves at their leisure. Owners Frank and Dana Trovato suggest you ask them about "behind home plate" Orioles tickets.

GRAMERCY MANSION
BED & BREAKFAST   **$$$**
1400 Greenspring Valley Rd., Stevenson
(410) 486-2405, (800) 553-3404
www.gramercymansion.com.

Nestled in the middle of the Green Spring Valley, just 20 minutes from downtown Baltimore and the Inner Harbor, the Gramercy Mansion Bed & Breakfast is a step back in time. The Tudor style mansion and estate, which dates from 1902, is set on 45 acres of bucolic countryside. Tim Kline, Gramercy manager/owner, and co-owner Anne Pomykala restored the mansion and its surrounding gardens.

This bed-and-breakfast and conference center has 11 stylish rooms, including two suites. The Cassatt Suite, a European Renaissance Retreat on the private lower level, features a garden terrace, king bed, sitting room with fireplace, and lavish bath with double whirlpool tub, separate two-person shower, and double vanity sinks. The Camelot Room is fit for royalty, featuring a Juliet balcony (you have to supply your own Romeo) with garden views, king bed, double whirlpool bath, and separate shower. Visit and you may discover you prefer the Blue Garden Suite, the Tower Room, or one of the other accommodations that can fill your life with romantic memories.

You may also take advantage of the Olympic-size pool and tennis court, stroll along a woodland trail, through the orchard, flower or herb gardens, or visit the organic farm.

INN AT 2920   **$$$**
2920 Elliott St., Canton
(410) 342-4450, (877) 774-2920
www.theinnat2920.com
If you prefer contemporary and chic in your bed-and-breakfast, then book your reservation at the Inn at 2920. Even the Web site is a pleasure to view. This five-unit home is a Canton row house and is decorated with works by local artists. Fans and open windows cool the rooms, although there is central air for those soggy Baltimore summer days. The usual amenities are available, including wireless Internet and rain showers, though phones are not available. Queen-size bed is in four of the rooms, though the "Bordello" room (the upstairs was a brothel for some time) has a king-size bed. Owners Warren Munroe and David Rohrbaugh are the dedicated hosts, and they promise "each and every guest a com-

plete bed-and-breakfast experience with superior accommodations and amenities, friendly service, and lasting memories."

SCARBOROUGH FAIR $$$
1 East Montgomery St., Federal Hill
(410) 837-0010, (877) 954-2747
www.scarboroughfairbandb.com
Barry Werner and Jeff Finlay run the Federal Hill bed-and-breakfast, which Ashley and Ellen Scarborough opened in 1997. It remains, as the Scarboroughs imagined it, a place where people from diverse backgrounds can gather to share everything from food to conversation to tips on the area they are visiting. This house, built in 1801, was a rehabilitated office building in the 1980s and now has become a six-bedroom guesthouse, about 2 blocks from the Inner Harbor. The previous owners put six months of work into converting the office building into a guesthouse, and their time was well spent. Each room has a different color scheme, Colonial- and Victorian-era antiques, and queen-size bed, with the exception of one room that offers two twin-size beds that convert into a king-size one. Each room has a private bath. Four rooms have a gas fireplace. A full breakfast is served in a 12-seat dining room. A greeting room and library, featuring a variety of books, is available to travelers.

When you're visiting Baltimore "just because" and are wondering what to do, let their Exploration Consultant create an itinerary for you.

THE WAYSIDE INN $$$
4344 Columbia Rd., Ellicott City
(410) 461-4636
www.waysideinnmd.com
Susan and David Balderson run the Wayside Inn the way your best imagination could conjure a warm, well-run bed-and-breakfast. The Luxury Pierpont Suite is touted as the newest room with yards of silk fabrics and hand-quilted bedding on a bed so high that you need a step to get up on it. Enjoy the in-room wood-burning fireplace (in season) and a wall-mounted plasma TV (you can ignore that if you wish). A romantic package includes dinner at Ellicott City's finest

restaurant, Tersiguel's French Country (do try the sweetbreads).

To recall the mid-1850s, the owners have maintained stately trees, flower gardens, and a small pond, giving the two-acre site a distinctly rural feel despite its closeness to urban life. One tradition of old inns that the Baldersons maintain is the keeping of lighted candles in each window to signal the availability of rooms and the welcoming spirit of its owners.

For antiques lovers, historic mill enthusiasts, and people looking for a place out of the mainstream, the Wayside Inn is a good bet.

i Baltimore's bed-and-breakfasts are busiest in May. The Preakness Stakes, the second leg of horse racing's Triple Crown, is the third Saturday of the month, and numerous college graduation ceremonies draw relatives and friends from near and far throughout the month. Reservations are hard to come by through September without advance planning.

THE WILDERNESS BED & BREAKFAST $$
2 Thistle Rd., Catonsville
(410) 744-0590
www.thewilderness.biz
Tucked at the edge of Patapsco State Park, The Wilderness seems like it's, well, nowhere. But it is, in fact, just a half-hour drive to downtown Baltimore or Columbia, and about five minutes to historic Ellicott City. Its Victorian charms and leafy three-acre setting make you feel a part of some place quiet and relaxing. The aroma of something sweet wafting in from the kitchen welcomes guests right away. A mix of comfortable furnishings and eye-catching antiques fill the sitting room, dining room, and three suites. Each suite has a separate sitting room and modern bath. If the outdoors beckons, there's a wide front porch, a screened porch in back, and a patio in the yard. Two resident cats keep an eye on guests.

RESTAURANTS

Known primarily for our shellfish — particularly crabs, oysters, and shrimp—Baltimore's culinary scene offers just about any cuisine you want. The scene includes innovative and traditional restaurants that offer five-star service and epicurean menus. On the other hand, we have some of the best casual, down-home food around.

Some restaurants still serve endangered species fish meals. If it's important to you, then ask about your particular aversion when you make your reservation.

To keep up with the Baltimore food scene, subscribe to the Downtown Partnership Baltimore e-mails and visit www.DineDowntownBaltimore.com for special menus, food-related events, and specials. Sometimes you might learn that Yankees umpires dine in Little Italy or Harbor East.

Baltimore has a winter and a summer restaurant week when 90 or more restaurants offer prix fixe lunches or dinners. This is a great time to try that restaurant that's always been tempting, but just not tempting enough. They really want to have fun and rename the days of the week to help you with Yumday, Chewsday, Winesday, Thirstday, Fryday, Platterday, and Dim Sumday, offering a "different kind of delicious daily."

In 2009 the three-course dinners were $30.09 per person, plus taxes, gratuities, and liquor. The winter week is toward the end of January and the summer week is in late August. You should reserve early because these programs are popular. Don't moan if you are late calling, though, because many of the restaurants have extended the week into two weeks because of the popularity.

If you mingle with the locals enough, you're sure to participate in the "best crab cake" discussion. Just after that comes the debate about who makes the best crab soup. I'm partial to cream of crab or she-crab soup. Others prefer vegetable and tomato-base (what do they know?). The 4th Annual Summer restaurant week in August 2009 kicked off with a Crab Soup Stakes. Set at the Harborplace Amphitheater, people were invited to sample soups from 10 of Baltimore's best restaurants and then vote for a favorite. Top honors went to Alizee on 4 West University Parkway for best Maryland crab soup and *Brightons* in the Intercontinental Harbor Court Hotel won for best cream of crab soup.

Baltimore is still a big small town and small neighborhood joints provide some of the best surprises. Friendly service, small and interesting menus, and a selection of local beers and artwork make these smaller, off-the-beaten-path places a great experience. At *Peter's Inn* in Fell's Point, the restaurant occupies the first floor of a small row house, and owners Bud and Karin change the menu weekly depending on what's fresh at the market.

No trip to Baltimore is complete without a stop at one of the many local diners, where some of the servers have waited tables for 30 years. We know they're great and that the waitresses may have had tall hair for a long time, but there was never any tall food served here. One of the best, *Bel-Loc,* has been around since 1964 and "suddenly" it's the in diner to visit because *Southern Living* magazine has named it the best diner of the south. We knew that.

There is a statewide smoking ban. That means absolutely no lighting up in any bar or restaurant.

Price Code

To further explain what to expect, we have included a price code for the restaurants listed. It isn't foolproof, but we have tried to offer a good average, meaning some meals cost more and some less. In general, it should give you a guideline to avoid sticker shock. The price code includes the cost of a dinner for two people, excluding appetizers and desserts, wine and spirits, taxes, and tips. Basically, it is the price of the entrees two people will have for the main meal.

$................. $15 and less
$$ .... $16 to $30
$$$ .... $31 to $40
$$$$ .... $41 and more

The restaurants are grouped alphabetically by cuisine.

If there is no town or city listed after the street address, that means the eatery is within the city limits. If a town or city follows the street address, it means you will be leaving the city.

Little Italy restaurants present a parking problem. Go early, get a place, and *mangiare*. Go late, take a cab or walk, or leave your car with a valet, enjoy. If you're lucky enough to find a street spot, remember to being quarters for the meter.

AFGHAN

THE HELMAND $$
806 North Charles St., Mount Vernon
(410) 752-0311
www.helmand.com
There's seemingly every type of food at this Afghan restaurant that's fewer than 10 blocks north of the Inner Harbor. For a reasonable price, you can dine on ravioli filled with ground beef and topped with a creamy sauce made of split peas and yogurt. Lots of meals have yogurt in them, including the pumpkin with garlic yogurt sauce. The atmosphere is really casual for this dinner-only restaurant that's open nightly. This is a Baltimore favorite, and it fills quickly.

AMERICAN

BURKE'S CAFE AND COMEDY CLUB $$
36 Light St.
(410) 752-4189
www.Burkescafe.com
Burke's Cafe, established in 1934, offers gigantic burgers, homemade soups, sandwiches, oyster stew, and salads. A favorite for visitors, many of whom stop by after an Orioles' game, is the Burke's onion ring, a large, tasty, breathtaking, and breath-killing appetizer.

On the comedy side, you may see Angel Salazar, Chad Daniels, and T (Todd) Rexx with performances on Thursday at 8 p.m., Friday at 7:30, 9:30, and 11:30 p.m., and Saturday at 7, 9, and 11 p.m.

Reservations are a good idea on weekend nights or if you plan to go before an event, but otherwise you'll be seated for breakfast, lunch, or dinner pretty quickly. The bar is known for its frosty mugs of beer and soda; it's also a good place to wait for a table. Burke's is open 7 a.m. to 2 a.m. daily. Parking is available at several parking garages within a block of the restaurant. Try the garage at the Gallery shopping area, or if it's late at night or the weekend, park on the street.

CHARLESTON $$$$
1000 Lancaster St., Harbor East
(410) 332-7373
www.charlestonrestaurant.com
Wherever Chef Cindy Wolf goes, so goes half the city, the half that eats out regularly and knows an inspired chef. Charleston is Wolf's home and she serves Southern food with a French accent or French food with a y'all drawl. Either way, it's worth the visit. A contemporary American restaurant set in Baltimore's Inner Harbor East development; this is the place to spoil yourself with rich, decadent food, phenomenal service, and an impeccable wine list. Educated servers guide you through the wine menu, which features more than 600 vintages. Everybody orders three to five courses here. The menu has only three prices, depending on those courses. The portions are large enough to thrill your taste buds and small enough to leave room for dessert. The seasons

rule here. Tomatoes will be spotlighted in summer; root vegetables in winter. Cheese courses and desserts are always a knockout.

Coffee Shops

Grind On Café
4607 Harford Rd., Hamilton
(410) 426-1161
www.grindoncafe.com
Owner Greg Bandelin wants his coffee shop to be your neighbor. Come for the local and organic coffee (with an emphasis on Zeke's), stay for a meeting, teach recycling by practice, buy some American-made non-toxic toys, enjoy the local artwork, and connect to the Internet through their Wi-Fi. Yes, they cater and prepare platters. Celebratory news on its own, the Grind On is open daily from 6 a.m. to 9 p.m.

Zeke's Coffee
3003 Montebello Terrace, Lauraville
(443) 992-4388
www.zekescoffee.com
Opening in 2006, after participating and being warmly received at the farmers' market trade, Zeke's offers a Charm City Blend that's also available in decaf or ½ and ½, a French roast (Colombian and Guatemalan beans), Herring Run roast, El Salvador Santa Rita, and about a dozen other blends. They also have organic coffees, several really nice tea blends, and brewing accessories. This is a family-run business with Thomas Rhodes the roaster and president and Amy Rhodes working the administration side. Zeke's is open Tuesday through Saturday from 10 a.m. to 6 p.m., and Sunday from 10 a.m. to 2 p.m.

CITY CAFE $$–$$$
1001 Cathedral St., Mount Vernon
(410) 539-4252
This is a vegetarian's delight because there is always a sandwich, pasta, and soup to try. Theatergoers are delighted because they can catch a pre-show dinner and make curtain time or stop by for dessert and coffee following the show. City Cafe takes up the entire first floor of a 1920s architectural gem that enjoyed a complete interior facelift in 2009. Executive Chef Chad Gauss shops local. The casual-dining experience includes outdoor seating at tables with umbrellas during the warmer months. Because of its location, it attracts a large neighborhood clientele from Mount Vernon who return often to try the latest creation on the menu. It's open daily. Since 1994 the restaurant, winner of several *City Paper* awards, has been serving breakfast, lunch, and dinner. There's also a coffee bar for your morning joe or last cup of the day, and a bar where the martini rules and you can order from the menu. Parking is available at meters, which must be fed until 6 p.m. Reservations are suggested for this restaurant, which can seat up to 170 people, particularly for the weekend brunch when the wait time is about 25 minutes. The restaurant is open Monday through Friday from 11 a.m. until last seating at 10 p.m. (10:30 p.m. on Friday), Saturday from 10 a.m. to last seating at 10:30 p.m., and Sunday from 10 a.m. to last seating at 8 p.m. Coffee shop hours are Monday through Friday from 7:30 a.m. to 10 p.m., Saturday from 10 a.m. to 10 p.m., and Sunday from 10 a.m. to 8 p.m.

i When you visit the City Cafe, in the coffee shop you order and prepay at the counter and a runner brings your food to you. Another option is to dine at the bar or be waited on at a table.

GERTRUDE'S AT THE BMA $$$
10 Art Museum Dr.
(410) 889-3399
www.johnshields.com
Round out your cultural experience at the Baltimore Museum of Art with a culinary experience at Gertrude's where John Shields, nationally acclaimed chef, cookbook author, and host of his own syndicated cooking program, gives life to his signature Chesapeake Bay cuisine. The restaurant is named for his German grandmother, Gertie. Shields changes the menu seasonally. When the weather is nice, you're invited to dine outdoors overlooking the sculpture garden. Tuesdays with Gertie are the best deals in town when the restaurant serves $10 and $12 entrees from the

regular dinner menu. Specially priced $18 and $24 bottles of wine are available. Reservations are really suggested for outdoor and Tuesday night dining. Wednesday night (after 4 p.m.) all bottles and glasses of wine are half price and BMA members still receive their usual 10 percent discount. Gertrude's is open for lunch and dinner Tuesday through Friday, with brunch also offered on Saturday and Sunday. It is closed on Monday.

i Gertrude's at the BMA has an annual two-day Kraut Fest, usually in early January that includes making pounds and pounds of sauerkraut in several large plastic containers. Regular business is deferred as there is live polka music and dancing. You can even find sauerkraut ice cream and German beer. This is sort of in honor of the large number of German immigrants who had moved to Baltimore by the mid-19th century, accounting for about a quarter of the city's population.

HELEN'S GARDEN RESTAURANT $$$
2908 O'Donnell St., Canton
(410) 276-2233
www.helensgarden.com
Located in Canton Square, Helen's Garden is a cozy, intimate cafe with a great wine list and an equally wonderful menu. This is the kind of place where you can either dress casual and get away cheap with a bottle of vino for less than $20 or you can show up in black-tie attire and have an elegant meal. Grilled fish entrees, particularly the tuna, are superb, and the weekend brunch menu is well loved by locals. Reservations are recommended. Open Tuesday through Saturday from 11:30 a.m. to 4 p.m. and 5 to 9:30 p.m. (open until 10 p.m. on Friday and Saturday). Sunday brunch is offered from 10 a.m. to 2 p.m. and dinner is served from 5 to 9 p.m. Valet parking is available Thursday through Sunday night at Linwood Avenue, on the west side of O'Donnell Square across the street from the fire hall.

ASIAN FUSION

ROY'S RESTAURANT $$–$$$$
720 B Aliceanna St.
(410) 659-0099
www.roysrestaurant.com
Yes, Roy's is a chain with two dozen restaurants in the continental United States, six in Hawaii, and one each in Japan and Guam. However, each local menu has about 50 percent Roy Yamaguchi signature recipes and the local chef contributes the other half. One of those well-known and dearly loved items is the Melting Hot Chocolate Soufflé. Order it when you place your entrée selection because they are made to order, not sitting under a heat lamp someplace.

Rey Eugenio, Baltimore chef since 2004, takes his inspiration from local availability and fresh seafood from the waters around Hawaii.

Something special happens frequently at Roy's. It could be a "Hulaween" bash with a prix fixe three-course dinner, games, prizes, costume contest, and arts and crafts for $35 per adult and $15 per *keiki* (child in Hawaiian). Chef Roy Yamaguchi periodically travels to the Mainland, even landing in Baltimore, as he did in August 2009 when three students (Jeff Sarzyuski, Lisa Davis, and Rachael Brosh) from Baltimore International College paired up with famed chefs to win a prestigious internship.

BEEF

CHAPS CHARCOAL RESTAURANT
(AKA CHAPS PIT BEEF) $
5801 Pulaski Hwy.
(410) 483-2379
www.chapspitbeef.com
Gus and Bob Creager started this "hole in the wall" in 1987 and it has been going strong ever since. It's been a highlighted stop when Charm City Cakes owner Duff Goldman took *Diners* host Guy Fieri to Chaps. It's totally possible that the same producer has worked on numerous shows because Anthony Bourdain and Adam Richman also visited. The bottom round beef is sliced thin, not "pulled" or "chopped." You can

ask for rare, medium, well, or a mixture. Throw on a little white onion and some tiger sauce (horseradish and mayo) and you're all set. You can order turkey, pork, corned beef, and sausage. The restaurant opens daily at 10:30 a.m. closing at 10 p.m. Sunday through Thursday and midnight on Friday and Saturday.

BISTRO

CORKS RESTAURANT $$$-$$$$
1026 South Charles St., Federal Hill
(410) 752-3810
www.corksrestaurant.com
Chef Jerry Pellegrino has an education in molecular biology that seems to serve him well in the food and drink industry. He pairs food and wine to some delightful and often unexpected results. The restaurant does have one of the largest and best selections of wine in the area. One of his passions is making sausage, and he has opened his kitchen to guests who make a variety of wet and dry sausages. In 2007, Pellegrino and restaurant partner Joel Shalowitz celebrated the restaurant's 10th anniversary, with a special menu with the original prices and foods from the opening days. Check the Web site for other special events.

Corks is open from Monday through Saturday from 11:30 a.m. until 11:30 p.m. Lighter fare is served until 1:30 a.m. Sunday brunch is served from 10 a.m. until 4 p.m. and the kitchen closes at 10 p.m. and the restaurant at midnight.

CHINESE

DING HOW $-$$
631 South Broadway, Fell's Point
(410) 327-8888
Fell's Point and Chinese food really don't seem like a likely match, but Ding How is apt to change your mind. At this restaurant in a historic part of Baltimore, you can find the usual Chinese favorites, lots of almost crispy vegetables, and local seafood specialties, including lobster, soft-shell crabs, and calamari. The restaurant is open Monday through Thursday from 11 a.m. to 10:30 p.m., Friday from 11 a.m. to 11 p.m., Saturday 11:30 a.m. to 11 p.m., and Sunday 11 a.m. to 10:30 p.m. You

can park on the streets of Fell's Point pretty easily. Dress is casual. Oh, they deliver.

CONTINENTAL

BRIGHTON'S ORANGERIE $$$
Intercontinental Harbor Court Hotel
550 Light St.
(410) 234-0550
www.harborcourt.com
Now the main restaurant in the Intercontinental Harbor Court Hotel, Brighton's has a bistro menu and a casual atmosphere that's perfect for an impressive business meeting lunch without all the pomp. Continental and local favorites, especially such seafood specialties as crab cakes and rockfish (a local favorite also known as striped bass) are the perfect companion to the great view of the Inner Harbor. This is one of the best places to see and be seen in the city.

Reservations are recommended at all times, for breakfast, lunch, dinner, and afternoon tea. During tea, scheduled between 3 and 5 p.m., a variety of homemade pastries and dessert fare is served with several types of tea. Brighton's is open every day but doesn't serve tea or dinner on Sunday. Valet parking is available, or you can park at the harbor and walk over.

PETER'S INN $$-$$$
504 South Ann St., Fell's Point
(410) 675-7313
www.petersinn.com
Owners Karin and Bud Tiffany run this small restaurant on the first floor of a row house, just a few blocks north of the hustle and bustle of Fell's Point. The place was known as a biker bar for many years (when Peter Denzer owned it). Now more a fine restaurant than a biker hangout, you'll find lawyers, doctors, actors, and "regular" people. Karin changes the menu weekly (except the salad, garlic bread, and steaks, which are a constant) based on what's fresh in the markets and keeps the offerings simple but exceptional.

Peter's is open Tuesday through Saturday for dinner only. Other important things to note: Peter's does not take reservations. You can park on the street or at meters.

DELI

ATTMAN'S DELICATESSEN $
1019 East Lombard St.
(410) 563-2666
http://attmansdeli.com

Attman's has been here since 1915, which translates to shortly after Noah's ark landed. It used to be part of a very competitive "Corned Beef Row," but Attman's is what remains. You can order the brisket, the white meat turkey, tongue, shrimp salad (no, it's not kosher), or bagel with Nova and cream cheese. Seriously, folks, they're great, but it's a deli on corned beef row. Go with the corned beef or the pastrami. Come back for the other stuff next time. A large stretch of the imagination might make you think of New York delis, but about the only similarity is you can order Dr. Brown's soda. You might even be able to find some Tulkoff's horseradish. The food's great, the prices are reasonable, and the sandwich might have enough meat on it to feed you for the rest of the week. Attman's is open Monday through Saturday from 8 a.m. to 6:30 p.m. and Sunday from 8 a.m. to 5 p.m. They'll even deliver with a $50 minimum purchase or ship anywhere in the world. I don't know about the anywhere, but probably that means anywhere you would probably want to ship.

DESSERT

VACCARO'S $
222 Albemarle St., Little Italy
(410) 685-4905
www.vacarrospastry.com

When dessert is calling you, it's time to head to Vaccaro's. This tiny little bakery and cafe in Little Italy knows just what you want. Tiramisu, crunchy cannoli filled with perfectly sweetened ricotta, three huge scoops of gelati (it's OK to ask for just one scoop), vanilla- or hazelnut-scented coffee, perhaps a liqueur-based after-dinner drink. It opens early enough for morning coffee and stays open late enough for opera and theater fans to cap off their night. If the tables are full and you don't want to wait (no reservations here), stop by the counter and take your treats home. On-street parking is usually easy to find for the after-theater crowd. Otherwise, be prepared to hunt or find your way to the garage around the corner. Vaccaro's is open daily at 9 a.m. From April through October, they're open until 10 p.m. and midnight (weeknights and weekends). They close an hour earlier from November through March.

DINER

BEL-LOC DINER $
1700 East Joppa Rd., Towson
(410) 668-2525

Said to be part of Barry Levinson's *Diner* inspiration, the Bel-Loc opened in 1964 and owner Bill Doxanas now claims three generations of one family who have worked there. Yes, there are neon signs, chrome stools, and pies made by Yia Yia Bakery. For their raisin bread French toast, they use bread from Grawl's bakery. You won't go wrong with the blueberry pancakes. So, we've known for five decades that this is the best diner around. Does it matter or make it better that *Southern Living* magazine agrees that this is the top diner in the south? The Bel-Loc is open daily from 6 a.m. to 11 p.m. The diner is near the Beltway and Loch Raven Boulevard, which explains the Bel-Loc name.

SIP & BITE RESTAURANT $
2200 Boston St., Canton
(410) 675-7077

Web site? You're kidding, right? This is a 24-hour diner where you can get a crab cake, Gyros, seafood, and just about anything else you'd want at 3 in the morning. No reservations accepted, no alcohol is served, and no credit cards are accepted. Just lots of atmosphere and some fairly good diner food. Closed Christmas day.

EASTERN EUROPEAN

ZE MEAN BEAN CAFE $
1739 Fleet St., Fell's Point
(410) 675-5999
www.zemeanbean.com

Whether you're out for a great first date, an eclectic menu, or award-winning borscht, Ze Mean Bean Cafe will fulfill your wish. This eatery with an East European atmosphere started with a specialty in coffee and desserts and has transformed into a totally satisfying dining experience. Ze Mean Bean, which opened in 1995, has perked its way directly into this century with a Web site that even lets you go through the nearly 100 wines in their list. There's even an Elk Run (Maryland) Gewürztraminer that they describe (under interesting whites) as "A sweet Gewurzt with aromas of lichee nuts." The restaurant is open Monday through Thursday from 11 a.m. to 11 p.m., Friday from 11 a.m. to 1 a.m., Saturday from 9:30 a.m. to 1 a.m., and Sunday from 9 a.m. to 11 p.m. with brunch served from 9 a.m. to 3 p.m. Live entertainment ranges from Latin folk to jazz to jazz with a Latin flair, and goes off into Russian traditionals and classic rock. Reservations are recommended. If you're interested in providing entertainment, send a CD demo and bio to Jim at the cafe. A three-course prix fixe dinner is offered every Tuesday for $19.95 per person or $29.95 with specially paired wines.

GERMAN

EICHENKRANZ   **$$$**
611 South Fagley St., Highlandtown
(410) 563-7577
www.eichenkranz.com
Eichenkranz has been offering true German food since it opened in 1894, and while ownership has changed a few times, with the latest owners taking over in 1992, the food has remained constant. Located off Fleet Street in Fell's Point, the restaurant offers four types of schnitzel—Wiener schnitzel, Jager schnitzel, schnitzel Holstein, and the Eichenkranz schnitzel, which features veal, shredded ham, and Swiss cheese. The casual atmosphere, which tends to draw lots of couples, is enhanced by a number of pictures of Germany retained from one of its original owners. The restaurant serves lunch and dinner every day. Reservations are recommended, even if you call on the day you wish to dine out, and parking is

free on a lot at the restaurant. There's a full bar, too. Check for Oktoberfest activities.

IRISH

AN POITIN STIL (THE STILL)   **$$**
2323 York Rd., Timonium
(410) 560-7900
www.thestill.net
When you are looking for an Irish pub you'll probably be real happy when you come across a Web site that's counting down the days until St. Patrick's Day. Chef Liam Hickey touts their Sunday brunch (11 a.m. to 2 p.m.) and you'll find traditional and perhaps some unorthodox Irish offerings (Irish nachos?) on the regular menu. Live music is available with a list of upcoming performers on the Web site. The dessert list—Irish cream cheesecake, homemade bread pudding, warm apple pie a la mode—tries to tell you ahead of time that you shouldn't indulge in too much dinner. The restaurant is open daily from 11 a.m. to 2 a.m. with menu service until midnight on weekdays and 1 a.m. on weekends.

i   At the Still look for a cheese/beer connection in the stout brie where the cheese wedge is dipped in stout beer–based batter. It's then fried and raspberry sauce is drizzled on top. Yes, dip the accompanying bread into the oozy goodness

JAMES JOYCE IRISH PUB
AND RESTAURANT   **$$–$$$**
616 South President St.
(410) 727-5107
www.thejamesjoycepub.com
Set in the up-and-coming Harbor East neighborhood, James Joyce has quickly become a popular spot for casual fare and live music several evenings a week. Baltimore has its share of Irish restaurants (no, not every one is listed here) but this one is notable for its convivial atmosphere and its varied menu. Traditional Irish fare is featured here, but the salads topped with meats and seafood are a delight, as are the hearty main courses available after 2:30 p.m. With so much

variety, you can eat cheap or you can splurge. There's a children's menu here. Valet parking is available in the evening. Parking is also available in the nearby garage.

| i | The 2900 block of O'Donnell Street in Canton, known as "The Square," has a number of great restaurants and bars concentrated on both sides of a small grassy park. If you're not sure what you're in the mood for, come here and walk around. You're sure to find something to please.

ITALIAN

AMICCI'S $$–$$$
231 South High St.
(410) 528-1096
www.amiccis.com
The High Street restaurant that opened in 1991 bills itself as "VERY" casual. The signature appetizer that's big enough to share or order for a meal, at $13.99 for lunch and $14.99 for dinner, is a round Italian bread loaf, brushed with garlic butter, toasted and filled with jumbo shrimp in a creamy scampi sauce. The restaurant serves beer, wine, and cordials. It's open Monday through Friday for lunch and daily for dinner. Reservations are a good idea, especially on weekends or summer weeknights.

DA MIMMO $$$$
217 South High St., Little Italy
(410) 727-6876
www.damimmo.com
Da Mimmo's offers a great selection of seafood, veal dishes, and the Italian specialties you'd expect from a Little Italy restaurant that's been in business since 1984. Shrimp dishes are among the best, while the collection of wines to choose from is equally impressive. Kosher dinners are available. Jerry and Elsa Burns entertain Tuesday through Saturday night in the Roman Cocktail Lounge and Aldo Locco performs on Sunday and Monday. The fine-dining atmosphere can be noisy; it just isn't a place for privacy. The vanity wall has photos of some of the famous who

have dined here including Johnny Depp, Faye Dunaway, Liza Minnelli, and Tom Selleck. Open daily for lunch and dinner. Reservations are an absolute must. Free parking is available.

SOTTO SOPRA $$$
405 North Charles St.
(410) 625-0534
www.sottosoprainc.com
If you're in the Mount Vernon cultural district, figure this eatery to be Little Italy North, a place where you can find some great homemade northern Italian fare. The chefs change every 18 months; the basics of osso bucco, carpaccio di manzo, vitello tonnato, and costata de vitello remain constant. Look for a special menu on Opera Night, a pairing of music and fine dining. Owner Riccardo Bosia shares your enthusiasm for good food and fine singing. Check the schedule.

JAPANESE

MATSURI $$
1105 South Charles St., Federal Hill
(410) 752-8561
www.matsuri.us
Bill Tien opened Matsuri in 1996 and the restaurant quickly became the go-to place for great sushi and items that aren't on every Japanese menu. When you're new to Japanese cuisine, try the Sapporo bento box dinner with the daily appetizer, California roll, and chicken teriyaki, and when you're ready to be a little more adventuresome, try the Kyoto bento box with appetizer, shrimp and vegetable tempura, and the chef's choice of four pieces of sushi. There's plenty of Japanese cuisine to go around here. Take the two-page sushi and sashimi menu. Served from a long, long bar, the options include tuna, salmon, sari clams, eels, and quail eggs. Among the favorites is the nabeyaki udon, broth-laden noodles topped with shrimp and fish cakes. The restaurant is open for lunch Monday through Friday from 11:30 a.m. to 3:30 p.m. and dinner Sunday through Thursday from 5 to 10 p.m. and Friday and Saturday from 5 to 11 p.m. Dress is casual, and reservations are important on weekend

nights, when the restaurant fills with regulars. Besides the great food, check for sports celebrities, visiting filmmakers, and political figures.

MEXICAN

BLUE AGAVE RESTAURANTE
Y TEQUILERIA $$
1032 Light St., Federal Hill
(410) 576-3938
www.blueagaverestaurant.com
Blue agave is the plant that produces the nectar of Mexico: tequila. The food magic is performed around the moles, an "elaborate concoction of spices, chilies, Mexican chocolate, and rich broth, thickened with ground toasted nuts, seeds, fried tortillas, or bread." All of their moles are made in-house with dried chilies that were hand-selected at farms in Mexico. As with Mexican restaurants, vegetarians can find a large selection of edible dishes on the menu. Lunch is available Thursday through Sunday, starting at 11:30 a.m. Dinner is served Tuesday through Sunday, starting at 5 p.m. Light fare is available until 12:30 a.m. on Friday and Saturday nights. Parking is on the street or in the Federal Hill Garage on West Street.

i The Blue Agave offers more than 130 premium tequilas, some of which are not available anywhere else.

PIZZA

BOP—BRICK OVEN PIZZA
800 South Broadway, Fell's Point
(410) 563-1600
www.boppizza.com
Somewhere after the best crab cake discussion comes the best pizza talk. Do you like thick or thin crust, sweet or tart tomato sauce, and pizzas with slices of cheese or shredded? Valid preferences.

BOP has a lot of fans who swear this pizza is the best, at least in Baltimore. You can watch as your pizza bakes in their traditional wood-fired brick oven that is kept burning 24 hours, and uses oak and maple that brings the oven to a temperature between 750⁰ and 900⁰. The tastes

and fragrances created by the heat of the wood fire produce a pizza that is vastly different to those cooked in a standard oven. You can build your own slice or whole pie with 52 toppings. Of course, you may just fall in love with the baked ziti pizza and never try another flavor or combination of flavors. Yes, there are sandwiches and salads on the menu. On their Web site are comments from George Carlin, Melissa Etheridge, Luciano Pavaratti, and Kevin Bacon.

BOP is open Sunday through Thursday from 11 a.m. until midnight and until 3 a.m. on Friday and Saturday.

i When you want to share the BOP pizza love, they will ship any 14" pizza on the menu to addresses in the United States

PUB FARE

THE BREWER'S ART $-$$$
1106 North Charles St., Mount Vernon
(410) 547-6925, (410) 547-9310
www.belgianbeer.com
Chef Dave Newman directs the seasonally changing menu in this pub, restaurant, lounge, and brewery that's said to be the "gayest non-gay bar in the city." Newman purchases produce from Baugher's, a family-owned farm in Westminster, and the Tuscarora Organic Growers Cooperative out of Hustontown, Pennsylvania. They brew their own fine beers on the premises and offer a selection of beers and fine wines from around the world. You can also find a great selection of Scotches.

i A brouhaha (hmm...brew-ha-ha?) arose in 2009 when a local newspaper said that Brewer's Art cooked their french fries in duck fat. No, no, no. They are cooked in canola oil. Vegetarians, take a deep breath and sigh of relief.

THE HIPPO
1 West Eager St.
(410) 547-0069
So many places in Baltimore (including a lot of banks and office buildings) were built as some-

thing and then converted into something else, that this building is a refreshing concept because it was built as a nightclub, the Chanticleer, in the mid-1930s. After serving as the prime entertainment spot, it became the One West Restaurant in 1961, and the Hippo opened its doors on July 7, 1972. It is believed to be the oldest gay nightclub, with the same name, in the country. Within the three rooms, the main dance bar is said to have one of the most progressive light shows on the East Coast. The saloon side is open daily from 4 p.m. to 2 a.m.

Selected Baltimore Firsts

In 1879 Constantine Fahlberg and Professor Ira Rensen of The Johns Hopkins University discovered saccharine, the first synthetic sweetening agent.

In 1848 William Young patented the first ice-cream freezer.

In 1891 Captain Isaac E. Emerson came up with the first formula for Bromo-Seltzer. The giant, 51' high blue replica of the Bromo bottle graced the Bromo tower building until the 1960s. The building now houses a fire station and art studios for visual and written artists.

In 1819 Thomas Kennett invented the first mode of preserving meats, fruits, and vegetables.

— Excerpted from *Baltimore—America's City of Firsts,* a pamphlet published by Baltimore Bicentennial Celebration, Inc.

SEAFOOD

BERTHA'S RESTAURANT & BAR   **$$**
734 South Broadway, Fell's Point
(410) 327-5795
www.berthas.com

If you followed the TV series *Homicide: Life on the Street,* you'll remember that Detective John Munch (Richard Belzer) bought a Fell's Point Bar and then he couldn't—or shouldn't—give up his day job. On a much more successful note, Tony and Laura Norris, musicians and music instructors from George Washington University in Washington, D.C., teamed up with a friend in 1972 to buy a decrepit bar in Fell's Point. A visit to a junk show uncovered a stained glass window dedicated to Bertha E. Bartholomew. They did give up their day jobs although they have returned to their first love as members of the Baltimore Mandolin Orchestra. He's a guitarist and she plays the mandolin.

Grab a stool, booth, table, or nook and enjoy the eclectic antiques- and tchotchke-filled room and the mussels. Live musical entertainment is available on Tuesday, Thursday, Friday, Saturday, Sunday, and the first Wednesday of the month. Scheduled performers and the bartender on duty will provide the entertainment. The crab soup is tomato based. Feel free to stop by the Bertha's shop and receive your free Eat Bertha's Mussels bumper sticker, a sticker that they say has been seen on all seven continents.

Bertha's is open Sunday through Thursday from 11:30 a.m. to 10 p.m. and Friday and Saturday from 11:30 a.m. until 11 p.m. The bar is open Monday through Sunday from 11:30 a.m. to 2 p.m.

G & M RESTAURANT AND LOUNGE
804 Hammonds Ferry Rd., Linthicum
(410) 636-1777
www.gandmcrabcakes.com
No Baltimore guide would be worth its paper and ink without including G & M and their crab cakes. They're spectacular. They're huge. Two of them with salad, sides, etc., are probably less expensive than I can buy the crab meat alone ($16.95 single, $23.95 double—good for at least one more meal at home). I promise myself every time I go there that I will order something else because if the crab cakes are that good, just imagine how good the seafood, chops, and other items are. I never waiver. I even suggest that people flying through

BWI Marshall allow enough time to catch a ride to the restaurant, order to go or have a meal, and then continue on their flight.

What has changed is the décor. It now has a two-story sports bar, multiroom dining hall, and the take-out counter. Just because you can't get to Linthicum doesn't mean you have to suffer. Go to the Web site and order the crab balls to be shipped to you.

OBRYCKI'S CRAB HOUSE $$$
1727 East Pratt St.
(410) 732-6399
As a visitor, the one place you'll probably go for steamed crabs is Obrycki's because "everyone" will ask where you had crabs and they'll be disappointed for you if you didn't try this restaurant that's been open since 1944.

When eating steamed crabs, be prepared to sit at a table covered with brown craft paper with paper towels and mallets at the ready. Obrycki's can be a cozy place for a crab cake, too. Brick and wood paneling make the room feel warmer, and with the friendly waitstaff here you're going to feel like family in no time.

Because they use only Chesapeake Bay blue crabs, Obrycki's is open only between March and November. Put together a hot, steamy day and some hot steamed crabs and realize the place can be really, really busy. Reservations, which can be made online, are a good idea at all times. The restaurant serves lunch and dinner, starting at 11:30 a.m. and continuing through to 10 p.m. Monday through Thursday, until 11 p.m. on Friday and Saturday, and to 9:30 p.m. on Sunday. Parking is available at a lot across the street. You can order crabs, crab cakes, etc., online or pick up a six pack ($69.95) at the airport.

TAHARKA BROTHERS ICE CREAM
1405 Forge Ave., Mount Washington
(410) 433-6800, (410) 685-5164
www.taharkabrothers.org
Formerly Sylvan Beach ice cream where your ice cream pleasure is their goal no matter which of the 19 or so flavors they make. Customers and employees alike tout the key lime pie, the gra-

ham cracker, salted caramel, and pumpkin. You can find them around town at civic functions and order a dessert of their making at Roy's of Baltimore, Maryland Club, Radisson Hotel at Cross Keys, City Café, Sotta Sopra. While they feed your tummy, they also feed the needs of at-risk young people by giving them jobs and teaching them entrepreneurial skills

During the winter, they're open Wednesday through Sunday from 2 to 8 p.m. During the summer they're open daily from noon to 9 p.m. and until 10 p.m. on Friday and Saturday nights. The Preston Street facility went on the sales block so they could raise funds to build a new ice cream factory. That might mean their ice cream will be in the freezer cases of your neighborhood grocery store.

WATERTABLE $$$$
Renaissance Harborplace Hotel
202 East Pratt St.
(410) 685-8439
Located in the Renaissance Harborplace Hotel, Watertable (with dynamite views of the Inner Harbor from the fifth floor location) has contemporary American cuisine, crab cakes, salmon, and tuna served every day in new and traditional ways. Save room for dessert because they're all made in the hotel kitchen. Remember to take your camera and arrive early (if possible) if you want a window table. Reservations are absolutely necessary; you can park in the hotel parking lot or walk over from the Inner Harbor area.

i Watertable Restaurant and Slow Food Baltimore partnered to kick off Slow Food's "Eat in Season Challenge" with a five-course local Farmstead Dinner, paired with Maryland wines. Speaking at the dinner were local farmers and vintners from Springfield Farms, Roseda Beef, Chapel Country Creamery, Woodhall Winery, Ivy Brand Farm, and more. The menu featured produce and meats from these and other growers, including Gunpowder Bison, Marvesta Shrimp Farms, South Mountain Creamery, and Basignani Winery.

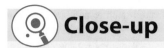 **Close-up**

How to Eat Crab

When you come to Baltimore, you should—religious and health reasons excused—try the Chesapeake Bay blue crab. You can have them in the hard shell, in the soft shell, crab cakes, and crab soup (red and white). Yes, the blue crab shell turns red when it's cooked. The easiest way to have hard crabs is to go to a crab house and have a really good friend pick the crab meat for you, right out of the hard shell, or be invited to someone's crab feast. Soft crabs are eaten with the shell intact and the whole thing fried or sautéed and stuck between two pieces of your favorite bread. In either case, this is a hands-on experience (there is a reason the tables are covered in brown paper). You should have a hammer and nutcracker or knife to open the claws and other tough shell parts of the crab. Plan on an afternoon or evening (or both) because eating crabs is a social event. Crabs generally are cooked in spices (think Old Bay or any "home" branded seafood spice mix you like) and sometimes in a beer-based liquid, with extra spices on the table. You will see people dunking the meat in clarified butter, vinegar, cocktail sauce, or just enjoying it plain. Soft shell crabs are much more expensive than hard shell because at best there are about three days between the start of the molting process and the hardening of the new shell.

Remember, you have relatively hot spices on your hands. Do not rub your eyes until after you have soap-scrubbed your hands! Also, water does not cut the spice. Either go for the beer or milk.

Crabs come in two genders (you figured that one didn't you?) and you can tell which is which by turning it over. If the "key" is shaped like the Washington Monument (in D.C.), then it's a male; if it looks like the dome, it's a female. Some will argue that males are tastier than females and some strongly believe the females are sweeter than the males. Female crabs molt or shed the shell 18 to 20 times and males about 21 to 23. You want the underside to be dark and grungy looking because that is a crab that's been around for a while and has grown into the larger shell that hardened after the molt. A sparkling white underside means the shell is new and the crabs won't be "fat." Yes, fat is an acceptable term for a full crab.

Crab soup comes cooked in a white sauce, as in cream of crab soup, and in a tomato base, generally referred to as Maryland style. There should be plenty of crab meat either way. **Maryland crab cakes** contain crab meat, a little mayonnaise, some powdered mustard, crab seasoning, egg, and a little filling that can be panko crumbs (my favorite), Italian bread crumbs, or something similar. When you see corn kernels and other veggie tidbits or anything other than those six ingredients, the restaurant is kidding itself and trying to kid you.

To get to the tasty meat, pry up the Washington Monument or the Capitol dome and, keeping it attached to the hard shell on the other side, remove the shell. Take your little knife and scrape off the lungs (those creepy looking things on the top of the crab). If you see some yellowish stuff (called mustard) between the two sides, you may eat that. Or not. Snap the legs and claws off of the body, split the body in half top to bottom and then remove the meat from each of the chambers. If you are concerned about what to remove first (shell or legs/claws), what you eat first (body or legs/claws), or what you put on your crabs, the only thing you have to worry about is how your host/hostess does it. Then, follow suit.

CAFE HON $$
1002 West 36th St., Hampden
(410) 243-1230
www.cafehon.com

Almost since its 1992 open, Cafe Hon became the focal point for the Hampden neighborhood. With

it's mix of its "Hon's Much Better Than Mom's Meat Loaf" and assortment of handmade pies, this isn't exactly a *Cheers* place, but then Cheers is in Boston and we're in Baltimore. Located in a 100-plus-year-old building that used to house a hardware store, the cafe is decorated in vintage and antique decor, with Formica tables and an antique chest for the liquor. The casual atmosphere is perfect for families and the neighborhood folks who make this a frequent gathering spot. Cafe Hon serves breakfast, lunch, and dinner daily.

THE KNISH SHOP   **$–$$**
508 Reisterstown Rd., Pikesville
(410) 484-5850
www.knishshop.com
Here's your kosher deli. You don't have to go to New York to enjoy the atmosphere and delicious meats. Where else do you have a choice of lean or full-cut corned beef? Where else can you order your Shabbos meals? A knish, an oven-browned and filled dough pocket, is the namesake and the attraction. The spinach knish draws constant raves, and the potato knish is another winner. An assortment of kosher specialty sandwiches is also available. The Knish Shop is open Sunday though Wednesday from 10 a.m. to 7:30 p.m., Thursday from 10 a.m. to 9 p.m., Friday from 10 a.m. to 7 p.m. It is closed on Saturday.

MT. WASHINGTON TAVERN   **$$**
5700 Newbury St.
(410) 367-6903
www.mtwashingtontavern.com
The building goes back more than 150 years, with lots of dark wood-paneled rooms providing that clubby feel. The eatery itself only dates from 1980. Indoor dining space upstairs includes the Chesapeake and Pimlico Rooms, decorated in hunting and lacrosse motifs. But if you yearn for the sun, ask for a table in the Atrium Room, a sun-drenched garden room with glass roof. The menu offers several seafood specialties, including crab soup with large, lump crabmeat, jumbo lump crab cakes, and a separate raw bar. If you like steak, they have it here—huge and juicy or petite and topped with crab and béarnaise.

Besides drink specials, this longtime popular hangout has free oysters on Thursday nights and free shrimp on Fridays from 5 to 7 p.m.

The restaurant offers lunch and dinner every day, with a Sunday brunch from 10:30 a.m. to 3

Flamingogate

For a couple of weeks in late October 2009, a battle cry arose from 36th Street, Hampden. Randall Gornowich, a graduate of the Maryland Institute College of Art, had created a huge pink flamingo from wire and cloth sometime in the early years of the 21st century. It was erected in front of the Cafe Hon and has been a landmark ever since. Proving that many good deeds don't go unpunished, the Department of General Services notified Denise Whiting, Cafe Hon's owner, that she needed a "minor privilege permit" to display the flamingo even though it is not at ground level and doesn't carry any advertisement. Whiting says it's "public art." As typical of Hampden, area residents were split between this beloved icon and tacky nuisance. Mayor Sheila Dixon entered the fray, expressing the hope that the issue could be resolved. That seems to mean, keep the bird, pay the fee. Then, on October 27, the lawn in front of City Hall was invaded by an army of plastic pink flamingos, claiming justice be served. Phew, an agreement had been reached that allowed Whiting to have her permit at a reduced rate with a pledge from the city to erect signs along the JFK that included the way to Hampden.

p.m. The bar is open until 2 a.m. nightly. The dining room is open Monday through Saturday from 11 a.m. to 11 p.m. and Sunday from 10:30 a.m. to 10 p.m. A late night menu is available until 1 a.m.

NIGHTLIFE

Baltimore's nightlife has always thrived, but it seems the choice of things to do has exploded in the last few years. Ten years ago, you might have had difficulty finding late-night revelry on a Wednesday night, but all that has changed. Cruise Cross Street in Federal Hill or Broadway in Fell's Point on any given evening, and you're bound to find bars, coffee shops, and music clubs filled with neighborhood friends. Flip through the latest edition of the *City Paper,* and you'll see pages and pages of concerts, theater performances, happy hours, and DJ sessions.

Such nationally recognized recording artists as Lake Trout and the Kelley Bell Band land here when they're not touring, and they frequently grace our music venues. Traversing Pratt and Lombard Streets on a Friday or Saturday night can be a traffic- and pedestrian-clogged hassle. But these crowds translate into packed clubs and restaurants, adding to the resurgence of Downtown nightlife. Power Plant Live! offers a number of nightclubs and restaurants in one square block. There are free outdoor concerts in the summer with popular national acts.

There is a wealth of jazz in the area, as one might expect of Billie Holiday's hometown. The city has also evolved a strong DJ culture, and the number of clubs featuring turntables attests to the talent that exists in our quarters. These DJs have a strong pipeline to the clubs in D.C., and you'll frequently find talent from the famous 18th Street Lounge and the ESL recording label spinning here. Baltimore even merited its own sound designation; when flipping through the record stacks in places like New York City, you may run across a heading called "Baltimore breaks."

Beyond the clubs and the bars, we have a strong allegiance to literature, and you'll find national chains and local literary spots stay open late. In this chapter you'll find a variety of offerings, ranging from the ideal dive bar to the high-end dance club. Most of these places exist in the city, although we have listed a few suburban hot spots. You can assume that all of the major hotels Downtown have some sort of adjacent bar for imbibing, so those have not been listed here. Neither have the chain clubs, like the Hard Rock Café, since those offer the same standard fare in every city.

Parking in Downtown basically comes in two varieties—on the street or in garages. Inner Harbor garages can run a couple of dollars an hour to $12 for the night. Outside of Downtown, most nightspots offer on-site parking, or spaces are available on nearby streets.

IMBIBING IN BALTIMORE

Maryland's alcohol laws are somewhat tricky. Municipalities, including Baltimore City and Baltimore County, have liquor boards that issue licenses for everything from full-service bars serving beer, wine, and alcohol to beer-and-wine-only establishments to places that allow people to bring their own but not purchase it at the facility.

To purchase or possess any form of alcohol in Maryland, you must be at least 21 years old—no

exceptions. Increasingly, bar, club, and liquor store operators are checking ALL patrons to make sure they meet the legal-age requirements. Failure to do so can cost them in fines and closure. As a result, be prepared to be asked to show proof of age, even if you are a few years beyond your 21st birthday. Bartenders sometimes card up to age 40 just to be sure. The waiters and waitresses who work at bars and restaurants serving alcohol are required to be trained to identify people who have consumed too much alcohol. Working hand-in-hand with the state's alcohol laws are increasing efforts to stop drunk driving. State, county, city, and marine police agencies have been making more drunk-driving arrests in recent years, fueled by the public's growing outrage over drunk-driving accidents and deaths. Officers in marked and unmarked cars often patrol areas known for their entertainment and tourism. During holiday weekends, the intensity of patrols increases, as do drunk-driving incidents.

If you plan to drink, bring along someone who will remain sober. A growing number of clubs offer designated-driver programs that enable people who pledge to remain alcohol-free to drink nonalcoholic beverages for free. Oriole Park at Camden Yards offers this program for all its home games. If you are a designated driver, ask when you enter the club if you're allowed to drink soft drinks or club soda for free.

If you need a taxicab, ask the bartender to get one for you. A number of clubs and bars have arrangements with taxicab companies that will get you where you need to be quickly and safely. Some tow truck companies also provide free towing, especially on holidays, of cars whose operators have consumed too much alcohol.

If you're staying in and plan on purchasing alcoholic beverages, remember that Baltimore City only allows beer, wine, or liquor sales in

i To help you stay on top of the local music scene, listen to Sam Sessa (*Baltimore Sun*'s after-hours reporter) and his Tuesday night "Baltimore Unsigned" show, of which he is the host on WTMD radio. Generally, Sessa features a live session followed by a sit-down interview. He has a loyal following (hey, how great will it be two or three or 10 years from now when you remember, "I heard that musician for the first time on Sessa's show and now it's Grammy Awards"?). For the moment, the best part of Sessa seems to be his golly-gee, gosh-darn charm. It's not that he's starstruck; he's just appreciative of good talent and his good luck.

liquor stores and most of them are closed on Sunday. Some bars offer carryout after hours and on Sunday, but be prepared to pay top dollar or plan to drive to an adjacent county, such as Howard or Anne Arundel, where liquor stores frequently stay open all weekend.

Feel Tipsy? Taxi rides, for up to $50, are available from 10 p.m. to 4 a.m. to those at least 21 years old who have been drinking at a restaurant or bar in Baltimore. Call (877) 963-TAXI for the service.

i When you want to go to church after a Saturday night out on the town, St. Vincent de Paul Church offers midnight Mass every Saturday night—although by then it's Sunday—in the historic church at the foot of the Jones Falls Expressway (just north of Little Italy) at 12:15 a.m. Everybody's welcome. Call (410) 962-5078 with questions.

BAY CAFE
2809 Boston St.
(410) 522-3377
www.baycafeusa.com
Located on the water in Canton, the Bay Cafe serves good food (like shrimp salad), but it is really known for its libations and great environment. The beach-themed space is the ideal location for cold cocktails and blended daiquiris on a hot, humid Baltimore day. Sit on the outdoor deck and watch the sailboats and tugs cruise by. Parking is available at a lot nearby.

BERTHA'S RESTAURANT & BAR
Lancaster and Broadway, Fell's Point
(410) 327-5795
www.berthas.com
The Fell's Point restaurant known for its mussels is also known for its live music. You can count on jazz or blues most Wednesdays, Fridays, and Saturdays. Bands play from 9:30 p.m. to close. The bar has a good variety of beers, including their own Bertha's Best Bitter, an English-style ale.

CAT'S EYE PUB
1730 Thames St.
(410) 276-9866
www.catseyepub.com
This Irish pub features a collection of flags from all over the world and live music every night, ranging from bluegrass to zydeco, jazz to Irish tunes. Two bars will keep your whistle wet, and a back room with games and chess tables—yes, chess tables—will keep your mind busy. Cover charges vary. They open their doors at noon every day.

CHESAPEAKE WINE COMPANY
2400 Boston St., Canton
(410) 522-4556
www.chesapeakewine.com
When you're a wine geek and even if you're a wine snob, you'll find company at the Chesapeake Wine Company. Friday night is live music. Tuesday is tasting time ($25 a person, no lectures, just good company and some knowledge). Wednesday is happy hour. Saturday is pairings or some other wine event. This is part of the Can Company complex, so if you're with the wine and your companion isn't, no problem. The hours are Monday through Wednesday from 11 a.m. to 9 p.m., Thursday through Saturday from 11 a.m. to 11 p.m., and Sunday from 11 a.m. to 6 p.m.

CLUB CHARLES
1724 North Charles St.
(410) 727-8815
www.theclubcharles.com
Look for ghosts, celebrities (John Waters, Nicolas Cage, Iggy Pop, Johnny Depp, to name a few), neon, and chrome as you retro to the '40s. The Art Deco–inspired bar is always a shoe-in as a great dive bar. It is open Monday through Sunday from 6 p.m. to 2 a.m. There's outdoor seating and a juke box for music.

COMEDY FACTORY
36 Light St.
(410) 547-7798
www.baltimorecomedy.com
About 2 blocks from the Inner Harbor the Comedy Factory brings in national and regional comedians including Todd Rexx (T Rexx), Angel Salazar, and Chad Daniels. Shows are scheduled for Thursday at 8 p.m.; Friday night shows are 8 and 10 p.m. and midnight; and Saturday shows are 7, 9, and 11 p.m. Tickets are about $17. Reservations are definitely suggested.

GRAND CENTRAL
1001/1003 North Charles St., Mount Vernon
(410) 752-7133
www.centralstationpub.com
The Grand Central boasts that it is Baltimore's best gay and lesbian entertainment complex. Entertainment of some kind is scheduled nightly, from a wet underwear contest ($3 cover—for wet underwear? hmm) to karaoke on Monday and Tuesday nights, The disco with its high-tech, industrial dance floor is open Wednesday through Sunday from 9 p.m. to 2 a.m. Sappho's Exclusive Ladies Lounge is Grand Central's newest space, above the disco, and has an outdoor deck overlooking North Charles Street, two pool tables, flat-screen TVs, and a comfortable upscale seating area.

i Good sources for up-to-the-minute nightlife activity are the "Live" section in the Thursday *Baltimore Sun,* a pullout section on what's going on for the weekend, or the *City Paper,* which offers an extensive collection of free events and outings in the area. The *Sun* is available everywhere for 50 cents. *City Paper,* which is published on Wednesday, is free and found in stores and on newsstands throughout the Baltimore area.

THE OTTOBAR
2549 North Howard St.
(410) 662-0069
www.theottobar.com
The Ottobar has been operating since 1997, although the first location closed and this one was opened in November 2001 in its place. It's bigger, cleaner, and more hospitable. When such groups at Meat Puppets, Rookie of the Year, Hawthorne Heights, and Art Brut mean something to you or you wish they did, then you and your

posse should visit the Ottobar. There's an upstairs venue and a downstairs venue and tickets can be purchased online.

ℹ️ If you want to find a lot of clubs in a small area, try Fell's Point. Within a 4-block-square area are more than a dozen watering holes and clubs whose entertainment ranges from hard rock to jazz to acoustic hits and dance music.

POWER PLANT
601 Pratt St.
(410) 752-5444, (800) 733-5444
www.cordish.com
The Power Plant and the Power Plant Live! venues are owned by the Cordish Company and are about two blocks apart, so you should make sure which one you want. The Power Plant is an old power plant that was closed, opened as an indoor Six Flags amusement park, closed, and has had another rebirth. The story goes that one reason the building survived is the extensive amount of copper used in the electrical generation process. They couldn't decide how to salvage the copper or there were other environmental problems, so the building stood. It is a mixed-use facility that includes the first ESPN Zone, Barnes & Noble, Hard Rock Café, Gold's Gym, outdoor dining (canal dining), and spectacular loft offices.

POWER PLANT LIVE!
Market Place and Water Street
(410) 727-LIVE
www.powerplantlive.com
Located at the intersection of Market Place and Water Street (not to be confused with the original Power Plant building on Pratt), Power Plant Live! is 2 blocks from the Inner Harbor, and has such restaurants, bars, and retail venues such as **Mondo Bondo, Babalu Grill, Maryland Art Place, Luckie's Tavern, Howl at the Moon,** and **Rams Head Live!** A free live music series takes place weekly on the Plaza stage from May through October with popular regional and national acts. Admission cover charge or minimum to the various establishments is governed by the individual bar and club.

GORDON CENTER FOR PERFORMING ARTS
3506 Gwynnbrook Ave., Owings Mills
(410) 356-SHOW
www.gordoncenter.com
The Peggy and Yale Gordon Center for the Performing Arts is almost nowhere near the center of town. Unless you think Owings Mills has a center. However, it is more than worth the drive to listen to international guitar night or come an hour early for the Christine Lavin and Don White concert and sit in the lobby knitting with Christine. Look for music, theater, dance, family programming, and films, many from your "yesterday" with audience members being appropriately attired. With only 550 seats, you might not want to wait until performance day to hope you can still get a ticket. The box office is open from Monday through Friday, from 10 a.m. to 4 p.m. and one hour prior to showtime.

Check the changing exhibits in the Joseph and Rebecca Meyerhoff Art Gallery. For those who just want a gallery tour, call Nancy Goldberg, (410) 356-7469, press 5.

ℹ️ Yes, the fountain and surrounding plaza at Power Plant Live! have been used in numerous TV shows and films, particularly and perhaps most effectively in a scene from *The Wire* that looked and felt a little bit like the scene from *The Conversation* with Gene Hackman.

J. PATRICK'S IRISH PUB
1371 Andre St., Locust Point
(410) 244-8613
In the heart of Locust Point is a quaint little neighborhood bar that is the self-proclaimed "Home of the Best Irish Coffee" in Baltimore. Their crab cakes have received rave reviews. Monday's traditional Irish music session is for beginners and intermediate players; Tuesday is with Laura Byrne and Jim Eagen; and Thursday is with Peter Fitzgerald. Live Irish music is performed on Friday, Saturday, and Sunday night. No cover is charged; on-street parking.

SHOPPING

The Baltimore region offers die-hard shoppers an eclectic mix of shopping experiences. For the most part, unique shops are listed, and then maybe a strip mall or two, and then the huge shopping malls.

The state's two largest malls are within a charge card of the city. Arundel Mills is a huge one-story outlet and regular shop mall with more than 200 shops and anchors, a few miles from BWI Marshall Airport. It's surrounded by a plethora of strip malls that may add another 100 stores. Coming in as the sixth largest mall in the country is Westfield Annapolis (off Route 50, west of Annapolis) and most people probably still call it Annapolis Mall, no matter how hard the Westfield people try to break us of that habit.

Baltimore's neighborhoods offer an appealing variety of mom-and-pop shops and boutiques. Fell's Point, Charles Street, Hampden, and Mt. Washington mix their shopping with charming streetscapes. Antiques Row on Howard Street is equally intriguing, with a patina of age covering the inventory of Potthast furniture, Stieff silver, and assorted tchotchkes. Many of these shops require that you ring the doorbell to gain access.

Farmers' markets abound with the city markets open all year while other temporary stands are seasonal.

Downtown offers shopping options at Harborplace and the Gallery; museum stores at the Science Center, National Aquarium, Reginald Lewis Museum, American Visionary Art Museum (maybe the most interesting of all the museum shops); and well, every tourist destination. It's an easy walk up Charles Street for a variety of small shops that offer prints and original art, fair-trade clothing, CDs, and jewelry, among other items. To the east, Harbor East, Fell's Point, and Canton are a short drive (or water taxi ride) away for galleries and specialty shops that cater to the young and young at heart. South of the Inner Harbor, Federal Hill's shopping isn't as concentrated, but Light Street offers a few shops plus the wonderful Cross Street Market, great for fresh produce and flowers.

All malls and shops are smoke-free in Maryland. If you light up, you'll be thrown out. Parking is free at all the suburban malls, even in garaged space, but in most shopping districts, you'll find on-the-street, metered parking or, in the case of Downtown malls and districts, pay parking

garages. Downtown garages usually charge a flat rate for the first hour or two and then "x" amount for every hour thereafter. Sometimes, it will be $3 for the first hour and $1.50 for every following hour, or it might be $1 for the first hour and $2.50 for every hour thereafter. In any case if you stay all day, you're going to be paying between $10 and $15 for parking. There are some special day rates if you park before 9 a.m. or after 5 p.m., but they vary. On the other hand, all of Downtown can be accessed by public transit, whether by bus, Light Rail, or subway.

It isn't possible or desirable to list every space with a cash register and merchandise in and around the city. You can find your way to the neighborhood grocery store, hardware hangout, and card shop. This list includes the larger malls, shopping districts, under-roof markets (farmers' markets), and then specialty shops and services, particularly those that have been around a few years and weathered financial ups and downs and style changes and other factors that can make or break a great shop.

MALLS

ARUNDEL MILLS
7000 Arundel Mills Circle, Hanover
(410) 540-5100
www.arundelmills.com
Since Arundel Mills opened in November 2000, it has become a popular destination for shopping, dining, and entertainment. The center includes more than 200 one-of-a-kind manufacturer and retail outlets, dining options (fast food to slow food), specialty retailers, and category-dominant stores.

Arundel Mills is located off I-95 and the Baltimore–Washington Parkway (Highway 295), heading south from Baltimore, via Highway 100 in Anne Arundel County. It is also just 2 miles west of the Baltimore–Washington International Thurgood Marshall Airport. There is plenty of parking available. Regular hours are Monday through Saturday 10 a.m. to 9:30 p.m. and Sunday from 11 a.m. to 7 p.m. Holiday shopping hours may extend later. Valet parking is available on weekends at the Cinemark 24 Theater entrance.

ℹ️ Lots of volunteers helped construct a 12' tall LEGO Christmas tree in early November 2009, as the new LEGO store opened. (Yes, there were LEGO-built presents underneath the tree.)

THE GALLERY
Pratt and Calvert Streets
(410) 332-4191
www.harborplace.com
Across the street from the Pratt Street Pavilion at Harborplace is The Gallery, four stories of glass that hold some of the more exclusive shopping opportunities in the area. The Gallery boasts more than 75 nationally known shops and eateries under a central skylight that makes you feel as if you're shopping in the National Arboretum.

The mall has its own underground parking, but there are also many lots nearby if that one should be full. Access to the parking lot is from Calvert Street, which is one-way north. The Gallery Garage offers both self-park (24 hours a day) and valet parking (5 p.m. to midnight Monday through Friday, 11 a.m. to midnight Saturday and Sunday).

HARBORPLACE
Light and Pratt Streets
(410) 332-4191
www.harborplace.com
The two Harborplace wings and The Gallery across Pratt Street are the places where most visitors will shop. There's food, entertainment, and souvenirs—sensible and ridiculous—from one end to the other. More than 10 million people a year visit the 130 shops, restaurants, and eateries, many of which feature outside tables that face the Inner Harbor. Boaters can pull their vessels right up to the dock and eat lunch at their choice of waterside cafes. Or they can get carryout and sit on their boats to watch the street performers at the Harborplace Amphitheater between the two glass pavilions.

The shops are as diverse as the eateries. Although the concept of this type of marketplace (think South Street Seaport in New York or Faneuil Hall in Boston) is a heavy dependency on locally owned and operated stores with little reliance on national chain outlets, there are several chain stores. So, look for Hats in the Belfry with fancy and everyday hats for men and women or the specialty Harborplace Store. A Five Guys hamburger stand is available, frequently considered the best burgers in the mid-Atlantic.

There is no parking at Harborplace and no free parking Downtown, unless you are extremely lucky and find that odd place on the street. If you're driving, consider The Gallery's parking, which is above Pratt Street on Calvert Street, or at one of the many meters or lots nearby. An hour's parking will cost $1 in quarters. Harborplace and The Gallery shops, restaurants, and eateries offer a $2 validation stamp for valet parking with any purchase.

WESTFIELD ANNAPOLIS SHOPPING MALL
2002 Annapolis Mall, Annapolis
(410) 266-5432
www.westfield.com/annapolis

With more than 240 stores, eateries, and entertainment options, you should be able to find anything you'd want in a regional mall. Check the Web site frequently or sign up for e-mail notices for information about specials. When you're planning to see a movie, you have to buy your ticket at the booth just past the food court and then take the escalator upstairs to the theaters. This is no big deal unless you've timed your arrival to within 30 seconds of the movie starting time. Wheelchairs and electric scooters are available at no charge, on a first-come basis. The kiosk is near Lord & Taylor. You must have a photo ID to borrow one. The mall is open Monday through Friday from 10:30 a.m. to 9 p.m., Saturday from 10 a.m. to 9 p.m., and Sunday from 11 a.m. to 6 p.m. Holiday hours have stores opening earlier and closing later.

i Stop by the Baltimore Washington Medical Center, storefront #407 (just inside entrance 4) for free educational seminars and screenings, from cholesterol to neck and back, to vascular. While you're there you can sign up to be a member of the Mills Milers, some 1,200 people who walk the climate-controlled mall every morning. No, not all 1,200 of them every day. Stop by between 7 and 10 a.m., Monday through Friday, complete the registration card and sign the release form. Call (410) 755-8773 for more information.

SHOPPING DISTRICTS

ANTIQUES ROW
800 block of North Howard Street, south of Read Street and a few blocks west of the Maryland Historical Society.
The Row—the oldest antiques district in the country—has been a factor in antiques collecting for more than 100 years and is still the place to find a wide range of specialty stores offering sterling silver and French furniture. Many of these dealers make their living selling to other dealers and decorators, but shops are still open to the individual buyer. There are more than 20 dealers on The Row and shops that specialize in ancillary services, such as restoration.

CANTON SHOPPING DISTRICT
Eastern Avenue to Conkling Street to the Waterfront to Chester Street
Canton is the waterfront area south and west of Highlandtown and east of Fell's Point. Look to the area around O'Donnell Square for specialty shops, beauty salons, pubs, restaurants, and gift shops.

CHARLES STREET SHOPPING DISTRICT
Charles Street, from Pleasant Street to Mount Royal Avenue
Farther uptown, both north and south of Mount Vernon Square and the Washington Monument, you'll find the Charles Street Shopping District. This area was home to the furriers, the saddleries, and the exclusive menswear shops. As the local demographics changed, so did the stores. Now the Charles Street corridor contains the shops that should keep you as current in fashion as you want to be. Wander your way through a dozen blocks of shopping, culture, and architectural wonders.

FEDERAL HILL SHOPPING DISTRICT
Along and between Light and South Charles Streets, south of Key Highway
Federal Hill Shopping District has its center at Cross Street Market and it has been enhanced by the neighborhood's renaissance. Look for gifts, clothing, antiques, collectibles, and some interesting restaurants.

FELL'S POINT SHOPPING DISTRICT
Broadway, from Eastern Avenue to Thames Street
Fell's Point Shopping District grew up at the foot of Broadway around the Broadway Market and has changed with the residential demographics. Look for collectibles, fashions, jewelry, and kitschy stuff.

i Unless you park at a paid meter or have a residential parking sticker, most on-street parking in Federal Hill is restricted to two hours. During baseball and football games, however, parking is prohibited altogether on many streets, and you can get a steep ticket. Be sure to read parking signs carefully.

HAMPDEN SHOPPING DISTRICT
36th Street, between Falls Road and Chestnut Avenue
www.hampdenmerchants.com
This shopping district, which runs for 4 blocks along 36th Street between Chestnut Avenue and Falls Road, has become a popular spot with quirky stores and street life. Look for vintage clothing, adult toys, souvenirs, books, chocolates, shoes, furniture, crafts, eating places, and much more.

HARBOR EAST SHOPPING DISTRICT
Aliceanna Street, from President Street to Caroline Street
When the Marriott hotel opened a few years ago, it perhaps heralded the dawn of Harbor East and its shopping. Look for tony shoes, handbags, clothing, swimwear, and other upscale merchandise.

HIGHLANDTOWN SHOPPING DISTRICT
East Avenue on the west to Haven Street on the east, along Eastern Avenue and Conkling Street
If there's a formal wear heaven, it's probably located here. Tuxedos, gowns, and gifts for every wedding couple can be found here.

MOUNT WASHINGTON SHOPPING DISTRICT
Kelly Avenue on the east to Smith Avenue on the west
Shops seem to reach north, south, over, and under the Kelly Avenue bridge. Look for restaurants, bakeries, clothing shops, and beauty salons. Also check out Sulgrave Avenue for shoes, collectibles, clothing, and a ceramic shop. Similar stores can be found on Smith Avenue.

OLD TOWSON SHOPPING DISTRICT
York Road, between Towsontown Boulevard and Joppa Road, Towson
Towson has one of the larger malls in the area, Towson Town Center, and is also the starting point of a shopping area that stretches to Perry Hall and Cockeysville. Old Towson, the area north of Towsontown Boulevard to Joppa Road, is a little shopping district all to itself.

THE VILLAGE OF CROSS KEYS
5100 Falls Rd.
(410) 323-1000
On the edge of Roland Park are upscale stores with some chain brand names and some independent boutiques.

UNDER-ROOF MARKETS

Baltimore's markets are our pride and joy. In continuous operation since the late 1700s, they provide a place to buy fresh foods, from garden lettuce to live crabs just off the boat, and serve as a central location for many neighborhood residents to meet and greet.

A contact number has been provided for Lexington Market, but if you need more information about the other markets, call Baltimore Public Markets at (410) 276-9498. The markets listed here, unless otherwise noted, are open 7 a.m. to 6 p.m. Monday through Thursday and 6 a.m. to 6 p.m. Friday and Saturday. The Avenue Market opens at 7 a.m. Monday through Saturday.

Bring cash. Many vendors do not accept credit cards.

AVENUE MARKET
1701 Pennsylvania Ave.
The Avenue Market opened in 1996 (replacing the 100-year-old Lafayette Market) as a showcase market for the African-American community. Conveniently located next to the Upton subway station, the Avenue Market has 15 vendors offering meats, produce, seafood, and baked goods.

BELVEDERE SQUARE
540 East Belvedere Ave.

Just off the junction of Northern Parkway and York Road, Belvedere Square has been attracting upscale foodies who come for organic soups and sandwiches, locally made ice cream, and a variety of fresh produce, seafood, cheeses, and prepared items.

BROADWAY MARKET
1640-41 Aliceanna St.
Broadway Market is not the oldest market in Baltimore, but it is in the oldest market building, dating from 1785. Look for prepared foods, produce, and seafood.

CROSS STREET MARKET
Cross Street between Light and Charles
www.southbaltimore.com
Cross Street Market is in the middle of the Federal Hill Shopping District, just south of the Inner Harbor. It's the neighborhood market for Federal Hill and surrounding South Baltimore and visitors to those areas. The 27 vendors sell flowers, imported wines, cheeses, candies, fried chicken, and oysters. The market is open 7 a.m. to 7 p.m. Monday through Saturday.

HOLLINS MARKET
26 South Arlington Ave.
Hollins Market, near Union Square, has 16 vendors selling meats, produce, poultry, seafood, baked goods, and prepared foods. It is closed on Sunday and Monday.

LEXINGTON MARKET
400 West Lexington St.
(410) 685-6169
www.lexingtonmarket.com
Lexington Market opened in 1782 in an area known as Howard's Hill, part of John Eager Howard's estate and donated by him for the purpose of creating a market. By the 1850s, when Baltimore was the second largest city in the United States, more than 50,000 people shopped here on market days. The two blocks of market space hold about 120 vendors of fresh and prepared food. Lexington Market is open Monday through Saturday 8:30 a.m. to 6 p.m. Light Rail and buses have market stops. There

are more than 4,000 parking spaces under roof. Parking is by the hour—$2 for the first hour and $1 for every additional hour.

NORTHEAST MARKET
2101 East Monument St.
www.bpmarkets.com
Northeast Market, started in 1885, near Johns Hopkins Hospital, has more than three dozen vendors who sell fresh foods and baked goods, with plenty of places to sit and eat. It's open Monday through Saturday 7 a.m. to 6 p.m.

BALTIMORE HIGHLIGHTS

Bakeries
DANGEROUSLY DELICIOUS
1036 Light St.
(410) 522-PIES
www.dangerouspies.com
When your sweet (or savory) tooth is yelling at you, it's time for a Dangerously Delicious pie. Then, it's up to you to decide if you want the chocolate peanut butter chess or white trash crème brulee, or one of the other creations of Rodney "The Pie Man" Henry. Also a devotee of rock and roll, you shouldn't be surprised if you walk in the store and hear some of the most talented musicians in the country performing. Dangerously Delicious is open Sunday through Thursday from 7 a.m. to 9 p.m., and Friday and Saturday from 7 a.m. to midnight. Yes, midnight.

You can also find Dangerous pies in Washington, D.C. at 1339 H St., NE, (202-398-PIES, www.dangerouspiesdc.com.

When farmers markets and other public gatherings are in season, you can find some pies at:
Goucher College, 1021 Dulaney Valley Rd., every other Friday
BMI (Baltimore Museum of Industry) Farmers' Market, 1415 Key Hwy., (410) 727-4808, Saturday
Green Spring Station Farmers' Market, Falls and Joppa Roads, Saturday afternoon, http://greenspringstation.com

Harbor East FRESHFARM Market, 1100 block of Lancaster Street (between South Exeter Street and Central Avenue), Saturday Baltimore Farmers' Market, Saratoga Street between Holliday and Gay Streets (under JFX Viaduct), Sunday

HOEHN'S BAKERY
400 South Conkling St., Highlandtown
(410) 675-2884
www.hoehnsbakery.com
This family-owned bakery has been sending forth great aromas and tastes since 1927 and they're still using the original brick hearth oven. Are you ready for some éclairs or cinnamon rolls? If it's baked and has a European or German background, you're sure to find it here. You need not bother going to their Web site, for it's just a landing page. Hoehn's is open Wednesday through Saturday from 7:30 a.m. to 6 p.m. It is closed Sunday through Tuesday. Cash only.

PATISSERIE POUPON
820 East Baltimore St.
(410) 332-0390
Chef Poupon has created as close to a patisserie as you will find west of Paris. Whether it's a fruit tart or a meringue lattice upon a lemony pudding, you'll be sure you've gone to French pastry heaven. Wedding cakes are made to be as memorable as your ceremony. The retail store is open Monday through Saturday from 7 a.m. to 6 p.m.

PIEDIGROTTA BAKERY
1300 Bank St., Little Italy
(410) 522-6900
www.piedigrottabakery.com
The reasons to visit Piedigrotta are as numerous as the pastries, breads, and cakes. Yes, they're delicious. You should know, however, that owner Carminantonio Iannaccone is credited—really and seriously—with creating the world's most popular Italian dessert, the tiramisu (pick me up) in Via Sottotreviso, Italy. After years of here and there and doing this and that, Iannaccone and his wife, Bruna, opened their shop in 2002. Everything is made from scratch with the best ingredients avail-

able. Iannaccone is also known for pioneering the expansion of the semi-freddo, a type of cake that is "not quite cake and not quite ice cream." The shop is now also open for sandwiches and salads, Tuesday through Saturday from 6:30 a.m. to 6 p.m. and Sunday from 6:30 a.m. to 3 p.m.

PUFFS & PASTRIES
830 West 36th St., Hampden
(410) 878-1266
www.puffsandpastries.com
Among the great treasures of "The Avenue" in Hampden is this relatively new (2008) pastry shop that uses fresh and local ingredients. According to the owner, Anisha Jagtap, it is a "butter only" shop and they do not use any shortening, margarine, or other butter substitute. Daily sweet specialties may include a local apple and English toffee tart or a lemon chiffon pastry. A fall savory could delight you with a combination of fall squash, bleu cheese, and roasted bacon flatbread. "Today's" special sandwich might be a three cheese grilled cheese sandwich with or without bacon. Acknowledging today's fascination with cupcakes, they do bake them, usually by special order only and then at a minimum of a half-dozen. Once in a while they are available in the store. They are open Monday through Thursday from 10 a.m. to 6 p.m., Friday and Saturday from 8 a.m. to 7 p.m., and Sunday from 11 a.m. to 5 p.m. Special orders may be picked up as early as 8 a.m. any day. Or, talk to them about delivery arrangements. They also sell Taharka Bros. ice cream.

Barbershops
FLOYD'S 99 BARBERSHOP
9050 Baltimore National Pike, Suite 102, Ellicott City
(410) 313-8420
www.floydsbarbershop.com
Floyd's is a growing chain of throw-back barbershops started by brothers Paul, Rob, and Bill O'Brien (the same O'Brien family that brings you Boog's BBQ at Camden Yards). It's supposed to remind you a little of Mayberry, but not too much. Their intent was a music-filled comfortable shop, with posters of hot bands and music artists

plastered on the walls, plasma TVs, and computers where you can log-on. They're offering a great haircut for men, women, and children, for a reasonable price. To top it off, everyone receives a mini shoulder massage. A basic cut will cost $19 and a kid's cut is $15. Greg Barba owns the Ellicott City franchise. Another Floyd's is located at 7313-I Baltimore Ave., College Park (301-403-2922).

They're open Monday through Friday from 10 a.m. to 9 p.m., Saturday from 9 a.m. to 8 p.m., and Sunday from 11 a.m. to 6 p.m.

THE QUINNTESSENTIAL GENTLEMAN
31 South Calvert St.
(410) 685-SHAVE (7428)
www.baltimorebarbershop.com
Enjoy Craig Martin's reinvention of the old-time barbershop. From a hot lather shave where you relax in the comfortable barber chair, have hot towels applied, have a pre-shave oil and hot lather to prepare your beard, and then a shave with a straight razor following the grain to the premium after-shave and ice-cold towel to soothe your skin and seal your pores, you will know you have had a shave that might make you think of the finer things we left behind in the last century. A shave can run you from $25 to $40 and a haircut from $25 to $55. You might even remember when a neck shave was on-the-house. You'll find it here where they hot lather your neck and finish with a hot towel. This is for walk-ins only and they suggest you arrive about five minutes before the half-hour so they can take care of you between appointments. Do remember to take care of your barber even though the service is gratis. There's also a shoeshine stand so you're in good shape from tip to toes. You can purchase razors, accessories, fragrances, and cigars at the shop or through their Web site. Quinntessential is open Monday through Friday from 9 a.m. to 7:30 p.m. and Saturday from 9 a.m. to 4 p.m.

Bookstores

ATOMIC BOOKS
3620 Falls Rd., Hampden
(410) 662-4444
www.atomicbooks.com

Atomic co-owner Benn Ray makes sure this store earns its "Literary Finds for Mutated Minds" reputation, with fiction, nonfiction, comics and graphic novels, stationery, zines, art and design books, action figures, film/TV/video games, music, and so much more. If you can't find what you want anywhere else, you probably should have shopped here first. The staff can be a little "independent" or "self-absorbed," so either know what you want or be pleased that they aren't constantly bothering you with offers of help.

i Join the Book Escape's Book Pass program ($50 annually except you receive a $50 store credit toward any non-sale purchases, so it turns out to be free). You receive 30 percent off in-stock new books, 20 percent off used books and new book special orders, and exclusive offers and coupons.

THE BOOK ESCAPE
805 Light St., Federal Hill
(410) 504-1902, (877) 576-8885
www.thebookescape.com
This tiny bookshop puts a premium on customer service while offering the latest best sellers and used and out-of-print books. They'll also order something if you can't find it on their shelves. Take a look at their Web site for their list of the Fantastic Fifty—50 noteworthy titles of all time, all in stock! Unlike many usedbook stores, the Book Escape seems to have all their titles in a computer data bank so that one book you want can be found! When you want to check out the armchair-worthiness of a book, snuggle into one at the store. Open daily from 10 a.m. to 6 p.m.

THE CHILDREN'S BOOKSTORE
737 Deepdene Rd., Roland Park
(410) 532-2000
www.thecbstore.com
Since 1978 this bright and airy shop has been specializing in only the best in children's books. Whether it's a classic by Roald Dahl or the latest Harry Potter, this place has it, along with shelves full of beautifully illustrated storybooks and those

related stuffed toys, books on tape and CDs, and cards and posters that encourage reading. It's a good place to come if you need a child's gift but have no clue or want something special. Check their calendar for author readings and signings. The store is open Monday through Saturday from 10 a.m. to 5:30 p.m.

The Book Thing

Perhaps you'll need a book for your return flight home? If you're visiting Baltimore on a Saturday or Sunday, stop by The Book Thing, where you can get your books for free. Baltimoreans give their already-read books to The Book Thing and The Book Thing gives them away. You can take as many books as you want. The doors are open 9 a.m. to 6 p.m. at their slightly worn "shop" at 3001 Vineyard Lane, just down the street from the corner of North Calvert Street and East 30th Street. Volunteers gladly welcomed.

Call (410) 662-5631 or check their Web site at www.bookthing.org for directions. Amazingly enough, there's parking on-site.

DAEDALUS BOOKS AND MUSIC
5911 York Rd., Belvedere Square
(410) 464-2701
Is there a remaindered heaven for books that don't sell? Yes, and it's called Daedalus. The store here, and a warehouse-type place in Columbia, 9645 Gerwig Lane (410-309-2730). Come here when you can't find that book or CD that you really wanted to add to your collection or that your best friend secretly wants (how many halo points will you earn when you find it?). They also have a catalog, and the Baltimore store has an evening speaker and film series and a children's story time on Monday mornings.

IVY BOOKSHOP
6080 Falls Rd., Mount Washington
(410) 377-2966
The Ivy Bookshop in Mount Washington is an independent bookstore that's an integral part of the community, particularly when they promote local authors with readings and signings. Although they carry a wide selection of books, look particularly for fiction, nonfiction, art, and cookbooks. The Ivy is open Monday through Saturday from 10 a.m. to 7 p.m., and Sunday from 11 a.m. to 5 p.m.

NORMALS BOOK & RECORDS
425 E. 31st St., Waverly
(410) 243-6888
www.normals.com
Normals has been around since 1990, buying and selling used and remaindered books, new magazines, and other good stuff. It's run by a collective of friends, former friends, and new friends, and has always been the place to go to when you needed a specific book. They'll do a search for you if it's not in the store. Normals is open daily from 11 a.m. to 6 p.m. Their buying hours are Monday through Saturday, from noon to 5 p.m. They are always looking for Eastern and Western philosophy, artist's monographs, Greek and Roman classics, hardboiled fiction, and so much more.

UKAZOO BOOKS
720 Dulaney Valley Rd., Towson
(410) 832-BOOK
www.ukazoo.com
First, Ukazoo, pronounced YOU-ka-zoo, doesn't mean anything. It was opened by brothers Jack and Seth Revelle. Locally bred and raised in Baldwin, the boys graduated from Loch Raven High School. You can find new and used books (and they know the inventory) with lots of out-of-print titles, comfy brown leather armchairs, and little group clusters. When you see a painting, photograph, or print on the wall that you really want to own, they're all done by local artists and are available to purchase. You can also find handmade clocks, journals, pottery, and Lichtenberg figures.

Check their schedule for sessions on creative writing, children's story hour, and game night (checkers, chess, backgammon, trivia, or bring your own favorite to the South Reading Room event). The store is open Monday through Friday, 9 a.m. to 9 p.m., Saturday from 9 a.m. to 10 p.m., and Sunday from 10 a.m. to 7 p.m.

i Ukazoo will buy your books when you have decided it's time to clean off your bookshelves and sell almost every book you've ever owned. They offer cash or store credit and you can bring your books in Monday through Saturday from 11 a.m. to 7 p.m. and Sunday from 11 a.m. to 6 p.m. Call ahead if you have boxes and boxes and boxes to sell.

Butchers

J. W. TREUTH & SONS, INC.
328 Oella Ave.
(410) 465-4650
www.jwtreuth.com
Treuth has been in the meat business for more than 100 years, and the family-owned business processes 100 cattle per day and distributes the beef to the Northeast and Mid-Atlantic region. They are the largest kosher distributor on the East Coast. A retail outlet lets you buy beef, pork, veal, lamb, poultry, lunch meats, and seafood from them. Or you can buy packages, including the grillmaster that includes two boneless sirloin steaks, four New York strip or Delmonico steaks, one rack of spare ribs, eight boneless chicken breasts, 24 ground chuck patties, and 16 hot dogs for $86.95. A hind quarter that's approximately 190 pounds is $2.69 a pound. Treuth is open Tuesday through Saturday from 8:30 a.m. to 5:30 p.m. It is closed Sunday and Monday.

CDs/Records

AN DIE MUSIK
409 North Charles St., Mount Vernon
(410) 385-2638
www.andiemusiklive.com
This store derived its name from a Franz Schubert composition from the early 17th century. It figures, then, that An die Musik specializes in classical, opera, jazz, and world music. Every member of the staff is an expert, and they welcome customer queries about obscure recordings. Check the Web site for the concert series. The store is open Monday through Saturday from 10 a.m. until 6 p.m. unless there's a concert and then they stay open later. It's open on Sunday from noon until 6 p.m.

SOUND GARDEN
1616 Thames St., Fell's Point
(410) 563-9011
www.cdjoint.com
Come here to buy and sell new and used CDs, DVDs, vinyl (LPs, new only), Blue-Rays, and video games. You can buy new DJ equipment, and listen to your newest performing sensation. The Garden opened in 1993 and is now said to be the largest music store in the area. They have a huge collection of cheap used CDs and DVDs. If you can't find what you want, they'll search and special order for you. Sign up for their e-mails and you're registered to win $100 shopping spree at the Garden. When you want to sell your music, movies, and games, stop by between noon and 9:30 p.m., daily. They pay 20 percent more for store credit than for cash. Sound Garden is open Sunday through Thursday from 10 a.m. to 10 p.m., and Friday and Saturday from 10 a.m. to midnight. They have another store in Syracuse, New York.

Clothing
Children's
CORDUROY BUTTON, FELL'S POINT
1628 Thames St.
(410) 276-5437
Infants, children, and toddlers are priceless. Clothing and amusing them, in style, may cost a little bit. However, the selection of well-made and designed clothing at Corduroy Button is worth your time and effort. You can be pretty sure, though, that you won't see a duplicate of your child when you're taking a walk, running errands,

or otherwise enjoying yourselves. And you probably will be the only one with that special birthday present. One Acorn and Apple Park are two of the featured lines carried here. Open Monday through Thursday from 10 a.m. to 8 p.m., Friday and Saturday from 10 a.m. to 9 p.m., and Sunday from 11 a.m. to 7 p.m.

Country/Western Wear

CAROL'S WESTERN WEAR
7347 Ritchie Hwy., Glen Burnie
(410) 761-1992
www.carolswesternwear.com
Since 1962, when square dancing was king and queen, through line dancing, and now beyond or back again, Carol's has carried the best in boots, outer wear, belts and buckles, hats, and everything else western. Among many lines, they carry Justin, Tony Lama, Nocona, and Lucchese boots. They are the state's number one dealer of Stetson and Resistol hats, Johnson and Held buckles, and Wrangler jeans. They also carry Los Altos boots and sponsored a trunk show of their newest products in the fall of 2009. They are open Monday through Saturday from 10 a.m. to 9 p.m., and Sunday from noon to 5 p.m. They have another shop at 9600 Fort Meade Rd. (Route 198), Laurel (301-317-4288).

Jeans

JEAN POOL
5616 Newbury St.
(410) 466-1177
www.baltimorejeanpool.com
Whether male or female, when you absolutely positively need the right pair of jeans, talk with Scott Wable, Jean Pool owner. Among the lines he carries are 1921, Stitch's, AG, Tag Jeans, Joe's Jeans, Fortune Denim, and James Dry Aged Denim. You can buy the belts, tops, and accessories here to perfect match your new jeans. Alterations are available. Swimming's fine at the Pool Monday through Saturday from 10 a.m. to 7 p.m., and Sunday from 11 a.m. to 4 p.m. During the winter, the Pool's open Tuesday through Saturday from 11 a.m. to 6 p.m., and Sunday from noon to 4 p.m. It's closed on Monday.

Men's Clothing

GIAN MARCO MENSWEAR
517 North Charles St.
(410) 347-7974
www.gianmarcomenswear.com
Italian, Italian, and more Italian. As in, Italian handmade ties, shoes, and suits. The owners go to Europe to find new designers and bring their finds back to Baltimore and you. Call, e-mail, or stop by the store for the latest fashion trends, colors, and fabrics. They thrive on your saying, "Show me something new and different that I'll be comfortable wearing." They're open Monday through Saturday from 9 a.m. to 6 p.m.

TOM JAMES OF BALTIMORE
17777 Reisterstown Rd., Suite 153
(410) 580-2022
www.tomjames.com
Part of an international chain that bills itself at the world's largest manufacturer and retailer of custom-made, luxury clothing, the personnel will provide wardrobe consultation about current trends, fit, pattern and cloth selection, and special events attire. They have more than 500 suit and 250 shirt fabric options, and they will come to your business or home to measure you or you can make an appointment to meet a tailor at the shop. Then, they do magical things to hide whatever tiny flaws your body may possess, whether it's one shoulder higher than the other or one arm longer. They also offer a selection of ready-made suits, sport coats, shirts, trousers, and formal wear.

VICTOR PASCAL CUSTOM TAILORS
22 Light St.
(410) 539-2500
www.victorpascal.com
The Paris-born tailor grew up around fashion, starting as a 14-year-old apprentice to his father, one of the city's top master tailors. He spent time in New York, working with Christian Dior, Ralph Lauren, and Adolpho before moving to the Baltimore area with his wife, Ann. Pascal personally measures and fits you and your lifestyle. He boasts that his suits are made with a canvas con-

struction and never with a glued fused process. Pascal purchases top quality end-of-bolt fabrics so he can pass the savings on to you. Although they're open Monday through Friday from 9 a.m. to 4 p.m., an appointment is suggested. They will occasionally open on Saturday.

Women's Clothing

DOUBLEDUTCH BOUTIQUE
3616 Falls Rd., Hampden
(410) 554-0055
www.doubledutchboutique.com
Anyone who's lived in the Baltimore area for a while and who follows the fashion scene has heard of Doubledutch. It's been praised as the best local boutique, best weekend clothes, best fun shoes, best inexpensive handbags, and an all-around best reason to shop in Baltimore (*Baltimore* magazine 2006). High praise that was well-earned. The store's motto is "modern lines & indie designs." Come here for clothing, accessories, shoes, bags, and cards and gifts. Among the lines are Wooden Ship, Built by Wendy, Grace Hats, Bubble Roome, and Erica Weiner. The store is open Monday through Thursday from 11 a.m. to 6 p.m., Friday and Saturday from 11 a.m. to 7 p.m., and Sunday from 11 a.m. to 5 p.m.

Eco-Friendly

BLUEHOUSE
800 Kenilworth Dr., Towson
Shops at Kenilworth
(410) 276-1180, (877) 276-1180
From plants and garden supplies to books, furniture, pottery, glassware, non-toxic water bottles, and so much more, all good for you and the environment. Owner David Buscher says their motto is "Healthy Living through Conscious Design." Every item is either reclaimed, recycled, and/or made of recyclable materials; uses alternative or managed resources; conserves natural resources; is locally made; is handmade; is organic, natural, or chemical-free; is durable, long-lasting, or collectable; or energy efficient. Some meet more than one of those requirements. You'll have one of those "oh, wow" moments when you see the Vinylux record bowl ($26), made from an old

LP record. Bluehouse is open Monday through Saturday from 10 a.m. to 9 p.m. and Sunday from noon to 5 p.m.

Flea Market

U.S. 1 FLEA MARKET
7540 Washington Blvd., Elkridge
(410) 799-8301
www.us1fleamarket.net
With 200 vendors indoors and another 70 outdoors, you could spend a weekend just going from one to the next at this flea market and maybe not make it all the way through. You can bargain-hunt for cheap clothes, furniture, art, cosmetics, toys, handbags, shoes, electronics, and whatever else you need. You're sure to hear, "I had one of those when I was growing up" at least once every 15 minutes. Plenty of eating choices, with an indoor food court and outdoor food vendors, and you can choose from tacos, pupusas, and fruit salad. The market is open Saturday and Sunday from 8 a.m. to 4 p.m.

Furniture

SU CASA
901 South Bond St., Fell's Point
(410) 522-7010
www.esucasa.com
Furnishing homes since 1999, Su Casa seems to be the one place to go when you have an unusual shape or size space to fill, whether you need a great sofa in a settee setting, or mixed materials dining room furniture. They also carry rugs, lamps, and accessories. Local deliveries, done by appointment, are free. Other deliveries have been made up and down the East Coast and west to wherever. Sign up for their mailing list so you know when they're having a warehouse sale. Pick up a queen bed for $400 instead of $850. A new dining room table could go for $250. Some of the items are discontinued merchandise and others are slightly imperfect current merchandise. Su Casa is open Monday through Friday from 10 a.m. to 9 p.m., Saturday from 10 a.m. to 10 p.m., and Sunday from 10 a.m. to 7 p.m. A second Su Casa is located at 8307 Main St., Ellicott City (410-465-4100) and another Su Casa venture,

PAD—Baltimore is located at 1500 Thames St., Fell's Point (410-563-4723).

Baltimore Treasure

Baltimoreans consider Potthast Brothers furniture a local treasure and snap it up when they happen upon it in any of the local antiques stores. The four Potthast brothers founded their furniture shop in 1892 after coming from Germany, where a fifth brother remained and continued to make furniture. The brothers' store was located on North Charles Street until it closed in 1975. With a staff of highly skilled craftsmen, they specialized in reproducing 18th-century styles and original Potthast designs. They made everything from dressing-table mirrors to side chairs to dining tables. If you're looking for something special from Baltimore, this just might be it (if you can find it).

Groceries

PENNSYLVANIA DUTCH MARKET
11121 York Rd., Cockeysville
(410) 316-1500
www.padutchmarket.com
Several Pennsylvania Dutch markets populate the region, including one in Annapolis, another in Laurel, and this one that's not far from Hunt Valley. Folks from Pennsylvania's Amish country bring their baked goods, beef and pork, and candies that compete for your attention with linens, quilts, and furniture. On Friday night, from 4 to 7:30 p.m., it's all you can eat with adults being charged $8.99 and children 10 and under charged $4.50. It's open Thursday from 9 a.m. to 6 p.m., Friday 9 a.m. to 8 p.m., and Saturday 8 a.m. to 4 p.m.

Hardware Store

FALKENHAN'S HARDWARE
3401 Chestnut Ave., Hampden
(410) 235-7771
This is the hardware store of the last century, or the movie It's a Wonderful Life, if it had a hardware store in it. Whatever screw or bolt or doodad you could possibly want or need will be here and the staff will know where it is so you don't have to walk the aisles. If you're going to be doing the fix-it stuff on Sunday, think about what you'll need before then because the store is closed on Sunday. It is open Monday through Friday from 8 a.m. to 6 p.m. and Saturday from 8 a.m. to 5 p.m.

Ice Cream

DOMINION ICE CREAM
1127 West 36th St., Hampden
(410) 243-2644
www.eatyourvegsiccream.com
Donna Calloway's "Eat Your Vegetables Ice Cream" uses the delectable dessert to help people meet their five-a-day requirement. (Hmm, does this start sounding like the tomato is a fruit/vegetable debate?) The varieties are MuscleUp (spinach ice cream), EagleEye (carrot), BoneyConey (tomato), Sweetie Pie Oh Mi (sweet potato), and they come with vitamins, minerals, amino acids, and antioxidants. Mix three flavors and you have a salad! They taste more of vanilla than veggies although the color reflects the fact that the entire vegetable is used from seed to peel, and they're raw so you don't lose the nutrients that would disappear if they were cooked. Yes, they also carry traditional and gourmet ice cream flavors (including sugar free and fat free), yogurt, soy varieties, fruit smoothies, milk shakes, malts, protein smoothies, and snoballs and sno cones.

Musical Instruments

TED'S MUSIC SHOP
11 East Centre St.
(410) 685-4198
Appropriately across the street from the Peabody Conservatory of Music, Ted's has been the place

to go to either rent or buy (or rent-to-buy) new and used instruments for more than 35 years. Ted's has every kind of instrument under the sun, and most of them hang from the rafters. From ancient African drums to electronic keyboards, Ted's pretty much has it all. The shop is open Monday through Friday from 9:30 a.m. to 6 p.m. and Saturday from 9:30 a.m. to 5 p.m. The shop is closed on Sunday.

Posters

GLOBE POSTER PRINTING CORPORATION
3705 Bank St.
(410) 563-3800
When you want a classic reproduction poster, whether from boxing or concert days, Globe is where you start. They've been printing these posters on 24-pound card stock since 1929. After working for the company since 1935, Joseph Cicero Sr. bought the business in 1974, bringing in his sons, Joseph Jr., Frank, and Bob. They replicate their original show posters using the original letter presses and inks. They sell retail only, with posters costing $29.95 each or $24.95 for six or more. They also sell T-shirts of some designs.

Shoes

MA PETITE SHOE
832 West 36th St., Hampden
(410) 235-3442
www.mapetiteshoe.com
When you're passionate about shoes and chocolates, revel in the combination found at Ma Petite Shoe where extraordinary shoes and indulgent chocolates come together under one roof. Stop by on July 14 for the annual Bastille Day festivities organized by entrepreneur and owner Susannah Siger. You can enjoy French music, and complimentary chocolate and homemade crepes courtesy of Sofi's Crepes. The store carries shoes for men, women, and children. The store is open Monday through Thursday and Saturday from 11 a.m. to 7 p.m., Friday until 8 p.m., and on Sunday from noon to 5 p.m.

Sports Gear

LIGHT STREET BICYCLES
1124 Light St., Federal Hill
(410) 685-2234
www.lightstcycles.com
Bikes are rented and sold here, from jogging strollers to adult trikes, from road and mountain bikes to distance and touring bikes. They carry Klein, Surly, Cannondale, and other national brands. Light Street Cycles sells and repairs bikes (not frame or metal repair work, though) and will build your bike for you or ship your bike when you move or go on vacation. They're open Monday through Friday from 10 a.m. to 6 p.m.

PRINCETON SPORTS
6239 Falls Rd.
(410) 828-1127
www.princetonsports.com
Since 1936, the family-owned business that Samuel and Lucille Davis started with their love of cycling has expanded to fill the needs of sports enthusiasts. Now, under the third generation of ownership, this is where you come when you need a custom-strung tennis racquet, a fine tune on your mountain bike clips, or help selecting the right skis. They can also help with your swimming and snowboarding gear, and accessories for all sports. Look for off-season sales. Open Monday through Friday from 10 a.m. to 8 p.m., Saturday from 10 a.m. to 6 p.m., and Sunday from noon to 5 p.m. Princeton Sports has a location in Columbia at 10730 Little Patuxent Parkway (410-995-1894).

Toys

SHANANIGANS TOY SHOP
5004-B Lawndale Ave., Wyndhurst Village
(410) 532-8384
www.shananiganstoyshop.com
From Air Hogs to Zoobs with several dozen other manufacturers in between, when you want a toy that's fun and maybe educational, you're sure to find it here. If, by chance, they don't have it, they'll order for you. Check their schedule for events that are sure to please you and your young ones.

Perhaps not quite as magical as *Mr. Magorium's Wonder Emporium,* but probably closer than anything else you'll find. Shananigans is open Monday through Saturday from 10 a.m. to 6 p.m.

Variety

HI'S VARIETY STORE
1727 Fleet St. (Fell's Point)
(410) 732-0952
Just as you can probably find a specialty coffee shop anywhere you go, there was a time when every town had a variety store. You could find oilcloth (red and white checkered pattern vinyl material with flannel backing that was used as a tablecloth that looked like fabric but didn't have to be washed), clothespins, greeting cards, and just about anything else you could want. Hi's has been around since the 1950s when Charles Wrocinski Sr. started the store. Pat and Charles Wrocinski, and their mother, Helen, help you with your Fell's Point history lesson as easily as they find something hidden treasure that you absolutely need to fix your old kitchen cabinet. Hi's is open Monday through Saturday from 10 a.m. to 7 p.m. and Sunday from noon to 4 p.m.

Wines

BIN 604
604 South Exeter St., Harbor East
(410) 576-0444
www.bin604.com
When you're looking for the perfect bottle of wine and you want someone to help you find it but you don't want to deal with wine snobs who make you feel so unworthy, talk with the wine geeks at Bin 604. They are not married to that old red-wine-with-red-meat and white-wine-with-fish-and-chicken thing. Tony Foreman, the wine guru, makes sure your intelligence isn't insulted and your wallet isn't destroyed. They have a bargain bin section that is devoted to "incredible finds" under $12 a bottle. Wine tastings are held regularly and binology classes let you learn about wines and meet people, and you can even have a private tasting session. Bin delivers within city limits for orders over $50 with a fee of $8.50 per address. Join the Bin 604 benefits club to earn your way to free tasting, stemware, and gift certificates to the restaurants. Open Monday through Friday from 11 a.m. to 10 p.m., Saturday from 10 a.m. to 10 p.m., and Sunday from 11 a.m. to 7 p.m.

ATTRACTIONS

As you should know by now, Baltimore has a full range of attractions. Regardless of your age and interests, you can see something you've never seen before or see something new as you view it for the 20th time. As each attraction is fighting for your time, money, and attention, each is reaching to entice as large an audience as possible. So, the *Baltimore Museum of Art* may seem like an "adult" attraction, but it has put forth a serious effort to entertain and educate children.

Several years ago, an eight-year-old boy and I spent a wonderful hour at an exhibit of French paintings. I asked him to adopt the pose of the person in the painting. OK, that was fun because they were not necessarily in your normal pose position. And, yes, he did behave a little silly after a while (which amused the guards and docents) but less so than if we'd looked at the paintings as French portraits. In other words, what's good for some children isn't necessarily good for adults. I've tried to list where there's something particularly interesting for children. That's not saying one has to be pre-pubescent or younger to be a child.

As one of the nation's oldest cities, Baltimore has an edge when people are looking for museums, historical sites, and attractions to visit. We have some museums that are one-of-a-kind. Some places cost a little bit, some a lot, and two—the *Baltimore Museum of Art* and the *Walters Art Museum*—ceased charging an entry fee in 2007. Whatever it is, you're pretty sure to find it in Baltimore.

Keep in mind that exhibits, operating hours, and admission fees change. It is always wise to check personally with an attraction you plan to visit. One great change in admission fees took place over the first weekend of December 2009 when more than a dozen museums and attractions participated in a Dollar or Less Days event sponsored by Downtown Baltimore. Among those participating were the American Visionary Art Museum ($1 Sunday), Babe Ruth Birthplace ($1 both days), Baltimore Maritime Museum ($1 admission per vessel on Sunday), Baltimore Museum of Industry ($1 both days), and Maryland Science Center ($1 admission both days excluding IMAX and traveling exhibit). When you're looking for a bargain and you don't want to mess with holiday-shopping crowds, keep the Dollar or Less Days event in mind.

AMERICAN VISIONARY ART MUSEUM
800 Key Hwy.
(410) 244-1900
www.avam.org

Remember when your mother put your kindergarten handprint turkey on the refrigerator so all the family could see how talented you were? Or did you do that for your child? Some of those hand-turkey artists have grown up to be self-taught artists, usually without formal training. You can see their works at the American Visionary Art Museum. Visionary art is said to "begin by listening to the inner voices of the soul, and often may not even be thought of as 'art' by its creator." In this spiraling, four-story gallery space you will discover inspirational creations made by extraordinary people. Perhaps the most-discussed item in the permanent collection is the 55' Giant Whirligig in the sculpture plaza. Entitled, "Life, Liberty & The Pursuit of Happiness," the sculpture was created by 76-year-old mechanic, farmer, and visionary artist, Vollis Simpson. The museum is open Tuesday through Sunday 10 a.m. to 6 p.m.

Admission is $14 for adults and $10 for seniors (60 and up) and students. Yes, there is a gift shop.

A new restaurant, Mr. Rain's American Fun House, opened at the museum in early November 2009. Owners Bill and Maria Buszinski and Perez Klebhan promise a "sophisticated and playful dining experience featuring iconoclastic Americana cuisine, cocktails, and farm-to-table philosophies." The menu will change seasonally. It is open for lunch Tuesday through Friday, brunch Saturday and Sunday, and dinner Tuesday through Sunday.

i Baltimore has many attractions that are unlike attractions anywhere else in the world. If you only have time to visit one place, the AVAM should be that place.

BABE RUTH BIRTHPLACE AND MUSEUM
216 Emory St.
(410) 727-1539
www.baberuthmuseum.com
For years the Babe Ruth Birthplace had way too much stuff. Contrarily, the old train station by Camden Yards was gorgeous space and nothing filled it. Voila! The Babe Ruth Birthplace and the Sports Legends Museum at Camden Yards are separate sports exhibitions but equal, or something like that. Although the Sultan of Swat made his name as a New York Yankee (*hiss!*), Babe Ruth was born in Baltimore on February 6, 1895. A museum now resides in the house (and two adjacent houses) where Ruth was born at 216 Emory St. The house almost came under the wrecking ball in 1968 until the mayor and the Greater Baltimore Council rallied to save the historic site.

Artifacts and photographs tell the story of a phenomenal life. Although much smaller than the behemoth in Cooperstown, this is a much more interesting museum about baseball and the Babe.

The museum celebrates Ruth's birthday each year on February 6 with free admission from 11 a.m. to 1 p.m. and a champagne toast and cake. It's open Tuesday through Sunday 10 a.m. to 5 p.m., November through March, and daily 10 a.m. to 6 p.m. April through October, with hours extended when the Orioles have a home game. Museum members have free admission. Otherwise, admission is $6 for adults, $4 for seniors, $3 (3-12) for children age 3 to 12, and free for those younger than age 3. A combo ticket with the Sports Legends Museum is $12 for adults, $8 for seniors, and $5 for children.

i A museum can be so much more than a museum. Baseball fans from California were visiting Baltimore while on a Sports Travel and Tours trip to see East Coast teams play. Each had been married before (and divorced) so they chose the Babe Ruth Birthplace to be married to each other. All the paperwork had been done, a bottle of bubbly obtained from the Lexington Market, and a local minister was enlisted to perform the ceremony. About two-thirds of the tour group joined them as witnesses as the ceremony was performed in the Babe's bedroom and the couple was treated to a recessional under raised bats.

THE B&O RAILROAD MUSEUM
901 West Pratt St.
(410) 752-2490
www.borail.org
The B&O Railroad Museum, which houses the largest railroad collection in the Western Hemisphere, reopened in 2006 following repairs needed after a 2003 snowstorm caused the roof to collapse. The museum looks better than ever. Train buffs will thrill to see some of the best historic trains in the world, and to ride the rails laid for the first trains. Children will love climbing aboard the trains and seeing the model trains. Between Thanksgiving and New Year's Eve, model railroad hobbyists bring some pretty extensive layouts to the museum. Seeing the model trains lets you relive the year you received your first train set.

Programs go beyond trains waiting to be seen or experienced. One of the most popular events is the turntable demonstration that shows how the museum moves locomotives and cars in and out of the 1884 Roundhouse. The B&O Railroad Museum's summer reading Program "I've Been Readin' on the Railroad" at the B & O Railroad Museum and the Ellicott City Station gives your readers a chance to win a free book and an engineer's outfit. Catch a restoration facility tour ($10 with admission) for a behind-the-scenes tour of the museum's restoration facility. Perhaps because "everyone" had a train set during early childhood years, one of the biggest events at the museum is the Festival of Trees that runs from late November through early January and has Baltimore's largest holiday celebration of toy trains and model railroading layouts.

The museum is open Monday through Saturday from 10 a.m. to 4 p.m. and Sunday from 11 a.m. to 4 p.m. The last admission is 30 minutes prior to closing time. It is closed for most major holidays. Admission is $14 for adults, $12 for seniors (60 plus), and $8 for children (2 through 12). A combination ticket that costs an additional $2 is available for the B&O Railroad Museum and the Ellicott City station about a half hour away by car. Visit the B&O Railroad museum on the first Tuesday of the month and pay only half-price admission.

i The biggest annual event for the *Constellation* these days takes place on a Friday afternoon in early September when she takes a ride to Fort McHenry and back to "turn around" so either the port or starboard side of the ship faces into the Harbor at least until next year when she's turned around again.

BALTIMORE CITY FIRE MUSEUM
414 North Gay St.
(410) 727-2414
www.museumsusa.org/museums/
info/1167039
This 117-foot tower was built in 1853 by the Independent Fire Company so volunteers could keep watch over the city. The building, inspired by Giotto's Campanile (Bell Tower) in Florence, Italy, was an operating firehouse for Engine Company No. 6 for more than a century. Today the museum offers a look back at early firefighting in cities and the Great Fire of 1904, which claimed no lives but destroyed about 70 blocks of Baltimore's central business district. The museum exhibits five pieces used to fight the 1904 fire, and film shot by Thomas Edison during the blaze. An Acoustiguide tour of the museum is available. Free tours are offered on Sunday from 1 to 4 p.m., Thursday from 9:30 a.m. to noon, and Friday from 6:30 to 9:30 p.m. or by appointment.

Harbor Pass

The Harbor Pass provides discount admission to five top Baltimore attractions for four days. For one price, you can visit the National Aquarium in Baltimore, the Maryland Science Center, Sports Legends Museum at Camden Yards, the Top of the World observation deck, and a choice of the American Visionary Art Museum or the Port Discovery Children's Museum. This pass doesn't include the dolphin show at the aquarium or the IMAX theater at the Science Center.

When you buy the tickets at least three days ahead of time, adults are $49.95 (25 percent discount) and children are $35.70. If you buy the pass at the visitor center, they're $56.85 for adults and $37.95 for children. They're good for four consecutive days and you must specify a start date. Buy them at the visitor center at the Inner Harbor or online at www.baltimore.org/harborpass. Call (877) BALTIMORE for information. The call center hours are Monday through Friday from 8:30 a.m. to 5:30 p.m. (Eastern time).

BALTIMORE HISTORIC SHIPS
301 East Pratt St.
(410) 539-1797
www.historicships.org

Here's where you can experience history on the water on so many levels. On Pier 1, you have the sloop-of-war USS *Constellation* (check the Plan of the Day for the next live firing of the Parrott rifle and the Powder Monkey tour). Walk over to Pier 3 to visit Lightship *Chesapeake* (check out the exhibit about canine friends) and USS *Torsk* (a Tench Class submarine that sank the last Japanese combatant ships of World War II). The U.S. Coast Guard Cutter *Taney* and the Seven Foot Knoll Lighthouse (one of the oldest Chesapeake screwpile lighthouses still in existence) are on Pier 5.

The Historic Ships are open different times on different days in different seasons and even then the hours are subject to change. In other words, check the Web site or call for specific information, particularly the last boarding time.

Admission prices vary according to the number of ships you want to visit. Captain (adult) is $10 for one ship to $16 for four ships. Reduced rates are available for Admiral (seniors who are 60 plus) and Midshipman (6-14 years) with Stowaways (5 and under) and military personnel with ID are free. Admission to the lighthouse is free for all.

BALTIMORE MUSEUM OF ART
10 Art Museum Dr.
(443) 573-1700
www.artbma.org

Maryland's celebrated art museum houses a permanent collection of more than 100,000 objects, ranging from ancient mosaics to contemporary art pieces. The Cone Collection features the works of Matisse, Picasso, Cezanne, van Gogh, Gauguin, Renoir, and others from the Modernist era, while the New Wing boasts post-1945 artwork, including a gallery of major works by Andy Warhol. The John Russell Pope Building has displays of furniture, decorative arts, paintings, and miniature rooms, while the sculpture gardens boast works by such artists as Rodin and Calder.

The museum and tiered sculpture garden are fully wheelchair accessible. Wheelchairs are available (lobby welcome desk) free of charge on a first-come, first-served basis. Sculpture Touch Tours for the blind and visually impaired, sign language interpretation, and selected foreign language interpretation for non-English speakers are available upon request. Call (443) 573-1818 for more information. Hours are Wednesday through Friday from 10 a.m. to 5 p.m. and Saturday and Sunday from 11 a.m. to 6 p.m. The museum is closed Monday, Tuesday, New Year's Day, July 4, Thanksgiving, and Christmas. Admission is free. Check the Restaurants chapter for information about Gertrude's, the in-house eatery. Free parking is available in two lots and metered parking is across the street.

On a weekend in mid-March on even years, the BMA has a Contemporary Print Fair where prints, drawings, photographs, and other works on paper from 20 dealers are featured and sold. Lectures are scheduled and you're invited to the family workshop to make your own prints. There is an admission charge for this event from $12 for BMA members to $30 for a weekend pass for non-members. Students with valid ID are free.

BALTIMORE MUSEUM OF INDUSTRY
1415 Key Hwy.
(410) 727-4808
www.thebmi.org

Located in the 1865 Platt Oyster Cannery building on the west side of Baltimore's Inner Harbor, this museum allows visitors to experience the industries that made the city one of the busiest ports in the nation. Founded in 1977, it is dedicated to remembering and sharing the industrial and technological heritage of the area and the people who created and worked in them. Learn about the long workdays at a belt-driven machine shop, a garment loft, a print shop, and aboard the historic 1906 steam tugboat the S.T. *Baltimore*. Life-size photos of children working in the industries help bring home the harsh conditions to today's children. The museum is open Tuesday through Sunday from 10 a.m. to 4 p.m. It is closed

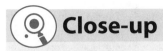

Close-up

The Cone Sisters

Etta and Claribel Cone, Baltimore sisters blessed with education, wealth, and extremely good taste, are largely responsible for the fabulous collection of Henri Matisse paintings now owned by the Baltimore Museum of Art. Etta bought her first work by Matisse during a visit to the Salon d'automne in 1905.

The sisters became one of his first patrons, collecting some 500 works by the French painter—the largest and most comprehensive collection in the world. Their 40-year acquaintance blossomed into friendship and when Claribel died in 1929, Matisse visited to extend his condolences.

The sisters bought paintings by American impressionist Theodore Robinson, Paul Cezanne, Paul Gauguin, Vincent van Gogh, and Pierre-Auguste Renoir; and there are144 works by Pablo Picasso in their collection.

In all, the Cone Collection at the BMA numbers some 3,000 items. Most of it is artwork, but the museum also has the sisters' personal library and archive, furniture, travel souvenirs, and jewelry.

The Cone Wing includes a virtual tour of their home with an exhibition of some of their things.

The sisters were 2 of 13 children born to German émigrés. Claribel was born in 1864; Etta in 1870. The family, who had lived in Tennessee, moved to Baltimore in 1871 to open a wholesale grocery. About 10 years later, they moved to an elegant apartment on Eutaw Place, located in what was a fashionable residential district and the center of a vibrant German-Jewish community. Etta and Claribel took an active part in the social scene of the day. Claribel studied medicine after high school, eventually doing advanced research at Johns Hopkins Medical School and becoming president of her alma mater, the Women's Medical College of Baltimore. Etta took on the responsibilities of running the family household.

Along with their friends Leo Stein and his sister, writer Gertrude Stein, both Baltimoreans, the sisters became passionate about travel and art. With the Steins, they traveled frequently to Europe and the Far East. In fact, Claribel remained in Munich for the duration of World War I. During that period she was deeply involved in her research and did not buy a single painting. Neither did Etta.

Beginning in 1922, the sisters' collecting began again in earnest. Though Claribel's collection emphasized the Matisse works, Etta focused more on works that explored the creative process. Their luxurious apartments in Baltimore were soon filled with memorabilia and great works of art. Etta promised the Baltimore Museum of Art her collection in 1940, with the stipulation that the museum promote a better appreciation of modern art in the city. The BMA got to work on that request right away. When Etta died in 1949, the art collections of both sisters were bequeathed to the museum.

on Monday and occasionally for a private event. Admission is $10 for adults and $6 for those age 5 through 18 and senior citizens. From June through October, you can shop at the farmers' market for fresh produce, Dangerously Delicious pies, and hand-crafted works.

BALTIMORE PUBLIC WORKS MUSEUM
751 Eastern Ave.
(410) 396-5565
www.baltimorepublicworksmuseum.org
When you want to know where your tax dollars are going, then head to the Public Works Museum. It was being renovated for most of 2009

and as great as it was before, it's even better now. Below the city streets lies a maze of pipes and drains moving our water and waste. Opened in 1982 in the historic Eastern Avenue Pumping Station at the east end of the Inner Harbor, this one-of-a-kind museum features the history of public works and the development of urban infrastructure. While it is a museum, it remains a working pumping station, with 30 million gallons of wastewater passing through here every day (OK, that might be too much information).

One highlight of the museum is the outdoor Streetscape, a model where guests can walk through the maze of pipes and drains that exist belowground. Children love the changing exhibits, with names like "What's Beneath the Streets?" and "The Rotten Truth About Garbage." There is also a computer room where games bring city works to life. The gift shop, though tiny, has some interesting items, all recycled. The museum is open Tuesday through Sunday 10 a.m. to 4 p.m. Admission is $3 for adults and $2.50 for seniors and children age 6 through 17.

BALTIMORE STREETCAR MUSEUM
1901 Falls Rd.
(410) 547-0264
www.baltimorestreetcar.org
You don't see or hear about streetcars these days, so it's interesting to visit the collection of them just awaiting their rebirth. This museum was founded in 1966 and traces the 104-year history, starting with the first horsecars in East Baltimore in 1859 through to the end of the streetcar era in 1963. Feel what it was like to ride a streetcar during a 1.5-mile round-trip ride aboard one of the restored streetcars. The museum offers operating layouts, displays, and a video on local streetcar history. It's open from noon to 5 p.m. Sunday year-round and Saturday and Sunday from June to October. Admission is $7 for adults and $5 for children age 4 through 11 and senior citizens, with a family maximum of $24. Admission includes unlimited rides on original Baltimore streetcars, access to the displays, and an audiovisual presentation of the streetcar history.

BALTIMORE TATTOO MUSEUM
1534 Eastern Ave.
(410) 522-5800
www.baltotat.com
When you can't get enough tattoo art on cable stations, then it's time to visit this museum. The art of body ink never went out of style in Baltimore. A full-service tattoo and piercing shop and a museum of classic tattoo art, this is the place to go for a lasting souvenir of your trip to Baltimore (you do not have to get a tattoo; however, you can buy temporary ones). They do everything from old school traditional to Japanese, Kanji, names, black and grey, portraits, flash off the wall, or custom-drawn designs. Open Monday through Saturday from 10 a.m. to 9 p.m. and on Sunday from 11 a.m. to 7 p.m.

i At the Baltimore Streetcar Museum, work has progressed on the snow sweeper as the staff and crew learned during early snowfalls in 2009 that the clearing abilities were great on the straight track, but not so great on the loops.

BALTIMORE–WASHINGTON INTERNATIONAL THURGOOD MARSHALL AIRPORT
I-195, Linthicum
(410) 859-7111
www.bwiairport.com
Airports have a nasty rap these days, whether it's expensive bland food or uncomfortable seating. So, it's nice to know that the folks at BWI Marshall are trying to make your time here as pleasant as possible.

Having said that, the airport has stopped the paging service. Hey, everyone has a cell phone or some portable communication device.

Services for the disabled are particularly good with TDD-equipped public phones throughout the facility and at the information desks on the upper level concourse B, lower level in the Southwest Airlines baggage claim 1-5 area, lower level concourse E, and the customer service center.

Visual paging monitors are available at the lower and upper levels at all concourses; call (410) 859-7111 to display a message.

Shuttle service to the parking lots and the BWI Amtrak railroad station can be provided by requesting a lift-equipped bus by calling First Transit at (410) 684-3346 to request a wheelchair accessible shuttle bus.

Unisex bathrooms are equipped for people with disabilities and can be used with or without an attendant. Two pre-security unisex bathrooms are to the right and left of concourse D security behind the airline ticket counters.

Aviation Safeguards serves Southwest, American, Delta, British Airways, and USA 300; for wheelchairs call (410) 981-1251.

Prime Flight Aviation Services serves AirTran, Continental, JetBlue, United, and USAirways. Request a chair at (410) 859-4444.

The Baltimore-Washington International Marshall Airport has an observation lounge between Wings B and C for children of all ages to enjoy the scenes of a busy airport. Large windows allow for viewing the action outside, there's a mockup of an airplane, a baggage train, and a gas truck for children to climb through and practice their flying and driving skills. On the second floor is an aviation exhibit that includes sections of a real airplane. You can't crawl into the cockpit, but you can look through the glass and push buttons to light up specific cockpit lights. It's the closest children can get to an airplane without shelling out big bucks for a seat on the next flight. A play area is adjacent to all this fun.

THE BASILICA OF THE ASSUMPTION
Cathedral and Mulberry Streets
(410) 727-3565
www.baltimorebasilica.org
The first metropolitan cathedral in the United States has been the mother church for Baltimore's Roman Catholic population since 1806. Designed by Benjamin Henry Latrobe, designer of the Capitol in Washington, the cathedral features a grand organ dating from 1821 and a high altar from 1822. The entire cathedral underwent a complete restoration that was completed in late 2006. The stained-glass windows were removed; the dark colors were replaced with cream, yellow, and rose. Galleries that were reserved for clois-

tered nuns and slaves were uncovered. Memorials to two of the cathedral's most beloved and famous visitors—Pope John Paul II and Mother Teresa of Calcutta—were added, as was a small museum, gift shop, and new access to the undercroft. Across the street from the Enoch Pratt Free Library main branch, this example of neoclassical architecture also holds the remains of Bishop John Carroll, America's first Catholic bishop, who placed the cornerstone. Guided tours are given on Sundays at noon and by appointment. The basilica is open Monday through Friday from 7 a.m. to 4:30 p.m. and from 7 a.m. until the conclusion of the 5:30 p.m. Mass on Saturday and Sunday. A tour request form is available on their Web site.

BROMO SELTZER ARTS TOWER
21 South Eutaw St.
(443) 874-3596
www.bromoseltzertower.com
After near total abandonment, the Baltimore Office of Promotions & The Arts created art studio space for visual and literary artists here. Among the 30 artists now calling this home are a playwright, oil painters, watercolorists, and photographers. Once a month, usually on the first Saturday, from 1 to 5 p.m., the artists' studios are open and you can visit with them, ask questions, and, of course, buy works of art. Refreshments and light fare are served.

CLARK'S ELIOAK FARM
10500 Clarksville Pike, Ellicott City
(410) 730-4049
www.clarklandfarm.com
OK, this place is outside the Baltimore Beltway. However, for generations of residents (and grandchildren of former residents), this is the place to see the storybook structures that the charming, sentimental, and determined Martha Clark and family rescued from the former Enchanted Forest Park, that enchanted from 1955 to the 1980s. This 540-acre farm tended by the Clark family for generations opened its doors to families several years ago with pigs and goats and calves willing to be petted and hayrides and pony rides

available. It's still a working farm. Generations of families went there to climb in Mother Hubbard's shoe and explore Cinderella's pumpkin coach. The Enchanted Forest is long gone, yet these memories (gee, I thought they were larger than that) continue to amuse. Storybook Time is on Tuesday and Thursday in June and July, held four times during each day. Admission is $4.50 per person. Hayrides and pony rides are an additional $2. The farm is open April through October 10 a.m. to 4 p.m. and is located by traveling Highway 29 to Highway 108 west; it's about 45 minutes from Baltimore.

CONTEMPORARY MUSEUM
100 West Centre St.
(410) 783-5720
www.contemporary.org
The Contemporary Museum is "dedicated to creating education programs and cultural experiences that reach an exceptionally wide range of constituents." Contemporary exhibitions and educational programs are on show at the gallery space on Center Street, just 1 block from the Maryland Historical Society and the Walters Art Museum. It is open Wednesday through Sunday from noon to 5 p.m. Call before visiting as it closes between exhibitions. The Contemporary has a suggested donation of $5 for adults and $3 for children.

THE DR. SAMUEL D. HARRIS NATIONAL
MUSEUM OF DENTISTRY
31 South Greene St.
(410) 706-0600
www.dentalmuseum.org
Although you're not supposed to look a gift horse in the mouth, you can get more than a mouthful of dental information at this museum dedicated to the history and development of dental science. Get ready for a brush with the world's first dental school, which opened on the campus of the University of Maryland at Baltimore in 1839. The museum building, which opened in 1904, houses collections of artifacts and educational exhibits dealing with the history and lore of teeth and dentistry.

The museum offers a look at the evolution of the toothbrush, temporary offices for a traveling dentist, and an interactive exhibition, "32 Terrific Teeth." The museum is open Wednesday through Saturday 10 a.m. to 4 p.m. and Sunday 1 to 4 p.m. Admission is $7 for adults, $5 for seniors, college students, UMB employees, and $3 for children 3-18.

i When you're looking for a tooth fairy pillow, as I did for months several years ago, head to the National Museum of Dentistry's gift shop. Or, you can find a molar-shaped toddler's stool, chattering walking lips and teeth complete with braces, or ice cubes shaped like teeth. The imagination is boggled.

ENOCH PRATT FREE LIBRARY
400 Cathedral St.
(410) 396-5430
www.prattlibrary.org
Since 1886 this branch has served as the central library for "The City That Reads," as former Mayor Kurt Schmoke once dubbed Baltimore. Among its more than two million volumes are extensive collections of writers Edgar Allan Poe and H. L. Mencken and a library of lyrics and sheet music for more than 100,000 songs. The library's benefactor, Enoch Pratt, set out to educate the common man by establishing this neighborhood library system, which has served Baltimoreans for more than 100 years. All the libraries in Maryland benefit from Pratt's gift, as it lends out its extensive collection to county library systems when requested. The nearly two dozen branches and bookmobile seem to have something happening every week. So, perhaps the real highlight of the library is the list of special events, classes, and meetings they sponsor at the main library and branches. In November 2009 you could have heard Taylor Branch discuss his new book *The Clinton Tapes;* taken a photographic tour of Roland Park with Denny Lynch; met with college admissions representatives to learn how to pay for college; learned advanced skills and techniques in Microsoft Word; and explored the photographs, letters, and other Poe memorabilia.

The central branch is open Monday through Wednesday 10 a.m. to 7 p.m., Thursday through Saturday 10 a.m. to 5 p.m., and Sunday 1 to 5 p.m. from October through May. Admission is free.

EUBIE BLAKE NATIONAL JAZZ INSTITUTE AND CULTURAL CENTER
847 North Howard St.
(410) 225-3130
www.eubieblake.org

Honoring Eubie Blake (1883–1983), the famous ragtime piano player and musical theater composer of *Shuffle Along* and songs "I'm Just Wild About Harry" and "Memories of You," the center's museum educates and explains the legacy of jazz greats from Baltimore, including Cab Calloway, Billie Holiday, Chick Webb, and Avon Long. Monthly exhibits in the gallery highlight renowned and aspiring artists. The museum is open Wednesday through Friday from noon to 6 p.m., Saturday from 11 a.m. to 3 p.m. and on Sunday by appointment. Admission is $5.

THE FLAG HOUSE AND STAR-SPANGLED BANNER MUSEUM
844 East Pratt St.
(410) 837-1793
www.flaghouse.org

Mary Pickersgill sewed by hand the 30-foot-by-42-foot flag that flew over Fort McHenry during the British bombardment in 1814. Built in 1793, this house was her home during her adult years. The adjacent museum commemorates the War of 1812 and features an audiovisual program about Pickersgill's life and her role in the war. Living-history programs are offered here on Saturday. The house is open Tuesday through Saturday 10 a.m. to 3:15 p.m. Admission is $7 for adults, $6 for seniors (55 and up) and military, and $5 for students (kindergarten through 12th grade). Free parking is available on Albemarle Street (pick up a pass from the visitor desk).

FORT MCHENRY NATIONAL MONUMENT AND HISTORIC SHRINE
2400 East Fort Ave.
(410) 962-4290
www.nps.gov/fomc

This place gives "The Star-Spangled Banner" its meaning. Three times an hour, a short orientation film *The Defense of Fort McHenry* is shown to introduce you to the park and its significance. The presentation closes with the playing of the anthem and the unveiling of the "flag [that] was still there." During the summer, rangers give talks daily and on weekends discuss living history in the fort. The Fort McHenry Guard performs drill, musket, and artillery demonstrations.

The Fort's position at the point of the harbor leading into Baltimore's port made Fort McHenry a strategic military site. The fort looks as it did that night in 1814 though displays recall its history through the Civil War and the two World Wars. Good times to visit are near sunset when visitors are asked to help lower the 30-foot-by-42-foot flag or for one of the twilight "tattoos" held in the summer. These combine music and historic military pageantry. The grounds offer a beautiful place to walk and see ships heading in from or out to the Chesapeake Bay. Remember to take a sweater or a jacket because the wind can be brisk.

In May 2009, the park service started building a new visitor center. The existing one, at 5,700 square feet, was built in 1964 to accommodate 250,000 visitors annually. The park visitor count now exceeds 600,000 and it's anticipated that it will hit one million in a few years. During the spring about 30-40 school buses arrive. These crowds have put a strain on the facilities and the patience of the visitors. Long lines form for information, the audiovisual program, the bookstore, and the restrooms. The new visitor center, at 17,200 square feet, is due to open before the bicentennial celebration of the War of 1812. The project is seeking Gold-level certification in the LEED Green Building Rating System.

The park is open every day except Thanksgiving, Christmas, and New Year's days from 8 a.m. to 5 p.m. Admission to the historic fort is $7 for adults (16 and up) and free for children younger than age 16. The entrance fee is good for seven days from the date of first use. You can buy a $30 annual pass that is good for the pass owner and any three adults in a single private non-commercial vehicle. The park also accepts various national park passes.

GEPPI'S ENTERTAINMENT MUSEUM
Camden Station
301 West Camden St.
(410) 625-7060
www.geppismuseum.com

One way to prevent "Mom" from trashing your old collection of whatever is today's really super hot collectible is to open your own museum, which is what it appears Steve Geppi has done. On the second floor of the old Camden train station (above the Sports Legends), local entrepreneur Geppi has installed a portion of his amazing collection of 6,000 or so comic books, animation cels, movie posters, and antique toys, arranging them by era. Audio commentary introduces visitors to each room. Interactive screens let comic book fans leaf through some of the classics or listen to music and radio programming from the World War II era. Perhaps what makes this a must-see is the presentation of items we remember from our own childhoods. The museum made an effort to include all kinds of items—cereal boxes, decoder rings, cowboy hats, *Star Trek* board games—that will trigger a memory from the past. Of course, many of these items are older than most of us: a 1568 broadsheet from Germany, comics of the 1930s, newspaper comic strips of "Yellow Kid" and "Buster Brown." In late 2009, Geppi featured a "Yellow Bricks & Emerald Cities" exhibit celebrating the 70th anniversary of *The Wizard of Oz,* which seemed to draw a lot of Friends of Dorothy.

The museum is open Tuesday through Sunday from 10 a.m. to 6 p.m. It's wheelchair accessible and parking is available on-site. Tickets are $10 for adults, $9 for seniors (55 and up), and $7 for children (5 through 18). Head to GEM on a Tuesday or Thursday and admission is half-price. Stop by on any Ravens or Orioles home game day and it's $1. Combination tickets with Sports Legends are available for $18 for adults, $15 for seniors, and $11.50 for students.

THE GREAT BLACKS IN WAX MUSEUM
1601-3 East North Ave.
(410) 563-3404
www.greatblacksinwax.org

The first and only museum of its kind, The Great Blacks In Wax Museum opened in 1983 to pay tribute to African Americans by exhibiting more than 100 lifelike statues in one place. You'll be standing next to Dr. Martin Luther King Jr., Supreme Court Justice Thurgood Marshall, Baltimore neurosurgeon Dr. Ben Carson, known for his lifesaving surgeries on infants at Johns Hopkins Hospital, and Kweisi Mfume, a former Baltimore congressman who took over the helm of the National Association for the Advancement of Colored People (NAACP). Yes, President Obama is present. A model slave ship offers an in-depth look at the slave trade that took place 400 years ago, while another gives a picture of black youths' contributions to the civil rights movement. Stop by the gift shop, where you can pick up everything from postcards to posters and tote bags.

Summer hours (July and August and February for Black History Month) are Monday through Saturday from 9 a.m. to 6 p.m. and Sunday from noon to 6 p.m. During most of the rest of the year, the museum is closed on Monday.

Admission is $12 for adults, $11 for college students and senior citizens, $10 for children 3 through 11. There is no admission charge for museum members.

HOLOCAUST MEMORIAL
Corner of Water, Gay, and Lombard Streets
(410) 752-2630

Near the Inner Harbor, this outdoor memorial and sculpture center is designed to remind visitors of the six million Jews murdered by the Nazis in Europe from 1933 to 1945. The memorial is open 24 hours a day. It was built in 1980 and was refurbished in 1997 and features two concrete monoliths that represent the boxcars used to transport Jews to the Nazi death camps. Railroad tracks surround the structure. The redesign, which involved the removal of a grassy hill, gives passersby along the Inner Harbor a view of the memorial.

JEWISH MUSEUM OF MARYLAND
Lloyd Street Synagogue
15 Lloyd St.
(410) 732-6400
www.jhsm.org

The Jewish Museum of Maryland (JMM) is said to be America's leading museum of regional Jewish history, was formed in 1960, and works to help restore family histories for people scattered during World War II. The museum seems to be constantly sponsoring activities for adults and children. One program combined love of history and biking with a tour of Jewish Baltimore from your bicycle seat. On the mostly flat 10-mile itinerary were several neighborhoods of South Baltimore, East Baltimore, and Bolton Hill, with stops at sites of Jewish interest. There was a registration fee of $20.

The Lloyd Street Synagogue was built in 1845 and was the first synagogue in Maryland. The second floor reopened for tours in September 2009 and the downstairs is due to reopen in the spring 2010 with a new exhibit, *The Synagogue Speaks*. Upstairs tours are given on Sunday and Tuesday through Thursday at 1 and 2:30 p.m. Private group tours are given Sunday through Friday at 9:30 a.m. Admission is free to members, $8 for adults, $4 for students, and $3 for children 12 and under.

LACROSSE MUSEUM AND NATIONAL HALL OF FAME
113 West University Parkway
(410) 235-6882
www.uslacrosse.org
Although on first blush it may seem that Baltimore goes crazy for Orioles, Ravens, and the flying Michael Phelps, lacrosse is firmly entrenched into many lives. If you love lacrosse, or if you know someone who does, stop here for a bit of history and a celebration of those who have made it the exciting sport it is. At the edge of the Johns Hopkins University campus, the museum has artifacts from the game as it is played now by men and women and from the way it was played in the past. (Equipment sure has changed over the years.) The museum is open June through January Monday through Friday from 10 a.m. to 3 p.m. From February through May, it is open Tuesday through Saturday from 10 a.m. to 3 p.m. Admission is $3 for age 16 and older, $2 for age 5 through 15, and free to any U.S. Lacrosse Member (bring your ID).

MARYLAND HISTORICAL SOCIETY MUSEUM
201 West Monument St.
(410) 685-3750
www.mdhs.org
The original draft of "The Star-Spangled Banner," the world's largest collection of paintings by Charles Wilson Peale and his family, and the nation's largest collection of 19th-century American silver are among the attractions in this independent museum and library of Maryland history. There's also a great collection of decorative arts and galleries with images depicting the Civil War and War of 1812. Of special childhood interest is their collection of 2,500 toys, dolls, and games, all played with by Maryland children. Yep, that's where your Toni doll went. Museum hours are Wednesday through Sunday from 10 a.m. to 5 p.m. The H. Furlong Baldwin Library hours are Wednesday through Saturday from 10 a.m. to 5 p.m. Admission is free to members, $4 for adults, $3 for seniors, students with valid ID, and children age 13 through 17, and $3 for children age 3 through 12. Admission to the library and museum is $6 for adults and $4 for students with ID. Parking is available in the Monument Street lot. Visit on the first Thursday of the month and the admission fee is waived.

THE MARYLAND INSTITUTE, COLLEGE OF ART
1300 West Mount Royal Ave.
(410) 669-9200
www.mica.edu
Art abounds all around The Maryland Institute. On the lawns, in the median strip down Mount Royal Avenue, and just about anywhere there is space to put sculpture. The institute also has four galleries with 60 to 90 exhibitions a year. Check the calendar for lectures, exhibit openings, concerts, and numerous related events.

MARYLAND SCIENCE CENTER AND IMAX THEATER
601 Light St.
(410) 685-5225
www.mdsci.org

The world of science comes alive with interactive exhibits and live demonstrations explaining light, mechanics, and sound. Hundreds of hands-on exhibits let you and your children explore science and how it affects our daily lives. DinoQuest is a room filled with life-size re-creations of the giant lizards that once roamed the earth.

The Davis Planetarium mixes stargazing with history and storytelling; and an IMAX movie theater features a five-story-high screen that shows films ranging from the Jim Carrey twist on *A Christmas Carol* (in 3D) to Van Gogh and his brush with genius to *Africa: The Serengeti*. Both of these special theaters are in addition to the normal admission fee.

Everything is interactive for happier, better educated children (and adults who want to be children again). Exhibits on the human body have been designed with children in mind: gross is cool here and educational. Dig for bones after staring up at the Giganotosaurus. Check out the displays that help us understand our place in the world and in space with images from the Hubble Space Telescope and the National Oceanic and Atmospheric Administration. Little ones have their own children's room where they can play with blocks, crawl around the Room to Grow area, or explore a Baltimore streetscape.

The Maryland Science Center is open October through March on Tuesday through Thursday 10 a.m. to 5 p.m., Friday 10 a.m. to 8 p.m., Saturday 10 a.m. to 6 p.m., and Sunday 11 a.m. to 5 p.m. From Memorial Day weekend through Labor Day, hours are Sunday through Thursday 10 a.m. to 6 p.m. and Friday and Saturday 10 a.m. to 8 p.m.

The IMAX Theater also has evening shows, and the observatory opens after hours on Friday nights for stargazing. Admission prices vary, depending on what you want to see. For the museum only, admission is $14.95 for adults, $13.95 for seniors, and $10.95 for children 3 through 12. Adding an IMAX film costs an extra $4 for all ages. Evening IMAX presentations are $8.

You may exit and return as often as you wish (in one day) after your admission has been paid and you're wearing the valid wristband for the day.

THE MARYLAND ZOO IN BALTIMORE
Druid Hill Park, 1 Druid Park Lake Dr.
(410) 366-LION
www.marylandzoo.org

The third-oldest zoo in the nation has more than 2,250 birds, reptiles, and mammals within its 160 acres. The zoo is divided into several sections including Africa Journey (chimpanzees, lions, and giraffes), the Children's Zoo, Polar Bear Watch. Programs such as Keeper Encounters, EdZOOcation classes, behind-the-scenes tours, and zoo camps teach children about endangered wildlife, their habitats, and life cycles. The programs change from day to day, so it's best to call for specific details. The exhibits and cages housing the animals have low sight lines designed to allow children of all ages to check out the action. The reptile house is a favorite, while the African Safari section offers an insight into life on another continent and is inhabited by elephants, chimpanzees, giraffes, and lions. The Children's Zoo focuses on animals that call Maryland home—from the hills and caves of the western part of the state to the waters and marshes of the Chesapeake Bay. The Children's Zoo, rated number one in the country, also includes hands-on KidZone, where children can hop across 6-foot-wide lily pads, perch in an oriole's nest, and jump over a frog.

Among the fairly recent additions to the zoo is Sampson the elephant who weighed in at 1,100 pounds and gained about 2.5 pounds a day for a very long time.

On hot summer days, shaded areas can be at a premium. Benches are available throughout the zoo, and almost every stretch is designed for stroller-pushing families and wheelchair users. Refreshments, including beverages, pizza, hot dogs, and snacks, are available at several locations. There's also a carousel (fee) in the Village Green section and a free tram to take people from one place to another. Free parking is available. You can also ride a camel for $5 from Memorial Day through Labor Day, feed a giraffe for $2 daily from 10:30 a.m. to 3 p.m., weather permitting.

The zoo is open daily, except on Thanksgiving, Christmas Day, and one Friday in June for an annual fund-raising event, from 10 a.m. to 4 p.m. It's completely closed in January and February. Adults are $13, seniors (62 plus) are $11, and children are $9 (2 through 11) and can be ordered online and printed. Then, you just go to the member entrance gate and avoid the lines.

i For $60 a year you can "adopt" a polar bear, an African elephant, or a penguin and receive a personalized adoption certificate, a plush animal, a fun fact sheet, and an animal photograph. Other animals can be adopted, too, although you won't receive the plush animal for your donation. You will also receive the zoo's quarterly magazine, an invitation for two to the Adopters Recognition Day held each spring, and your name on the Web site's recognition page. Perhaps the best part, though, is you don't have to feed or clean up after your adopted animal.

NATIONAL AQUARIUM IN BALTIMORE
Pier 3/501 East Pratt St.
(410) 576-3800
www.aqua.org

There's a National Aquarium in Baltimore and a much smaller one in Washington, D.C., at the Department of Commerce building, both now run by the same management. This section is about the one in Baltimore. You can come visit, meander your way through the huge tanks, and almost feel like these fish are swimming around you and you don't even need your SCUBA gear. There are so many other things to do here, though, depending on the time of the year and other factors.

Among the options might be a Tots and Tales session for children on Wednesday morning where you can learn about aquatic animals through story and song. You can start your day with an exclusive, insider's look at the dolphins. Start with a continental breakfast, talk with the trainers, explore the facility, and then see the dolphin show.

The building was designed by Chermayeff, Sollogub & Poole, Inc. who also designed the

aquarium in Chattanooga, so, yes if you've seen both you'll know why they look similar.

Sharks, dolphins, puffins, stingrays, poison dart frogs, piranhas, electric eels, and reef fish are just some of the 14,000 or marine creatures from the four corners of the globe at the National Aquarium in Baltimore. The aquarium also houses a rain forest (the glass pyramid on top of the building). Perhaps you saw Margaret, the Brazilian Hyacinth Macaw on a television show, not for her preening abilities or her royal blue feathers and yellow face, but about endangered species. Maybe you thought, hmm, a macaw at an aquarium. Well, yes, up in the rain forest.

Take the elevator to the top and start walking down the ramp. You'll see exhibits about several habitats, ranging from tidal marshes along the coast of Maryland to the dense tropical foliage of a South American rain forest. Level 5 offers the Tropical Rain Forest, where careful observers can view colorful birds, golden lion tamarinds (monkeys), red-bellied piranhas, and lizards. Other treats at the aquarium include a 1,300-seat aquarium that hosts daily dolphin shows.

On level 4 you can see one of the aquarium's exhibits that re-creates a section of the backwater Amazon River tributary and the forest that it seasonally floods. Along a 57-foot-long acrylic wall, you can see schools of tropical fish, giant river turtles, dwarf caimans, caiman lizards, and a giant anaconda. Level 4 also has the Atlantic Coral Reef, where you are surrounded by a rainbow—hundreds of vividly colored tropical fish.

Level 3 has the shocking electric eels and entanglements of a giant Pacific octopus. Patient people in this gallery are rewarded by the sight of tiny jawfish that live in small burrows that they dig.

On level 2, Mountains to the Sea, you can trace the water cycle from a freshwater pond in the mountains of western Maryland through the Tidal Marsh, into the Coastal Beach, and out into the waters of the Atlantic shelf.

Then, on level 1 you can see stingrays and small sharks in a 265,000-gallon pool and Animal Planet Australia: Wild Extremes. Children of all ages love the new "4–D" movie theater on level 1.

Time your visit right and you can see SCUBA divers feeding the fish.

Tickets are $24.95 for adults, $14.95 for children age 3 through 11, and $23.95 for seniors (ages 60 and up). The dolphin show and 4-D Immersion Theater that lets you see behind the scenes cost an extra couple of dollars and a package of all three is $29.95 for adults, $19.95 for children, and $28.95 for seniors. Besides the fact that an annual membership helps the aquarium, it makes financial sense if you're going to be a frequent visitor. As an example, the Family Plus membership cost $199 and includes admission for two adults and up to six of your unmarried children 21 and under living in your household and named on the membership. You also receive admission for one guest per visit and two one-time-use tickets. Tickets are available online at www.aqua.org and at www.ticketmaster.com, with a 95 cents per ticket service fee. Groups of 15 or more receive a discount. Visiting hours vary by day and season, roughly 9 a.m. to 5 p.m., with longer hours on Friday and in the summer. Arrange for an early or post 3 p.m., Friday evening, when the crowds are lighter. The aquarium closes 90 minutes after the last admission.

If you're driving, plan to park in one of the downtown lots or use the Inner Harbor Garage/Landmark Parking, 100 S. Gay St. that welcomes cars and vans. Print the parking certificate on the Web site for a discount certificate that's good for $3 off the maximum daily rate. You must redeem the certificate at the aquarium's information desk.

The three gift shops—aquarium, dolphin, and shark—mean you can find memories anywhere. Or, you can shop online.

OBSERVATION AREA
Dorsey Road, Linthicum
(410) 859-7111
www.bwiairport.com
This is another observation point at BWI where you don't have to pay a parking fee. An outdoor parking area lets you watch plane takeoffs and landings. Located to the south of one of the airport's busiest runways, the parking area provides children of all ages with an up-close view of

planes in motion. The planes fly about 200 feet over the site. You'll also find a playground area. During the summer months, stop there to enjoy hot dogs, snowballs, and other refreshments. The area is part of a 12½-mile scenic trail that encircles the airport property.

ORIOLE PARK AT CAMDEN YARDS
333 West Camden St.
(410) 547-6234
www.theorioles.com
After decades of building multipurpose arenas that weren't totally suitable for football or baseball, and years of trying to play a great game in an outdated Memorial Stadium, Baltimore finally had its brand new "retro" park baseball stadium. Oh, there were a few problems, soon fixed. Other cities visited and learned from this experience. Where Baltimore had "chiropractic" seats along the third base line, the Stadium at Arlington "corrected" the problem and ended up with a chiropractic section along the first base line. This stadium is so much more than a baseball playground. It was even one of the parks used by the teams in the movie *Major League II.*

So, the Os haven't been winning the games we'd like them to. In fact, being excited that they didn't lose 100 games in the 2009 season says all that needs to be said.

The Os started something that should be adopted by every team. It's a scalp-free zone outside Gate F (corner of Camden and Russell Street, across from Pickle's Pub). That's where you go, as much as two-and-a-half hours prior to all home games if you have tickets to sell or want to buy for today's game (and sometimes tomorrow's game) and be assured that you will pay no more than face value. Oriole's management monitors the area but does not participate in the sales. Usually, sellers are season ticket holders who aren't going to be attending the game. Buying a ticket on a game being played because of a rain-out is really easy and usually provides the best seats for the least amount of money. Trying to buy a ticket when Boston or New York is the opposite team is super tough because half the stadium is filled with fans from those cities. They travel south because it's easier to buy tickets for these games than back home. Also, don't worry about the tickets being adjacent to each other. Usually, there's enough room to move around and be together once you're inside the park.

This made a lot of sense when all 40,000-plus seats had been sold and scalpers were getting 10 times the face value. It makes sense today even with sparser attendance numbers.

Located under the green tent behind the center field bleachers on Eutaw Street is **Boog Powell's BBQ.** During practically any Orioles home game, Boog Powell, the former All-Star first baseman, can be found signing autographs and stirring up some of Maryland's finest barbecue beef and pork. Additionally, Boog's BBQ is available on the Club Level behind home plate.

Stop by for an autograph and a photo op with Boog, or talk with Ann Marie O'Brien who's been running this operation for years. Yes, she's part of the O'Brien family that runs the Floyd's 99 Barbershops, with a location in Ellicott City.

Baseball is king for 81 games each year, and sometimes more than that if the Os go into play-off season. However, you can tour the stadium daily from mid-February through mid-December, except on days with afternoon home games. Tour tickets can be purchased either online, or at the main box office windows, located at the north end of the ballpark's warehouse. Private tours can be arranged. You can purchase tickets in advance or on the day of a tour from the ticket office in the ballpark warehouse adjacent to gate H. Tickets are $7 for adults and $5 for children younger than age 12 and seniors. Parking is free during the weekends when the team is away. There is lot parking available during the week for $5. It's best to call ahead for details. Tickets are sold in advance or the day of the tour, subject to availability. Call the Tour Information Line at (410) 547-6234.

The old B&O Railroad warehouse runs along Eutaw Street behind the right-field seats. The seven-story brick building, built around the turn of the century, is the longest warehouse building on the East Coast; it extends an amazing 1,016

feet, although it is only 51 feet wide. That means that, if stood on end, it would be taller than New York's Empire State Building. So there.

At 439 feet from home plate, the warehouse is a long shot away for a batter. Despite the distance from home plate to offices, the powers that be decided with the right wind speed and direction, etc., it might be possible for a ball to come crashing through the windows. Shatter-proof glass was installed, at considerable extra expense. As of 2009, no player has hit the warehouse during a game. Ken Griffey Jr., then the Seattle Mariners' star outfielder, nailed it during the home-run derby the day before the 1993 All-Star Game, which was hosted by the Orioles in their year-old stadium. It bounced on the Eutaw Street walkway and jumped into an open window in the public relations office. As you walk among the shops and offices along Eutaw Street beside the warehouse, look down and you'll see round, bronze markers where home runs have landed as players continue to tee up for the warehouse. Inside the ballpark, the field is set 16 feet below ground level, giving the park a more intimate feel than its predecessors. Conveniently located about 6 blocks west of the Inner Harbor, on land a block from where Babe Ruth, the Bronx Bomber himself, was born and raised, the stadium integrates the skyline and feel of today's Baltimore with some of the classic features of old ballparks. Steel, rather than concrete, trusses and an arched brick facade call to mind bygone playing grounds like Ebbetts Field in Brooklyn and Shibe Park in Philadelphia. Other distinctive features, some copied at Jacobs Field in Cleveland, Turner Field in Atlanta, and the Ballpark at Arlington in Texas, include an asymmetrical playing field and low outfield walls. On every aisle is a reproduction of the logo used by the Baltimore Orioles of the 1890s, a National League team that won consecutive pennants from 1894 to 1896. The seats designated for wheelchair users were created for this park and have been copied and used in ball parks constructed since 1992.

Camden Yards even welcomes rain. The field features Professional Athletic Turf, an irrigation and drainage system below the natural grass that ends rain delays about 30 minutes after the rains stop. The field can remove as much as 75,000 gallons of rainwater from the field each hour. Because the grass is shallow-rooted, it has to be watered twice daily. When there's a day home game, the water drained from the rain is used to back-water the grass.

Recent renovations included replacing the entire playing surface and changing the field dimensions of the ballpark. Home plate was moved about 7 feet closer to the backstop, bringing fans closer to the action, providing better sight lines from hundreds of seats, reducing obstructions near the foul poles, and increasing safety for spectators behind home plate.

The foul line measurement increased from 318 feet to 320 feet in right field and from 333 feet to 337 feet in left. The center field distance increased from 400 feet to 406 feet and the deepest part of the ballpark, left center field, increased from 410 feet to 417 feet. The foul poles were repositioned and the left-field pole from Memorial Stadium from 1954 through 1991 was installed. The Memorial Stadium foul pole is shorter (70 feet) and required a smaller support structure that allowed more fans in the lower club and upper decks to have an unobstructed view of the field. The Orioles have used the original right-field foul pole from Memorial Stadium since Camden Yards opened in 1992.

The bleacher seats in right field and center field are really good seats, although you're looking over the shoulders of the outfielders. Standing-room-only tickets, which enable spectators to watch from an outfield porch in right field or to fill seats left unoccupied, are another bargain. You'll also notice the 72 luxury boxes, where movers and shakers can watch the game, sip champagne, and eat from expensive platters. They're great seats and great eats when you can get them, but don't hold your breath.

The club level is the place to be if you want to be treated like royalty but can't afford to own a luxury box. In these seats, just a few feet higher than the Press Box, waiters and waitresses will get your hot dogs, turkey sandwiches, or crab cakes. With so few rows, you also don't have a lot of

people walking back and forth for snacks, beer, or bathroom stops. Another advantage of club seats: there is access to indoor facilities with air conditioning, a bar, and TV lounges.

When leaving Camden Yards by Light Rail you can do at least two things to help ensure a seat. One, aim for the front or rear of the car instead of trying to board in the middle. Or, take the train away from where you're headed (going north when you want to go to Cromwell Station) and get off at the first or second stop, then board the train headed south, which probably will be empty or relatively empty until it arrives at the Convention Center or Camden Yards stations.

Some legends hang around forever and some need a little tweaking. Wild Bill Hagy (June 17, 1939–August 20, 2007) seems to be part of the later. During Memorial Stadium days, Hagy could be found in upper deck section 34, leading the "roar from 34." He was easy to spot because he led the "O-R-I-O-L-E-S" chant during the late 1970s and early 1980s. The 6'2" cab driver from Dundalk wore sun glasses, a "wild" beard, and a straw version of a western hat. Periodically, he would lead the cheer from the top of the dugout. It's said he led his last cheer three weeks before his death, in Cooperstown, New York, at Cal Ripken's Hall of Fame enshrinement ceremonies on July 29, 2007. Hagy died suddenly at 68 at his home in Arbutus. The Os distributed #34 T-shirts on T-shirt Tuesday on June 17, 2008.

Fast forward to 1989, while still in the old stadium, when "Robo Vendor" Perry Hahn, a long-term beer seller who created a device that lets him open and pour two beer cans in six seconds. The little motor and can opener thing runs around the cans and voila! Hahn calls it the Tandem High Speed Can Opener and he spent about $4,500 developing it. He started his quest for more efficiency during the '89 season, at Memorial Stadium, when crowds were huge and staff was small. His electrical engineering degree from the University of Maryland helped. Yes, you're shaking your head in agreement, and then, oops, the beer containers are plastic and, well, maybe it was just a day late and a dollar short. Undaunted, apparently, Hahn can still be selling beer at Camden Yards, the Preakness, and at other sporting events.

Just as Cal Ripken Jr. set a record, octogenarian Ernie Tyler earned his longevity record by working as the Orioles' umpire attendant every day from 1960 until July 2007. He missed the game so he could attend Ripken's induction into the Baseball Hall of Fame. The umpire's iron man couldn't and wouldn't refuse baseball's Iron Man's invitation. Tyler's job description includes rubbing mud onto baseballs before each game to rough them up. He sits near the Os dugout during the game, retrieving foul balls and delivering new balls to the umpires.

Camden Yards has people or organizations present the National Anthem. They don't sing it. It could be a way to protect themselves in case someone decides to do something people might think less than orthodox. The fans have a tradition of accenting the "Oh" in "Oh, say does that Star-Spangled Banner yet wave," which is thought to reflect the Orioles and the flat way Baltimoreans pronounce the vowel; they do this at Baltimore Ravens games too. Anyone interested in performing the National Anthem prior to an Orioles game should send a resume outlining past singing performances, along with an acapella version of the National Anthem. Please direct this correspondence to Baltimore Orioles, Attn: Ballpark Entertainment Department, 333 West Camden St., Baltimore, MD 21201.

PHOENIX SHOT TOWER
801 East Fayette St.
(410) 605-2964
www.baltimore.to/ShotTower/index.html
www.carrollmuseums.org/home.html
The Phoenix Shot Tower was constructed in 1828 where, as the name suggests, lead shot ammunition was made. Molten lead was poured through colanders at the top of the shaft, fragmenting into pieces, which became round before falling into vats of water to cool. This 234-foot structure, which was in use until 1892, was the tallest building in the United States until 1846. Through a light and sound show, you learn how the shot was made for pistols, rifles, and even larger

molded shot for cannons. No, you aren't allowed to climb inside and it isn't air-conditioned so it can get quite warm in summer. This is one of a handful remaining shot towers in the country. The others are in Virginia, Iowa, Wisconsin, Ohio, Pennsylvania, New York, and Connecticut.

i If you want the Oriole Bird to visit you at your seat, just select the inning (from a list of options) and donate $75 to the Os Charitable Foundation. The Bird brings a goodie bag to help celebrate. Requests should be made at least a day in advance by calling (888) 848-BIRD. For $25, you can have a birthday, anniversary, marriage proposal posted, or military personnel return on the scoreboard. Call (888) 848-BIRD or visit www.orioles.com at least 48 hours in advance to schedule your scoreboard surprise. Requests cannot be taken the day of the game. Fans may also sign up for future games in the Fan Assistance Centers by providing the celebrant's name, address, age/years married, the date of the game, and the name and daytime phone number of a contact person in case the Orioles have a question.

PORT DISCOVERY
35 Market Place
(410) 727-8120
www.portdiscovery.org
Since opening its doors on December 29, 1998, Port Discovery, the child-powered museum, is one of the ultimate experiences in fun and learning for children and their families in the Baltimore area. Designed in collaboration with Walt Disney Imagineering and a team of educators, Port Discovery takes education and entertainment to a new level and brings a new vision to the idea of a children's museum. Located in the historic Fishmarket Building, Port Discovery is one of the largest children's museums in the country. On Meet and Greet Street free fun and entertainment, including live performances and special exhibits, is offered. In Kidsworks, children can crawl, jump, slide, swing, and swoosh through a three-story

urban tree house. MPT Studioworks allows children to watch TV and learn how it works. There is also a learning library designed to enhance the museum experience.

Port Discovery is open from October through Memorial Day on Tuesday through Friday from 9:30 a.m. to 4:30 p.m., Saturday 10 a.m. to 5 p.m., Sunday noon through 5 p.m. The museum is closed on Thanksgiving day, Christmas Eve and day. Admission is $12.95 for age 2 and older.

Harbor Park Garage offers discounted parking on weekends. It's attached to Port Discovery's building with easy access from Lombard Street or Market Place. Please pick up a validation at the museum box office. Or, you can take the subway to the Shot Tower/Market Place stop, just outside the museum's doors.

PRIDE OF BALTIMORE II
Inner Harbor
(410) 539-1151
www.pride2.org
When it's in port, this replica of an 1812 clipper privateer ship offers great insight into the 19th-century-style Baltimore clipper ships that plied the waters of the Chesapeake throughout the century. The *Pride II* has sailed all over the world, extending a dose of Baltimore charm and history wherever it docks. It's usually at sea more than half of the year. Hours vary for tours, which are conducted by the paid and volunteer staff that man it during journeys. No admission is charged. Call in advance to see when the boat is in dock. The *Pride* offers sailing trips around the Baltimore harbor and between Baltimore and Annapolis (one-way only). They cost $45 to $65.

Pride of Baltimore II replaced the *Pride of Baltimore* that was sunk off Puerto Rico in 1986, taking her captain and three crew members with her. Both ships were built in the Inner Harbor.

REGINALD F. LEWIS MUSEUM OF MARYLAND AFRICAN AMERICAN HISTORY AND CULTURE
830 East Pratt St.
(443) 263-1800
www.africanamericanculture.org

We land at BWI Thurgood Marshall Airport. We hear about Frederick Douglass. If we've lived through enough of earth's rotations, we remember such names as Cab Calloway and Chick Webb. We can Google or do a Wikipedia search and learn something about these people. However, through the exhibits of African-American history and accomplishments, the Lewis Museum is designed to inspire children and the rest of us by telling their stories and accomplishments. The exhibitions about politicians and artists, religious leaders, and athletes are people-oriented, with memorabilia and stories of individual Marylanders. The three major galleries focus on family and community; labor (including slavery); and art and intellect. Some exhibits are harrowing, just as some portions of African-American history are harrowing, but most exhibits relate stories of great achievement. The exhibits appeal mostly to older children and adults. The museum's goal is to reach out to children and inspire them to achieve their own dreams. Admission is $8 for adults, and $6 for children age 8 and older and seniors. The museum is open Wednesday through Saturday from 10 a.m. to 5 p.m. and Sunday noon to 5 p.m. During the summer, the museum stays open Thursday night until 8 p.m. A parking garage is available across the street from the museum.

Special performances, films, art activities, and education sessions are held during Kwanzaa.

SCHOOL 33 ART CENTER
1427 Light St.
(410) 396-4641
www.school33.org
Housed in an old schoolhouse, the School 33 Art Center has fostered contemporary art in this city since 1979, working to connect the public to contemporary artists. An eco-friendly outdoor garden—fed by a rainwater collection system—is just one example of the center's commitment to improve inside and out. Administered by the Baltimore Office of Promotion and the Arts, its gallery space mounts 18 shows a year featuring the work of local artists in its three galleries. The center's Studio Artist Program provides inexpen-

sive studio space for working artists, while afford-able, year-round classes and special weekend workshops taught by professional artists bring art to the masses. Each fall the center sponsors the Open Studio Tour, which takes us around the city and allows us to peek into the magical spaces where the artists create their work. The gallery is open Wednesday through Saturday from noon to 6 p.m.

SHERWOOD GARDENS
Between Stratford, Highfield, Underwood, and Greenway Streets, Guildford
Guildford Association Executive Office
(410) 235-3752
With about 80,000 tulips and other spring flowers planted around the six acres of this garden, you don't have to go to the airport to think you're in the Netherlands. Peak blossom times are late April and early May, so sharpen your photogra-phy skills and you can fill your entire year with blossom photos. Sherwood is wonderfully tran-quil the rest of the year, so bring a blanket and picnic and enjoy. An abundance of annuals are planted each year for your summer enjoyment. The gardens are open daily from dawn to dusk, with no admission charge.

SPORTS LEGENDS MUSEUM AT CAMDEN YARDS
Camden Station
301 West Camden Street
www.baberuthmuseum.com
On the ground floor of and below the old Cam-den Yards railroad station is where you'll find lots of sports stuff. Compare your height to Cal Ripken Jr., try on a uniform, and catch some interesting newsclips. If you love sports—any sport, baseball, lacrosse, horseracing—this is your place. This is the home of the Maryland Athletic Hall of Fame and the Orioles Museum with shrines to the Bal-timore Colts and Johnny Unitas; tributes to such baseball greats as Cal Ripken Jr., Babe Ruth, and Jimmy Foxx; and memorabilia from girls soccer teams, college sports programs, the Preakness, and baseball's Negro Leagues. The museum is open Tuesday through Sunday 10 a.m. to 5 p.m.

November through March and during baseball season daily 10 a.m. to 6 p.m. (until 7:30 p.m. on home game days). Tickets are $10 for adults, $8 for seniors, and $6.50 for those age 3 through 12. Combination tickets with the Babe Ruth Birth-place and Museum are available and discounts are given to visitors with tickets for the Oriole Park stadium tour. A discount coupon is available on the Web site, too. A combo ticket with the Sports Legends Museum is $12 for adults, $8 for seniors, and $5 for children. The top floor is home to the Geppi Entertainment Museum.

TOP OF THE WORLD OBSERVATION LEVEL
World Trade Center
401 East Pratt St.
(410) 837-8439
www.viewbaltimore.org
The 27th floor of the World Trade Center in Bal-timore offers a stunning 360-degree view of Bal-timore's skyline. Stationed binoculars and photo maps enhance the experience, offering a detailed look at the Inner Harbor and the surrounding city. The Top of the World Observation Level is open from mid-March through mid-September from 10 a.m. to 6 p.m. (check for later hours). For mid-September through November, it's closed on Monday and Tuesday. November through March, it's only open Friday, Saturday, and Sun-day. Admission is $5 for adults, $4 for seniors (60 plus), and $3 for children (3 through 12). Security measures require searches of purses, briefcases, packages, and backpacks. For your convenience, the Trade Center staff suggests that you leave nonessential items at home or in your hotel. Remember the Observation Level is part of the Harbor Pass ticket.

THE WALTERS ART MUSEUM
600 North Charles St.
(410) 547-9000
www.thewalters.org
Walk in the front door and say thank you to William and Henry Walters who left their art collection to the city. The Walters collection is one of only a few worldwide to present a com-prehensive history of art from the third millen-

nium B.C. to 20th-century Europe. This collection is renowned in the cultural community for its breadth of pieces, including a rare sarcophagus from second-century Rome, Fabergé eggs, Greek sculpture, medieval ivories, Art Deco jewelry, and so much more. The museum also plays host to major traveling exhibitions, such as a show featuring works by Edouard Manet. Children can be fascinated by the Chamber of Wonders that includes trays of exotic insects, a stuffed alligator, and playing checkers or chess in the Knights Hall. Personally, I'm in awe of the restoration work they do. You can catch a "behind-the-scenes" look at what the conservators are doing through a 4' by 5' viewing window that was cut into the room. You can interact with the conservators with questions and conversations.

Free docent-led tours of the permanent or special exhibition are usually offered on Sunday at 2 p.m. Other tours, audio tours, scripts, and touch tours are available from the Visitor Services Desk. Call ahead if you have a special need. The museum is open Wednesday through Sunday 10 a.m. to 5 p.m. Extended hours may apply for special exhibitions. Admission is free except for occasional special exhibits.

From October through June, the Walters sponsors a free First Friday series from 5 to 9 p.m. They feature live entertainment, music, activities, light snacks, and a cash bar. The theme will relate to one of the collections or exhibits.

Yes, there is a gift shop.

WASHINGTON MONUMENT
Mount Vernon Place
**(410) 396-1049, (410) 396-0929,
(877) BALTIMORE**
www.promotionandarts.com

The view from the top of the first architectural monument to honor George Washington is worth the climb—228 steps (but who's counting?). It's 178' tall and has a free museum on the ground floor that helps explain the monument's history and construction. The climb is $1 and there's no age limit (young or old), but it is not an easy climb and there's no place to rest. There is no room for strollers, and your backpack loaded with infant is going to be heavy in no time. Beyond being able to say you climbed it, thus eliminating something from your bucket list, the sights from atop the monument are breathtaking.

The tower can be climbed Wednesday through Sunday from 10 a.m. to 4 p.m. and on the first Thursday of the month from 10 a.m. to 8 p.m.

On the first Thursday of December, at about 5:30 when offices are shut down, the city plays host to the official lighting of the monument with entertainment, fireworks, and refreshments. The St. Patrick's Day parade start here, and the flower mart is here.

ANNUAL EVENTS

Baltimore is a happening place. From family backyard crab feasts to Artscape (our yearly arts and crafts fair that draws crowds of more than one million), we have fun wherever and whenever we can. The attract locals and tourists and contribute to the 80,000 jobs that are associated with area tourism and $1 billion in taxes.

This list provides highlights of some of the more popular and some of the unusual annual events. It is by no means a complete list of every happening. Check the *City Paper,* the city's most-widely distributed free paper. About one-quarter of its pages list what's scheduled. *Baltimore* magazine does likewise on a monthly basis. Or, if you have a particular interest, check the Web site of the particular event organization and ask to be placed on its e-mail distribution list.

Three Web sites offer relatively up-to-the-minute information about area events and attractions; the Baltimore Office of Promotion serves as our city's party planners, and it maintains a comprehensive calendar of Baltimore events at www.promotionandarts.org. The Maryland Office of Tourism has a statewide calendar that highlights activities throughout Maryland at www.visitmaryland.org. Finally, Visit Baltimore keeps a list of happenings at **www.baltimore. org.**

Most festival and event locations are user friendly; therefore, they are wheelchair accessible and bathrooms of some sort are on-site. If an event does not have a bathroom, the listing should indicate that. Although some listings may indicate an event is free, some will have a fee that is current as of this writing.

Some events, including the Friday night series, run weekly for months. Rather than list each event for every week it's scheduled, the listing will say "continues through . . . ."

JANUARY

FRIDAYS AFTER FIVE
National Aquarium
Pier 3/501 East Pratt St.
(410) 576-3800
www.aqua.org
Come and party with the fishes every Friday night from mid-September through early March. Admission is only $8 after 5 p.m. and maybe you can find your ichthyologist soul mate.

EDGAR ALLAN POE BIRTHDAY CELEBRATION
Westminster Hall and Burial Grounds
Fayette and Green Streets
(410) 396-7932
http://poecelebration.tripod.com

Throughout the entire weekend closest to Poe's January 19 birthday, Poe House sponsors a celebration in honor of the life and works of Edgar Allan Poe. Events vary from year to year and may include theatrical presentations of Poe's stories, musical renditions of his poems, a bagpipe tribute, and a graveside toast—after dark, of course. More than 1,000 people attend the celebration.

REVEREND DR. MARTIN LUTHER KING JR. BIRTHDAY CELEBRATION PARADE
Parade route follows Martin Luther King Jr. Boulevard, between Eutaw and Russell Streets
(877) BALTIMORE
www.promotionandarts.com
Baltimoreans love a good parade, so the city takes to the streets in honor of Reverend Martin Luther

King Jr.'s birthday. Many of Baltimore's own living legends participate in the parade, including past civil rights activists and prominent community and political figures. Floats, marching bands, choirs, and dancers add to the festive commemoration.

FISHING EXPO AND BOAT SHOW
Maryland State Fairgrounds
2200 York Rd., Timonium
(410) 838-8687
www.fishingexpo.com
With all the fishing options in the state, it makes sense that the East Coast's largest fishing expo is held here each year in mid-January. Bass, saltwater, and fly-fishing retailers sell their goods as boat companies and fishing supply manufacturers display their latest toys. Seminars and demonstrations help reel in the crowds, and patrons can try their hand at pulling in a live trout. Discount coupons for admission are frequently offered on the Web site. Prices are $8 for adults and $4 for children (10 through 14).

HORSE WORLD EXPO
Maryland State Fairgrounds
2200 York Rd., Timonium
(301) 916-0852
www.horseworldexpo.com
Marylanders love the field as much as the stream, and our state boasts an impressive history of steeplechase and horse races. This event, usually held mid-January, is a must for horse lovers. Hundreds of vendors sell a plethora of horse products and services for every breed of horse and every discipline of riding. A parade of breeds, educational seminars, and demonstrations are scheduled throughout the three-day event. Admission is $10 for adults and $5 for children (7-12) ; All activities are indoors and heated. Parking is free.

FEBRUARY

BLACK HERITAGE ART SHOW
Baltimore Convention Center
1 West Pratt St., Baltimore
(410) 521-0660
www.aavaa.org

February is Black History Month and it's celebrated with numerous events including an exhibit of the country's best African-American visual and performing artists. Held the second weekend of the month, the African American Visual Arts Association brings together lecturers, jazz and gospel singers, and poets for a showcase of contemporary arts and crafts. Admission is free.

THE ACC CRAFT FAIR OF BALTIMORE
Baltimore Convention Center
1 West Pratt St.
(410) 583-5401, (800) 836-3470
www.craftcouncil.org/baltimore
When you visit and shop at this juried craft fair sponsored by the American Craft Council, you will be meeting face-to-face with the artists (700 plus) because they are required to be there. Exhibitors are selected from applicants from across the country. All items must have been made in the United States. Choose from ceramics, glass, wood, metal, jewelry, fiber, and leather. The ACC Craft Fair is usually held over a weekend in late February but sometimes meanders into early March, so call for exact dates. Admission is $14 for adults, and there is a two-day pass that can be purchased for $20. Children younger than age 12 get in free.

MARCH EVENTS

ST. PATRICK'S DAY PARADE AND 5-K RUN
Downtown city streets
www.irishparade.net
The Sunday closest to the annual Irish holiday includes a parade and a 5-K Shamrock Run through Downtown. The 5-K starts at 1:35 p.m. and concludes with a party, prizes, and awards. The parade forms in Mount Vernon at the Washington Monument and steps off around 2 p.m., heading south on Charles Street. Thirty Irish organizations, 20 marching bands, pipe and drum corps, and politicians wind their way through the city heading east on Pratt Street and disbanding at Market Place. Pre-registration is required for the race with entry fees starting at $25 depending on how early you register. Watching the parade and the race is free.

MARYLAND DAY
Maryland Historical Society
201 West Monument St.
(410) 889-4488
Whether or not your birthday falls on March 25 or somewhere near there, you can join state and city officials who celebrate the anniversary of the state's founding.

LUNCH WITH THE ELEPHANTS
Lexington Market
400 West Lexington St.
(410) 685-6169
www.lexingtonmarket.com
One of Baltimore's most exciting annual events, "Lunch with the Elephants," takes place in Lexington Market's south parking lot on Wednesday when the Ringling Bros. and Barnum & Bailey elephants dine on the world's largest stand-up vegetarian buffet of 1,100 apples, 2,000 bananas, 1,000 carrots, 30 loaves of fresh Italian bread, and big juicy watermelons.

Baltimore is the only city in the country to host this annual event annually.

APRIL EVENTS

JOHNS HOPKINS UNIVERSITY SPRING FAIR
Homewood Campus,
Johns Hopkins University
(410) 516-7692
www.jhuspringfair.com
The Spring Fair is a three-day event planned, organized, and run exclusively by Johns Hopkins students, and it attracts members of the student body and community members from Baltimore and Washington, D.C. The fair features food, music, art vendors, carnival rides, children's shows, and activities.

MAY EVENTS

FLOWER MART
Mount Vernon Square
Under the Washington Monument
(410) 323-0022
www.flowermart.org

The Second Sundays Antique Markets

The Second Sundays Antique Markets bring out dealers and antiquers to the Broadway Market Square in Fell's Point from 8 a.m. to 5 p.m. every second Sunday April through October. About 50 dealers bring their wares, with buyers coming from all over the city and beyond. The Preservation Society, a nonprofit organization formed to maintain the character of Federal Hill and Fell's Point, sponsors the antiques markets.

Put on your nicest hat (you know, the one with all the flowers—there's a contest) and head down to the Washington Monument for a day of flowers, lemon sticks, crab cakes, and the sounds of children singing. The Flower Mart closes a section of Charles Street the first weekend in May and fills the area with 200 tables laden with crafters' wares, bedding plants sold by local charities, and lots of other garden goodies. Concerts by local schoolchildren are held throughout the celebration.

ALMOST FAMOUS BALTIMORE KINETIC SCULPTURE RACE
American Visionary Art Museum
www.kineticbaltimore.com
Since 2001, kinetic sculptures (and their owners/constructors/operators) from across the eastern United States have convened at the American Visionary Art Museum for the East Coast Championship race. A kinetic sculpture is an amphibious, human-powered work of art custom built for the eight-hour race that covers about 15 miles across pavement, the Bay, and through mud and sand. This "race" provides a year's entertainment after what's probably taken at least a year to assemble the craft.

Baltimore "Bike Jam"

Bike Jam 2009, a full day of high-caliber pro-am cycling, was held Sunday, May 17, in Patterson Park. It featured The Kelly Cup Pro Race, Bike Jam 2009 features games, bike safety, live music, and other family summer fun. This annual event is free and open to the public and runs all day, 8 a.m. to 5 p.m.

Baltimore Bike Jam is the mid-Atlantic's largest cycling festival now in its 12th year at historic Patterson Park near Baltimore's famed Inner Harbor. The event includes Maryland's only pro race on the National Race Calendar, and Baltimore's largest pro-am cycling race, The Kelly Cup. These races are sanctioned by the U.S. Cycling Federation (USCF), thus attracting professional and amateur racers from the mid-Atlantic and throughout North America. Past BikeJam races have included former Olympic and Tour de France participants. More than 8,000 spectators and 1,200 participants were expected in 2009.

Highlights of the event include:

Pro Road Racing

Recreational Bike Ride (12- and 31-mile rides)

Cycling Stunt show

Interactive Village

Bike & Health Expo

Food & Live Music

Kids Activity Pavilion

Kids Bike & Safety Rodeo (noon to 1:45 p.m.)

Live Music Stage (bands play from 12:30 until 5p.m.)

Assorted cycling vendors

Kid's Helmet Give-Away (CareFirst / BlueCross has donated and will distribute 250 kids' cycling helmets)

Bike Jam promoter and participant Dr. David Scharff, Mercy Medical Center internist, has served as president of Lateral Stress Velo, a bicycle club and racing team from Baltimore. LSV includes mountain bikers and road bikers, and the club is a member of both National Off Road Biking Association (NORBA) and the United States Cycling Federation (USCF).

For information regarding entry fees for BikeJam cycling races, visit www.bike jam.org.

MARYLAND FILM FESTIVAL
Locations vary
(410) 752-8083
www.mdfilmfest.com

This four-day festival is Maryland's own Sundance, bringing world-renowned filmmakers and movies to Baltimore, usually the first weekend in May. The festival presents more than 120 foreign and domestic feature films and shorts. Admission to one film is $10, a three-show pass is $20, and an all-access pass for the entire event is $175 to $250, depending on how early you buy the pass.

THE PREAKNESS PARADE AND PREAKNESS WEEK
East on Pratt Street to Market Place
(877) BALTIMORE, (410) 837-3030
www.preaknesscelebration.org
The Preakness Parade (held the Saturday before the Preakness) begins Preakness Week, a celebration in early to mid-May that often includes a hot-air balloon ascension, outdoor concerts, schooner races, benefit galas, fireworks, and more, and culminates in the running of the Preakness Stakes

THE PREAKNESS STAKES
Pimlico Race Course
5201 Park Heights Ave.
(410) 542-9400
www.preakness.com
The third Saturday in May marks the annual running of the Preakness Stakes, the second leg of horse racing's Triple Crown, held here since 1909. Gates usually open at 8:30 a.m. for the infield, which is the area inside the track. Infield seats are popular because you are right at eye level with the horses, seats are less expensive, and because it's a great all-day picnic. The track has imposed seriously strict regulations against alcoholic beverages and the types of coolers you can bring into the track.

As soon as the Preakness winner has been declared official, a painter climbs to the top of the replica Old Clubhouse copula to paint the weather vane. Using the colors of the winner's silks, the jockey and horse will remain there until a new winner is declared in the next year's Preakness. The silver Woodlawn vase was created by Tiffany and Company in 1860 and is said to be the most valuable trophy in American sports. The winner receives a replica while the original generally resides at the Baltimore Museum of Art (it's brought to the race track under heavy guard).

BALTICON: MARYLAND REGIONAL SCIENCE FICTION CONVENTION
Marriot Hunt Valley Inn
(410) 563-2737
www.balticon.org

The Preakness

When you look at the infield on television, it looks as if infielders are trapped, since the races run around them; but, in fact, there is a tunnel under the track that allows you to come and go as you please, but why would you want to go? Concession stands, betting windows, and the all-important portable toilets are available for infielders. The clubhouse, which is under roof, is the most posh seating, and guests dress for the occasion. (If you purchase a clubhouse seat, don't go in jeans.) Racing begins at 10:30 a.m., but the Preakness goes off at around 6:05 p.m. and is the next to last race of the day. For standing-room-only, clubhouse admission is $25 and the prices increase for better seating up to $575 (and more). If you like this year's seats and you want them again next year, you must submit your application by early January. Parking can be difficult and starts at $45 and goes up and up. Traffic backs up for miles, so give yourself plenty of time to get there if you're driving and wear your walking shoes. Sometimes you can find less expensive parking on someone's front lawn, but you might have to walk more than a mile. However, public transportation is available, including Light Rail and MTA Preakness buses.

Black-eyed Susans!

- The Black-eyed Susan cocktail, as served at Pimlico Race Course, where the Preakness, the second leg of horse racing's Triple Crown, is made with one part Cointreau, one part Mount Gay Rum, one part vodka, and equal parts of orange and pineapple juice. This is topped with a lime wedge.

- Black-eyed Susans (the state flower) don't bloom until at least a month after the race, so the flowers used in the cascades are daisies or chrysanthemums that have the centers painted with black lacquer. Three people spend two full days creating the 18″ x 90″ blanket that adorns the race winner.

Authors, publishers, editors, artists, scientists, musicians, and other sci-fi and fantasy stars gather for this four-day event that has more than 300 hours of multi-track programming. See the art show, dealer's room, concerts, dances, and more. Ticket prices vary by when you purchase them, ranging from $48 (by February) to $60 at the door.

JUNE EVENTS

LATINO FEST
Patterson Park
(410) 563-3160
www.eblo.org
The Latino Fest is a celebration of folk music, dance, arts, and crafts from all of Central and South America. Groups perform folk music of the Andes, Latin jazz, and salsa. Arts and crafts displays and demonstrations include handcrafted pottery, silver from Peru, and woolens from Ecuador and Bolivia.

GAY PRIDE FESTIVAL
Various locations
(410) 837-5445
www.baltimorepride.org
In June, the Gay, Lesbian, Bisexual, and Transgender Association of Baltimore sponsors a weekend celebration to which all are invited. On Saturday a Gay Pride Parade heads north on Charles Street, through the Mount Vernon neighborhood, and disbands at Eager Street for a rowdy block party. The festivities continue on Sunday with a festival at Druid Hill Park with live music, ethnic food, and more than 100 booths full of information, arts, and crafts.

JULY EVENTS

BALTIMORE'S FOURTH OF JULY CELEBRATION
Inner Harbor
(877) BALTIMORE
www.promotionandarts.com
Wherever you find a place, whether it's on top of a hotel, at the Inner Harbor, or visiting a friend on Federal Hill, the July 4th fireworks seems more appropriate in Baltimore because this is where Francis Scott Key penned the lyrics to "The Star-Spangled Banner" and you get to see fireworks in the sky and maybe reflected in the water. The free show begins at 9:30 p.m.

ARTSCAPE
West Mount Royal Avenue, beginning south of North Avenue
(877) BALTIMORE
www.artscape.org
Artscape is a city-sponsored free event that is the country's largest public arts celebration. Strung out along Mount Royal Avenue from The Maryland Institute College of Art, bending around in front of the Lyric Theatre and around the Meyerhoff Symphony Hall are hundreds of arts and crafts vendors and food vendors. You'll find potters, woodworkers, glassworkers, ironworkers, and painters. Look for theatrical productions, poetry readings, and lots of music. Take Light Rail to avoid driving and parking.

MARYLAND OKTOBERFEST
5th Regiment Armory
Howard and Division Streets
(410) 522-4144
www.md-germans.org

Yes, the Oktoberfest is held in July. The doors open at noon, and the oompahs start at 1 p.m. Polka until you drop or just sit at the communal tables and drink, eat, and sing. German imports—sauerbraten, sauerkraut, schnitzel, and a gazillion types of wursts—are there for the gobbling. There's also a wine garden for those who have trouble with hops and barley. Crafts and souvenirs are available. Oktoberfest is usually held the second weekend of the month. Admission is $6 for adults and $5 for seniors. Children under 12 are free when they're with a paying adult.

BILLIE HOLIDAY VOCAL COMPETITION FOR WOMEN
CAB CALLOWAY VOCAL COMPETITION FOR MEN
Meyerhoff Symphony Hall
(410) 752-8632
www.promotionandarts.com

As part of Artscape, the city honors jazz greats Billie Holliday and Cab Calloway by searching for emerging vocal talent in the mid-Atlantic region through funding, exposure, and recognition. Admission to the show is free and open to the public, but tickets are required and available in advance and on the day of the show. Only two tickets are allowed per person.

AUGUST EVENTS

MARYLAND STATE FAIR
Maryland State Fairgrounds
York and Timonium Roads, Timonium
(410) 252-0200
www.marylandstatefair.com

For 11 days in late August and early September, the state of Maryland puts its best feet forward as Marylanders bring their best pigs, cows, chickens, quilts, jams, pies, wine, honey—you name it—to try to win a blue ribbon. The midway games of chance

are there and rides fill young and old with thrills and pleasures. Admission is $8 for adults, $6 for seniors (62 plus), and $3 for children (6 to 11). Ride tickets are $1.25 each and you can figure up to six tickets for some rides. Take the Light Rail, Timonium stop, or the No. 9 bus and don't even think about driving or trying to find a parking space.

ℹ A lemon stick is a fresh lemon that has a peppermint stick as a straw. When you're eating one, keep squeezing the lemon. It helps secure the peppermint stick and ensures you're sucking juice, not pulp. When the end of the stick in the lemon starts to melt, take it out, turn it over and start again.

SEPTEMBER EVENTS

THE IRISH FESTIVAL
Maryland State Fairgrounds
York and Timonium Roads, Timonium
(410) 747-6868
www.irishfestival.com

Fill up on Irish champ (potatoes and onions) and Guinness while tapping your feet to the lively music of the Irish folk groups that perform continuously on stage. You'll find the usual souvenirs to buy, and some educational opportunities, such as a lecture on 20th-century Irish literature. The festival, held in mid-September, is sponsored by Irish Charities of Maryland, Inc. The entrance fee is $10 for adults, $8 for seniors, $5 for children (12-17) and active military personnel with ID card.

BALTIMORE BOOK FESTIVAL
Mount Vernon Place
Charles and Monument Streets
(877) BALTIMORE
www.baltimorebookfestival.com

More than 150 International and local authors gather at this festival to celebrate the book and written word. The spoken word can be heard on eight stages while celebrity chefs give cooking demonstrations. There's also live music, theater, food, and projects for children, and plenty of opportunity to talk with your favorite author,

OCTOBER EVENTS

FREE FALL BALTIMORE
7 East Redwood St., Suite 500
(410) 752-8632, (877) BALTIMORE
www.freefallbaltimore.com
More than 70 cultural organizations present more than 300 free events at numerous venues during October. You can listen to music, attend museum exhibitions, hear lectures, participate in workshops, and just enjoy the many benefits of Baltimore. Some programs require reservations. See the list of activities on the Web site.

FELL'S POINT FUN FESTIVAL
www.preservationsociety.com
Showcasing the nautical history, enduring charm, and vibrant spirit of one of Baltimore's oldest downtown neighborhoods, the Annual Fun Festival in early October features a flea market, crafts and vendors, plus five stages of live music and entertainment and activities for children of all ages. Indulge in delicacies and libations from all over the world, available on every corner.

SCHOOL 33 ART CENTER OPEN STUDIO TOUR
1427 Light St.
(410) 396-4641
www.school33.org
Baltimore's visual artists—they're brilliant, inspired, and dazzling—have their works on display for the annual open studio tour. Check the Web site so you know which artists you want to visit, where the studio is located, and what time those studios are open. You'll find everything from paintings, sculpture, photography, art glass, art jewelry, lampwork, beads, acrylics, oils, and the list continues.

BALTIMORE MARATHON
M&T Bank Stadium
And various locations around town
(410) 605-9381
www.thebaltimoremarathon.com
The marathon, known officially as the "Baltimore Running Festival—Under Armour Marathon," brings out hundreds of serious and not-so-serious runners who participate in a marathon (minimum age is 16), half-marathon or team relay (minimum age is 14), 5K (no age restrictions), and the Kids Fun Run (12 and under). Registration is $80 to $100 depending on how far ahead you register. The route goes through interesting parts of town, which you either drive by too quickly or don't go near at all.

i About a week after the Baltimore Marathon, there is a tent sale at the Falls Road Running store, 6247 Falls Rd. (410-296-5050). You can buy official race gear at discount prices and purchase a second (or third) race shirt. If you won an award on race day, you can pick it up then.

CHOCOLATE FESTIVAL
Lexington Market
400 West Lexington St.
(410) 685-6169
www.lexingtonmarket.com
Lexington Market turns into a chocoholic's fantasy land as it hosts its annual Chocolate Festival where Baltimore's finest chocolatiers and bakers offer everything from truffles to fudge to chocolate strawberry shortcake. The gluttonous can enter a range of chocolate-eating contests. Visitors can enjoy a great mix of live music, good food, children's entertainment, and cooking demonstrations throughout the event.

ZOOBOOO
The Maryland Zoo
1 Druid Park Lake Dr.
(410) 366-LION
www.marylandzoo.org
If you've ever wondered how you trick or treat at the zoo (do the penguins or camels have the best treats?), then you can have your questions answered at ZooBooo. Come costumed for the contest, be ready to make spooky things, and venture into the haunted barn, if you dare. Face painting, crafts, giveaways, entertainment, and food are available. Entrance to ZooBooo is the regular zoo entrance fee of $15 for adults and $10

for children (2 through 11) and $12 for seniors (65 up). Some activities have an extra charge. The entrance fee includes the Children's Zoo.

NOVEMBER EVENTS

GREEK FESTIVAL
Annunciation Cathedral
24 West Preston St.
(410) 727-1831
www.greek-fest.com
Greek food (homemade and served in their dining room or under the tent), including mousssaka, pastitsio, spanakopita, lamb shanks, hand-carved gyro, and more. Live music, dance performances, jewelry, children's activities, silent auction, and vendors.

CHRISTMAS IN HAMPDEN
700 block of West 34th Street
www.Christmasstreet.com
Since 1951 there's been a miracle on 34th Street, in Hampden. The residents string up thousands of Christmas lights, stretching them across the street, lining their roofs, and covering every square inch with color. Then they fill their yards with every kind of Christmas decoration they can think of: inflatable snow globes, musical trains, blinking angels, nativity scenes and, a popular favorite, the hubcap tree. It's all kitschy. And it's definitely fun. The display goes up Thanksgiving weekend and lasts until New Year's Day. Cars drive through the display; or when the weather's nice, Baltimoreans park nearby and walk to see the decorations.

HOLIDAY FESTIVAL OF TRAINS AT THE
B& O (CONTINUES THROUGH DECEMBER
AND JANUARY)
B & O Railroad Museum
901 West Pratt St.
(410) 752-2490
www.borail.org
Baltimore's largest holiday display of toy and model train layouts debuts during this traditional holiday festival. Train rides and photo opportunities with Santa are available every weekend after

Thanksgiving up through the weekend before the Christmas holiday. Among the organizations displaying their train sets are the Washington, D.C. Metropolitan Area LEGO train club, the Baltimore Area American Flyer club, the Western Maryland Historical Society "HO" scale modular group, the Baltimore Area NTRAK club, the National Capital Trackers, and the Japan Rail Modelers of Washington, D.C.

DECEMBER EVENTS

DOLLAR OR LESS DAYS
(443) 573-2837
This program, usually the first weekend of December, entices you to stay downtown or come downtown to dine, shop, and see attractions and museums that have reduced admission prices. Special discounted parking rates are available at participating garages.

WASHINGTON MONUMENT LIGHTING
Mount Vernon Square, 600 North Charles St.
(410) 396-0929, (410) 752-8632
The annual Lighting of the Washington Monument is held the first Thursday in December. The event features local entertainers, food, and a dazzling fireworks display. The holiday village, with food and crafts vendors, operates in the Mount Vernon's West Park, starting at 5:30 p.m., the stage entertainment begins at 6 p.m., and the Monument Lighting and fireworks display starts shortly before 7:30 p.m. (Times subject to change.)

BALTIMORE'S NEW YEAR'S
EVE SPECTACULAR
Various locations downtown
(877) BALTIMORE
www.promotionandarts.com
Baltimore rings in the New Year in a big way—and all without alcohol. Started a few years ago, there are live music and countdowns around the Inner Harbor and Fell's Point. The party begins at 9 p.m. and culminates with fireworks at midnight. All outdoor events are free. The subway, Light Rail, and buses generally operate until midnight or one hour after the fireworks.

THE ARTS

Baltimoreans are passionate about the visual and performing arts. Whether it's professionally operated regional theater or a Broadway road trip, Baltimore provides a willing and eager audience. During July and August, many of the community theaters focus on new scripts as they present the works of entrants in the Baltimore Playwrights Festival. This listing provides information about the major professional theaters and a few of the older or unique regional and community theaters and groups. For information about the visual arts venues, check the Attractions chapter.

PERFORMING ARTS

Music

BALTIMORE SYMPHONY ORCHESTRA (BSO)
Joseph Meyerhoff Symphony Hall
1212 Cathedral St.
(410) 783-8000
www.baltimoresymphony.org
In the 2007–2008 season, the BSO named Marin Alsop as music director, making the BSO the first major American orchestra to do so. During her year as a music director designate, Baltimoreans fell in love with their new Maestra whose concerts are a delight. The BSO concerts may be a series of all of Beethoven's symphonies, Soulful Symphony with an emphasis on African-American musicians, Symphony with a Twist for young adults, and a series at the Music Center at Strathmore, 5301 Tuckerman Lane, North Bethesda (Montgomery County). The Meyerhoff Symphony Hall is the BSO's permanent home.

i The BSO Holiday Spectacular, the last two weeks of December, with help from the Baltimore School of the Arts, usually includes an appearance by the high-kicking tap-dancing Santas. To many, that is worth the experience all by itself.

CONCERT ARTISTS OF BALTIMORE
1114 St. Paul St.
(410) 625-3525
www.cabalto.org
Since 1987, founder and artistic director Ed Polochick has organized a group of professional chamber orchestra musicians and vocal ensembles to present engaging, accessible classical music programs throughout the state. The group, which ranges from duos to a full cast of 70 musicians, performs operettas, pops concerts, and classical favorites in a number of venues around town. Performances are frequently followed by informal question-and-answer sessions with the audience. Tickets for adults start at about $20, depending on the event, the venue, and the seat location.

PIER SIX CONCERT PAVILION
731 Eastern Ave.
(410) 244-1131
www.piersixpavilion.com
The tent on the Inner Harbor just beyond the National Aquarium is the site for many pop, blues, and rock concerts during warm weather. Many national and international acts have played here, including the B-52s, the Goo Goo Dolls, Linda Ronstadt, and B.B. King. Summer concerts can be steamy, so dress appropriately. Tickets are available at the Pier Six box office, though it's open only on show days, and at Rams Head at either location in Baltimore (410) 244-1131 or Annapolis (410) 268-4545 or at Ticketmaster outlets. Or go online to the Web site piersixpavilion.ramsheadlive.com or www.ticketmaster.com.

Movies under the Stars

What could be better on a warm summer night than a movie under the stars? Both the community of Little Italy and the American Visionary Art Museum schedule them.

In Little Italy the movies usually have an Italian theme—*Moonstruck* is a regular—and they are shown on the side of a building over a parking lot on summer Fridays when it is finally dark enough. The neighbors bring their children and their chairs (and their bug spray) for a night out.

In Federal Hill, the museum shows movies on the side of its building and Baltimoreans spread their blankets on the hill. The museum also stays open until 9 p.m.—with free admission after 5 p.m.—and also schedules an activity for families to go along with the movie's theme. Everybody is invited to both.

RAMS HEAD LIVE
20 Market Place, Power Plant Live!
Restaurant: (410) 244-8856
Box Office: (410) 244-1131
www.ramsheadlive.com
You never know who'll play next at Rams Head Live. It could be Ice-T or Pat Benatar, India.Arie or Weird Al Yankovic, or maybe an up-and-coming band. All sorts of acts come to play in this 26,000-square-foot concert hall/tavern/restaurant. Although Rams Head's Annapolis and Rehoboth Beach locations are all about music and food, music has been number one here since its opening in December 2004. Food is served here, of course, but people are coming for the music. The schedule is posted on the Web

site, and tickets run anywhere from $15 to $60, depending on the act. It's big, it's loud, and it draws a crowd.

Professional Theater

ARENA PLAYERS
801 McCulloh St.
(410) 728-6500
www.arenaplayersinc.org
Arena Players is the nation's oldest continually performing and historically black community theater. Begun in 1953, its first production was William Soroyan's one-act drama *Hello Out There*. By 1961 the company had found its permanent home and has since reshaped the space to create a modern theater. Five plays are presented every season, with productions by such playwrights as William Inge, August Wilson, and Lorraine Hansberry. The young actors of Youtheater also perform four times a year, usually a lavish musical such as *The Lion King* or *Once on This Island*. Tickets are about $15.

BALTIMORE THEATRE PROJECT
45 West Preston St.
(410) 539-3091
www.theatreproject.org
The Theatre Project brings to Baltimore some of the best, cutting-edge, fringe theater in the country, maybe the world. Its founder started the theater in a run-down building with makeshift seating and passed a hat at the end of the performances. Today's space is much more professional; the seats are comfortable and you can buy a real ticket or even a whole subscription. In a recent season, theologian Dietrich Bonhoeffer and Albert Einstein's dreams were the subjects of two plays. Circus, women's empowerment, and dark comedy were among the choices, too. As long as you're out for a cultural event, stop by the John Fonda Gallery to see the works of contemporary visual artists. Works may include paintings, drawings, sculpture, photography, or fiber arts. Except for special events, theater tickets generally are $20 for adults, $15 for seniors and artists, and $10 for students.

Making the Cut

Film and television making is a big business in the Baltimore area where the SAG (Screen Actors Guild) and AFTRA (American Federation of Television and Radio Artists) chapters have the third largest membership in the country, after Los Angeles and New York. Among the movies and TV shows/pilots shot here were *Die Hard 4: Live Free or Die Hard, Enemy of the State, He's Just Not That Into You, Ladder 49, My One and Only, Past Life, Something the Lord Made,* and *Syriana*.

These productions call for a large number of background (extras) people to fill the scenes showing people sitting on a park bench, walking to and from an office, sightseeing, or participating in electioneering and voting. Becoming a background worker is neither difficult nor expensive. You most likely will not retire on background pay. It is long hours and boring. Yet, you'll have an experience to talk about for the rest of your life.

Go to the following Web pages and check how they like to be approached. Send an e-mail, snail mail your information, attend an open house, and then, wait.

Here are some of the local casting companies: **Betsy Royall Casting,** www.betsy casting.com (Baltimore); **Pat Moran and Associates,** www.PatMoranAndAssociates.com (Baltimore); **Carlyn Davis,** www.extrasnow.com (Falls Church, Virginia); **Central Casting,** www.centralcastingusa.com (Baltimore and Washington, D.C.).

CENTERSTAGE
700 North Calvert St.
(410) 332-0033
www.centerstage.org
CenterStage is the State Theater of Maryland and has been in business for 45 years. The theater is in the Mount Vernon neighborhood, just 2 blocks east of the Washington Monument, in what was once the building for Loyola College and Preparatory School. The building was donated by the Jesuits in 1974. There are two theaters in the building, the Pearlstone Theater and the more intimate Head Theater. The larger Pearlstone has 541 seats with excellent sight lines from every seat. CenterStage mounts six shows every year—some Broadway, some classic, some more avant-garde. A recent season featured Sondheim's *A Little Night Music* and August Wilson's *Joe Turner's Come and Gone.* There are also always offerings by new writers as well. Children under 5 are not permitted unless the show is specifically advertised for all ages. Sascha's Express in their Mezzanine Café serves light dining before each performance. Irene Lewis is the company's resident director. The season runs from October to June, but the theater is never really dark.

CHILDREN'S THEATER ASSOCIATION (CTA)
1055 Taylor Ave., Suite 200
(443) 901-0835
http://ctabaltimore.org
Children's Theater Association has been a Baltimore fixture since 1943 and is the oldest theater for young people in the state. CTA offers three public performances every year for general audiences at the Baltimore Museum of Art Theater, and performances in schools and community settings. The season runs from September through May. Recent performances include such educational pieces as Stay Tobacco Free and Teddy Roosevelt. CTA also offers acting classes to students throughout the year at the Loch Raven Library, 1046 Taylor Ave.

HIPPODROME THEATRE AT THE FRANCE-MERRICK PERFORMING ARTS CENTER

12 North Eutaw St.
(410) 837-7400, (410) 547-SEAT (Ticketmaster), (800) 551-SEAT, (410) 752-7444 (accessible seating and services)
www.france-merrickpac.com
www.broadwayacrossamerica.com

The Hippodrome (or the Hipp), a historic theater from vaudeville days underwent a $62 million renovation and reopened on February 10, 2004, dropping the curtain on the Morris Mechanic Theatre that had maintained Baltimore as a vibrant theater town as best it could until it just wasn't good enough. Jeff Daniel, an early figure in the theater's revitalization, has returned as its new executive director. It's been said that part of his mission is to bring the bigger, more impressive shows, and to book other performers, including concerts and gospel shows, to help expand the theater's appeal. The thinking, of course, is along the lines of "when the tide comes in, all the boats rise." When more people stay or come to the Westend then there will be more things for them to do (restaurants, shops, services), which will bring more attractions and people. Good thinking.

LYRIC OPERA HOUSE

140 West Mount Royal Ave.
(410) 685-5086
www.lyricoperahouse.com

The Lyric presents about two to three dozen productions a year, ranging from the *Nutcracker* to *Rent*. You can see a Broadway road company production one week and national comedy acts the next. The Lyric was built in 1894 and today seats 2,564 (1,000 orchestra, 206 boxes, and 1,358 balcony seats). Although its antique facade has been replaced by a more modern front and a gallery-type outer lobby, the theater remains as it was built, including perfect acoustics and excellent sight lines, even for those in the last row. The old lobby, which is now the inner lobby, has been renovated to look as it did when the theater first opened—which is to say, spectacular. The theater and its continuing history are part of Baltimore's pride.

The Lyric also has helped fill the vacuum caused by the Baltimore Opera folding. The Lyric has had a smattering of extraordinary opera performances. In a warm homecoming moment (or two), the Opera New Jersey production of Bizet's *Carmen* included many Baltimore Opera chorus members in the New Jersey cast. Earlier in the season Renee Fleming was set to perform a recital of art songs and arias with pianist Gerald M. Moore.

For additional opera information and a full calendar of operatic productions in the area, check the Baltimore Concert Opera Web site, www.baltimoreopera.com.

COMMUNITY THEATERTHE BALTIMORE THEATRE ALLIANCE

100 East 23rd St.
(410) 662-9945
www.baltimoreperforms.org

The Baltimore Theatre Alliance (BTA) is an invaluable resource to the 43 community and regional theaters in Baltimore that are its members. BTA gives member theaters a central clearinghouse for theater information, actors, and technicians. For instance, once a year, BTA holds major auditions to which all member theaters send representatives. If a theater needs a lighting tech for a particular play, it calls BTA. If you are a lighting tech who wants work at the community-theater level, you can get on the list by sending your resume to BTA. When you want to see a show, visit the Web site for a calendar with the company name, production, location, box office phone number, and opening and closing dates.

THE CHARLES THEATER

1711 North Charles St.
(410) 727-3456
www.thecharles.com

This is our city's premier cinema for international and rare films. Housed in a renovated 108-year-old Beaux-Arts building, The Charles has five screens, most with stadium seating. The lobby is spacious and comfortable and it attaches to the adjacent Tapas Teatro cafe, which is the perfect spot for a pre-movie meal. Every year The Charles helps host the Maryland Film Festival and on Sun-

The Hipp

Although pre-Broadway try-outs can be scheduled at the Hipppodrome (and that probably is still a goal), the bread and butter is the touring road company shows. In December 2009, the Hipp was the first theater on the tour of Dreamgirls. Fiddler on the Roof with Topol, Young Frankenstein, In the Heights, Stomp, The 39 Steps, and Mama Mia were other shows on the 2009-2010 season. Individual and season tickets are available through www.broadwayacrossamerica.com that requires you to sign up (no charge) before it lets you know how much tickets are. Perhaps you can find a way around that or perhaps it doesn't bother you.

The renovation of the Hippodrome was considered a catalyst for the renewal of 18 blocks around the theater in Baltimore's Westside. Adjacent buildings provided a stage house, lobbies, retail box office, administrative, offices, loading dock, and flexible multi-purpose spaces.

The France-Merrick Performing Arts Center offers a variety of accessibility services to assist patrons on enjoying events at the center. Accessible seating is available for all performances at the France-Merrick Performing Arts Center. Accessible seating, audio description, and ASL signed interpretation services are available. All inquires regarding accessibility services should be made in advance by calling (410) 752-7444.

Inner Circle subscriber parking is at the Baltimore Grand Garage (5 North Paca St., 410-706-6603) with 81" of clearance. The garage is directly connected to the theater and is open 24 hours a day. Other parking lots, surface and multi-story, are available nearby. Central Parking, 7 North Calvert St. (410-986-0336, www.parking.com) has a clearance of 9'4" if you need additional height. There are almost two dozen city parking lots operated by Central. Make sure you're parked in the one you want and that you remember where it's located.

The Box office is open Monday through Friday from 11 a.m. to 3 p.m.; on performance days, the box office hours are extended to first intermission.

days it offers a film series called Cinema Sunday, which begins with a simple brunch of bagels, coffee, tea, and includes a speaker after the film. Doors open at 9:45 a.m. for brunch and conversation. The film begins at 10:35 a.m. Tickets are $6 for matinees (any show before 6 p.m.) and $8 for evening presentations.

THE ROTUNDA CINEMATEQUE
711 West 40th St., Hampden
(410) 235-5554
www.senator.com
This independent theater, a sister to the hallowed Senator, shows a mix of classic and newly released movies on two screens at this refurbished old movie house. Tickets are $6 for matinees (before 6 p.m.) and for seniors, students, and children (all day). Evening tickets are $8. Children younger than age five are not admitted except for the occasional children's flick. Plenty of free parking is available behind the Rotunda.

THE SENATOR
5904 York Rd.
(410) 435-8338 (theater), (410) 435-9892 (office)
www.senator.com

A Summer for Playwrights

When most theaters would typically be going dark, Baltimore's non-professional theaters are gearing up for a summer of original plays. The Baltimore Playwrights Festival takes over theaters from all corners of the city—and neighboring suburbs.

About 10 plays, all written by local writers, are produced. Dramas, comedies, musicals, one-act plays, and full-scale productions are submitted for judging by members of local theater companies. Some get a reading, and ultimately the final plays are chosen for production. Theater staff members also attend the public readings so they can decide which play they want to produce.

A play usually runs two to three weeks, with runs scattered throughout the season so theater lovers have a chance to see as many as they want. All this drama ends with an awards ceremony in September. But the best part has to be the chance to see so many new plays in just a few weeks.

The schedule is posted at www.baltimoreplaywrightsfestival.org in April or early May, just in time to order a subscription—or just see what's going to be playing this summer. Baltimore Playwrights Festival is headquartered at Fell's Point Corner Theatre, 251 South Ann St. in Fell's Point.

For mainstream movies with ambience, you'll want to go to The Senator, which is just south of Northern Parkway on York Road. Though average size for a neighborhood theater when it was built, it now is counted among the largest in greater Baltimore, with seating for 900 and a screen about 40 feet tall. Its 1939 Art Deco ambience is intact and preserved for posterity, right down to the etched, oval, blue-glass mirror over the water fountain and marble stalls in the ladies' room. Listed on the National Register of Historic Places and named one of the best movie theaters in the country by USA Today, The Senator is still a first-run house. It has had the distinction of being host of world premieres of many of the movies that have been made here in Baltimore. Outside the theater is a Baltimore-style walk of fame, where stars and producers have their names in the cement.

Admission is $10 for everyone. Children younger than age five are not admitted unless the film showing is a children's movie. However, babes in arms are never admitted.

TOBY'S DINNER THEATRE
Best Western Hotel
5625 O'Donnell St.
(410) 649-1660, (866) 99-TOBYS
www.tobysdinnertheatre.com
Toby's Dinner Theatre has been a fixture in nearby Columbia for nearly 30 years and now founder Toby Orenstein brings her mix of musical theater and a hearty buffet to this unlikely spot, a hotel off I-95 beside a hotel, truck plaza, and bus station. The season is ambitious, with plays year-round. In its opening season in 2006–2007, Toby's produced Fiddler on the Roof, Grease, and Dreamgirls. Productions change every two to three months. Everybody will find something they like on the buffet, including the sundae bar. Sunday plays begin with brunch. Tickets run about $45.

PARKS AND RECREATION

Meander through Baltimore and you're sure to be delighted with all the green space. Every community has a park, a playground, school fields, or some kind of green space that allows for getting out among trees and grass. Recent (at least the last 30 years) credit goes to the state for its Program Open Space that targets one-half of 1 percent of all real estate sales to protecting and enhancing with green areas.

The funds are also used to buy land for state parks and state forests. Maryland has 47 state parks and forests, areas where people can take part in activities ranging from hiking and biking to hunting and camping, swimming and boating to birding and fishing. About a third of these areas are within the Baltimore area. The state has about 2,000 campsites and 120 full-service and camper cabins that are available from May 1 through September 30 through a central number (888) 432-2267 or online at www.dnr.state.mud.us. Call the specific park for information about camping the rest of the year.

A few parks within the city limits deserve special attention.

PARKS

DRUID HILL PARK
Druid Lake Drive near I-83
(410) 396-6106
The park, the first large municipal park in the city and one of the largest inner-city parks in the country, surrounds the Maryland Zoo in Baltimore. Development started in 1860 (Manhattan's Central Park was started in 1858), with the lake construction beginning in 1863. The lake's dam is supposed to be the largest earthen dammed lake in the country. The Baltimore Zoo was created because people started donating animals to the park. Also within the grounds are the Baltimore Conservatory, the Palm House, tennis courts, public swimming pool, fields, and trails. Birding is particularly rewarding here.

FEDERAL HILL PARK
Key Highway at Battery Avenue
Overlooking the Inner Harbor, Federal Hill offers one of the best views of the Inner Harbor. There's a playground, a small basketball court, and an open section for throwing a ball or a Frisbee. For a real walking workout, try climbing the 100 steps from Key Highway to the hilltop a few times. Benches are available for a post-workout rest. Park on the street or at the harbor and walk over.

GWYNNS FALLS PARK/LEAKIN PARK
Edmondson Avenue at Hilton Parkway
Franklintown
(410) 396-7931
www.gwynnsfallstrail.org
Spread out among several miles of land along the Gwynns Falls, this park offers hiking, biking, bird-watching, sightseeing, and relaxing spaces. It serves as a stop on the Gwynns Falls Trail. Formed to protect the Gwynns Falls from development all around it, it's filled with grass, trees, and other natural amenities that provide a strong contrast to the nearby housing. You can access the park from a variety of sites along Edmondson Avenue. Leakin Park, a portion of the facility, offers tennis courts, a track, abundant parking, and a ropes course, which tests even the best athletes with climbing, balance, and endurance testing. The ropes course is operated by the city and several other agencies, primarily for children in summer camps and school day trips.

PATTERSON PARK
Eastern and Patterson Park Avenues
Friends of Patterson Park
27 South Patterson Park Ave.
(410) 276-3676

Patterson Park is one of the city's oldest parks and provides a welcome respite from the demands of city life. Within its 137 acres are sports fields, an ice-skating rink, tennis courts, a 60' tall pagoda (tours on Sunday from noon to 4 p.m.), a lake where you can fish (you should have a license), jogging/running trails, a fountain, two playgrounds, summer swimming pool, winter skating rink, and so much more. Open areas where the bothers of urban living seem to take a backseat await you when you head toward East Baltimore's crown jewel of parks whose centerpiece is the 1890 Pagoda. There's even a small stadium, named Utz Towardowicz after the person who gave the funds for it, that hosts baseball and softball competitions. Parking is available on the streets surrounding the park.

i The October Barcstoberfest (Baltimore Animal Rescue and Care Shelter) helps raise funds to treat abused animals and to help with pet adoptions. The highlights are the Strut Your Mutt Walk and the pet costume contest. Visit www.baltimoreanimalshelter.org for more information.

RECREATION

Departments and Centers

Baltimore City
BALTIMORE CITY RECREATION CENTERS
3001 East Dr.
(410) 396-7900
www.ci.baltimore.md.us

Baltimore City operates 61 recreation centers throughout the city. The programs range from after-school activities, including study groups and tutorial sessions, to more recreational offerings and summer camp programs.

The recreation centers also operate such programs as baseball, softball, lacrosse, tennis, table tennis, pool, swimming, football, and track and field for toddlers, children, adults, and senior citizens in recreation and therapeutic care. Indoor sports are played within the centers, either in gyms or activities rooms, in schools and on fields at schools and parks. More sedate programs, including crafts, art, painting, and dance, are also offered.

The fees for these programs vary, with most costing less than $20 for a full season in a sport. Call to receive a schedule of the activities available.

i Most of the larger hotels in the area have relationships with fitness centers or have their own facilities so you can easily find a way to exercise, even in the worst weather.

Boardsailing
BALTIMORE AREA BOARDSAILING ASSOCIATION
(410) 315-8481
www.windsurfbaba.org

The membership association organizes regular competitive boardsailing events with prizes. Membership for a year is $20 for an individual or a family and runs from April 1 through March 31.

Dancing
CHARM CITY SWING
charmcityswing.com

Charm City Swing is operated by a U.S. Naval Academy math professor and a doctor who met while swing dancing in 1999. Learn swing dancing at the Austin Grill, 2400 Boston St. in Canton and the Vietnam Veterans Hall off Holabird, 6401 Beckley St. You can start with videos posted on the Web site or look to YouTube. Classes are $10 or $80 for eight weeks of lessons.

GREATER BALTIMORE SWING
DANCE COMMITTEE
www.baltimoreswing.org

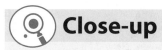 Close-up

Where to Take Pets

Baltimore's Charm City moniker extends from the way it treats people to its ability to accommodate pets, especially dogs. The area offers a variety of locations where Fido can run, walk, or sense the outdoors. All of the places can be just as rewarding for you, the one with the leash. When you take the four-footer, remember that all jurisdictions require that pets be leashed.

All jurisdictions require that pets be cleaned up after, and these requirements are maintained with fines ranging from $5 to $15 for violators.

Watch out for ticks. Small deer ticks can lie in the woods around Baltimore, so it's a good practice to check your pet (even if you're using the most advance tick collar) and yourself and remove any ticks immediately.

Not everybody's dog is as friendly as yours, and not everyone is as willing to experience the ritualistic love/hate relationship between pets on first encounter. Make sure the person with a pet ahead or behind wants your dog rubbing elbows or whatever else before you allow it.

Unless otherwise noted, the following sites are within Baltimore City limits. No admission fee is charged at any of these locations.

In the northeast **Herring Run Park** at the intersection of Harford Road and Argonne Drive is a 4-mile-long area along the watershed for Lake Montebello. It has easy-to-follow trails and provides dogs and owners with lots of cool sights, smells, and sounds. A playground, restrooms, and parking are all on-site.

Robert E. Lee Park at Lakeside Drive and Hollins Avenue offers a meeting place for single dogs, cats, and humans. Set along Lake Roland, dozens and dozens of dogs roam this park or take a plunge. On a warm afternoon or on weekends, it's the place to be.

In the Northwest area **Druid Hill Park,** at the intersection of McCulloh Street and Druid Hill Avenue, check the open fields for people and pets. This area outside The Maryland Zoo in Baltimore is perfect for a quiet picnic with a loved one and pet. In the back area of the park, away from the on-street parking, are tree-lined trails although the open areas are large enough to accommodate even the most rambunctious dogs.

This nonprofit group hosts dances on the second Saturday around town. Lessons precede the dances. Tickets are $12 and $15. Check the Web site for details.

THE FRIDAY NIGHT SWING DANCE CLUB
8520 Drumwood Rd.
(410) 583-7337
www.fridaynightswing.com
The Friday Night Swing Dance Club promotes swing, Latin, and social dancing in the greater Baltimore area. It encourages dancers of all levels to participate and has weekend dances that are regularly attended by 300 to 400 people. Sessions are generally $12 and that includes light refresh-

ments. With more than 6,800 people on the mailing list and more than 3,500 on the e-mail list, this is one of the largest dance groups on the East Coast.

Fencing

THE CHESAPEAKE FENCING CLUB
201 Homeland Ave.
(410) 532-7445
www.chesapeakefencing.com
Just north of the College of Notre Dame in North Baltimore, this club offers open practice Monday nights, with supervised junior practice Monday, Thursday, and Saturday evenings for children age 6 through 12 years. Foil, saber, and epee les-

sons are conducted by Moniteur Ray Gordon by appointment and for a varying fee.

Golf

Private golf clubs abound in the suburbs and usually the only way you can play on one of them is to join the club or be asked to join a foursome by a club member. Public courses, however, are nearby, not necessarily as challenging, and certainly a lot less expensive. You can buy a Player Card for $20 a year that's good for discounts on greens fees and benefits at the five Baltimore municipal courses, Mount Pleasant, Clifton Park, Forest Park, and Carroll Park. All five courses offer a 9-hole only early-bird special during the first hour of operation. You start on the back nine and you can still be at work on time. The listings for each course include the cost of greens fees for one player. All courses listed have pro shops with clubs, tees, and other essential and nonessential golf equipment. For more details, check the Web site, www.marylandgolf.com.

CARROLL PARK GOLF COURSE
2100 Washington Blvd.
(410) 685-8344
www.bmgcgolf.com
This course is the closest to downtown Baltimore. It's a good course to walk, featuring eight par 4 holes and four par 3s. The course's newest hole, the 232-yard No. 4, requires a low, down-the-middle approach to set you up for a slight right dogleg. For an afternoon golfer looking for a quick game, this course can be completed in about two hours, even when it's busy. A round costs $11 to $18. Cart rental is $6 per person and pull carts are $3.50.

CLIFTON PARK GOLF COURSE
2701 St. Lo Dr.
(410) 243-3500
www.bmgcgolf.com
This Baltimore City–owned course has been good for beginning and intermediate players, because the 5,714-yard course has no water and had a few trees. As a way to enhance your

visual appreciation, improve the environment, and maybe challenge you a little bit more, more than 100 trees were planted on October 3, 2009, as part of the 7th Annual Ricky Myers Day of Service and Baltimore City's TreeBaltimore action plan. Greens fees range from $8 for juniors to $30 for adults, a good bargain for people in the city, especially golfers who like to walk. The cost is the same whether you ride or walk. Giving this par 70 course an urban flavor are the several roads that run nearby (all of which are out of bounds). Golf pro Mark Paolini offers lessons, while the course provides practice greens, a restaurant, and a snack bar.

FOREST PARK GOLF COURSE
2900 Hillsdale Rd.
(410) 448-4653
www.bmgcgolf.com
What is said to be the largest sand trap on the East Coast at the number 2 green and covering three-fourths of the green (about 120' by 10'), according to the operators here, is something to admire. You do not have to become intimately familiar with it. The mega-bunker on this 5,815-yard course used to be a water hazard but was covered with cement and sand some years ago. The 18th hole features a par 5 double-dogleg, forcing you to avoid the slice for two successive shots; if you can't, you're in big trouble trying to make par at 71. A round costs between $8 for juniors to $35 depending on what day and time you want to play. Tim Sanders offers golf lessons at the course. A snack bar and shower facilities are available.

i Advance notice needed to reserve tee times varies from two to seven days. Make sure you do it as soon as possible, especially for Friday and weekends.

MITCHELL'S GOLF COMPLEX
301 Mitchell Dr., Reisterstown
(410) 833-7721
www.mitchellsgolf.com
A nine-hole executive course, the Golf Complex draws beginners and good golfers alike, most

of whom want a quick golf fix. The toughest holes are No. 5, which is a 150-yard water shot that looks much easier than it is, and No. 14, a 205-yard par 3 shot over a pond. The facility also features batting cages, three miniature golf courses, and a driving range to keep the children or others busy while you hit the links. Nine holes on weekdays are $12 ($8 for seniors) and $18 for 18 holes. Weekends, the fee is $15. You can rent a golf cart ($8 per person), pull cart ($3), or even the golf clubs ($10). There is also a snack bar.

MOUNT PLEASANT GOLF COURSE
6001 Hillen Rd.
(410) 254-5100
www.bmgcgolf.com
Municipal doesn't mean easy. Arnold Palmer won his second PGA tournament, the old Eastern Open in 1956, and Sam Snead also won on this 6,003-yard course. In 2008, it was ranked the 12th best municipal golf course in the United States, according to *Golfweek Magazine*. This par 71 is set on rolling hills and tight fairways. On a breezy day, the back nine can be a duffer's nightmare. It's one of the busiest courses in the area; 85,000 rounds of golf are played each year, so reservations are necessary. Greens fees run from $10 to $44 (pre-noon on weekends). Golf pro Jim Deck provides lessons. A snack bar is on-site.

Gymnastics
GERSTUNG
1400 Coppermine Terrace
Mount Washington
(410) 337-7781
www.gerstung.com
In northern Baltimore City, Gerstung offers gymnastics programs and movement education to children from 1 through 13 years of age in a large

building off Falls Road near I-83. Skills classes are also presented to children age 5 through 13. Dance classes and rock climbing are also available. Call for rates and information on special summer programs.

Horseback Riding
Maryland is horse country, so horseback riding opportunities abound. The *Equiery* is a monthly publication about and for the equestrian community. Pick it up at tack shops and feed shops. See more information at www.equiery.com or (410) 489-7826. The Maryland Horse Show Association provides information about the horse community and can be reached at (410) 591-0380 or www.mdhsa.org.

Running
BALTIMORE AREA TRIATHLON CLUB
www.tribmore.org
This local organization offers support to athletes who like to run, swim, and bike fast. Track workouts are held weekly and their Web site includes area races.

BALTIMORE ROAD RUNNERS CLUB
P.O. Box 9825
Baltimore, MD 21284
(410) 377-7327 (24-hour hotline)
www.brrc.com
For more than 30 years, this club has promoted running for recreational and competitive runners. Some members run occasionally, others are marathoners. Some runs are 100 meters long and others 10 or 20 miles. Relays are on the schedule, too. Some events have no fee; others are minimal depending on whether or not you're a member. Membership is $25 for an individual and $30 for a family.

ON THE WATER

Since settlers first encountered what is now Baltimore, a main attraction has been its waters, hundreds of big and small tributaries to the Chesapeake Bay. Beautiful rivers, gentle and serene coves, an open harbor, and streams perfect for spending time with a fishing pole or a rudder in hand—these are some of the area's most respected and protected resources for anglers, boaters, windsurfers, and personal watercraft operators.

If you're looking for a place to fly fish, the Gunpowder River offers one of the best trout streams on the East Coast. If you're eager to practice steering a catamaran, try the rivers lining eastern Baltimore County. Their many coves and inlets offer calm and shallow waters that enable the novice or the most experienced skipper to practice his or her skills.

If you want tidal waters, the Chesapeake Bay and some of its larger tributaries provide what you're looking for. If you seek nontidal waters, some of the rivers flowing in eastern Baltimore County are your best bet.

SAFETY ON THE HIGH SEAS

With water comes responsibility, and Maryland's Natural Resources Police (a division of its Department of Natural Resources) keeps a close watch over the surrounding waters to make sure participants follow these rules and regulations. They are joined by marine police teams from Baltimore City, Baltimore County, Howard County, and Anne Arundel County and U.S. Coast Guard units from Curtis Bay, an area near the Inner Harbor on the Patapsco River.

The number of people boating in Maryland has been on the rise in recent years, with explosive growth in the personal watercraft category. And remember that people are not the only living things out there

WATERWAYS

The Chesapeake Bay

The origins of the world's largest estuary, the Chesapeake Bay, date from the last Ice Age, more than 20,000 years ago, when a colder climate prevailed on earth. Back then, sea level was more than 300 feet lower than it is today.

Now, the bay has an average depth of 21 feet, with its deepest point in the middle bay, near Bloody Point, where it drops to 174 feet. The bay is 195 miles long, and it draws water from a 64,000-square-mile area, extending to the headwaters of the Susquehanna River, 441 miles away from its mouth in the northern bay in Otsego, New York. Water flowing from New York to Pennsylvania to Maryland makes its way to the bay. At 4,000 miles the Bay's shoreline is longer than the shoreline of the Pacific Ocean on the West Coast. Really.

The bay's 55-foot channel makes it a favorite for shipping companies sending ore, vehicles, coal, and other materials from all over the world to the port of Baltimore and Hampton Roads, Virginia, which is closer to the Atlantic Ocean and Baltimore's competitor to the south.

Because of the intense amount of commercial traffic, operating recreational vessels on the bay can be more challenging than on some of the rivers. Keep in mind that the larger commercial vessels always have the right of way because of their size, which prohibits them from being able to maneuver easily in the channel. In foul weather, give them a wider berth and heed their horn blows.

In addition to larger vessels, the bay's depth can be a hazard. Shallow waters with unpredictable shifts, especially in side creeks, can run you aground. Furthermore, dredging of channels isn't always done as often as necessary, and sometimes the depths reflected in maps can be fluid, to say the least.

Weather conditions can also challenge boaters. Sudden changes in weather are frequent in summer, although variances occur in spring and fall, too. The bay tends to offer good boating weather most of the time, however sudden storms can bring high winds, heavy downpours, and rough seas in areas where the sun was shining brightly just a few minutes prior. Keep an ear to the radio to monitor situations as they develop, and when signs of possible trouble appear, heed them quickly. Don't wait for the storm to hit—act beforehand.

If you're planning to fish for striped bass (rockfish), you'll want to be in the deeper waters of the lower bay rather than northern sections. The fish seem to favor the deeper areas, with Bloody Point being among the best sites for them. You also might want to talk to other mariners to see where they're hitting. Just watch out for the occasional fish tale, designed to keep you out of their special spot.

Middle River

An active boating area near Baltimore, Middle River is home to a number of marinas, waterfront restaurants, and boatyards. The river has several creeks, including Galloway, Frog Mortar, Stansbury, Dark Head, Hopkins, Sue, Hog Pen, Norman's, and Seneca Creeks. These creeks provide quiet, calm, and protected waters where waterskiing, swimming, and personal watercraft are allowed. Crabbing and fishing are frequent activities of residents and visitors to the area. Bass, carp, and catfish are frequent visitors to these waters. On weekends and holidays, a 6-knot speed limit is enforced upstream of Galloway Point.

Back River

Back River is between Middle River and the Patapsco River, an area that used to be home to a

Numbers to Know

- If you experience marine problems, contact the **Maryland Natural Resources Police,** (800) 419-0743, or use Channel 16 VHF on your on-board radio.

- For general information from the **Department of Natural Resources,** call (877) 620-8DNR

- **Boating emergencies,** channel 16 VHF (monitored by Coast Guard, city, state, and county police)

- **Coast Guard Search and Rescue,** (410) 576-2525

- **Baltimore County Fire Department,** 911 or (410) 887-5974

- **Baltimore County Police Department,** 911

- **Maryland Natural Resources Police,** (410) 260-8881 or (800) 628-9944

- **Local Weather,** (410) 936-1212

- **Coast Guard Station Curtis Bay,** (410) 576-2625

- **Coast Guard Station Stillpond,** (410) 778-2201

- **Coast Guard Boating Safety Hotline,** (800) 368-5647

- **Coast Guard Auxiliary Flotilla boating class,** (800) 336-BOAT

great deal of industry and still shows signs of the industrial age. The river is home to a number of recreational anglers and boaters who moor their boats along the shorelines. Back River has a poor reputation in the area because of the Back Water Treatment Facility, which can offer a pungent aroma.

Despite this problem—far larger in reputation than in reality—the river is a peaceful getaway from the more widely used Gunpowder, Middle, and Patapsco Rivers.

As this is a favorite place for crabbers, trying to negotiate around the crab lines or the people checking them can sometimes test the navigational skills in best of us. The area supports the same bass, carp, and catfish populations as its fellow rivers to its north.

Selected Baltimore Firsts

In 1788 the Chesapeake was the first American vessel to raise the colors of the United States above its billowing sails.

Our Constellation was the first ship to capture an enemy ship after the Revolution in 1797.

Isaac McKim of Fell's Point built the first clipper ship, the Ann McKim, in 1833.

The first steamship made wholly of American steel, the DeRosset, was registered here in 1839.

—Excerpted from *Baltimore—America's City of Firsts,* a pamphlet published by Baltimore Bicentennial Celebration, Inc.

Patapsco River

The Inner Harbor overshadows the Patapsco River by name and opportunity, but in spite of this, the river claims its own recognition. Many of the area's finer marinas are in the Inner Harbor, Fell's Point, and Canton areas, where big-ticket boats dock during weekends and summer nights.

Preparation is the key process when you're planning to take your boat to the Patapsco and Inner Harbor areas. To reserve a space, contact the Baltimore Harbormaster's office at (410) 396-

3174. The larger your boat, the more advance time you need to reserve a docking space.

i Tide Point, a former Procter and Gamble Plant built in the 1920s, recently benefited from a $67 million redevelopment. Located on the harbor in South Baltimore, the office park has a lovely waterfront promenade replete with Adirondack chairs for lounging. Grab a cup of coffee from the nearby cafe and enjoy Baltimore's working waterfront.

Boating

Give Baltimoreans a body of water larger than a puddle, and they'll try to sail or motor a boat over it. Especially popular are the Chesapeake Bay, the Susquehanna, Gunpowder, and Bush Rivers, and the Middle and Patapsco Rivers (see the Waterways section for more information).

What follows is a roundup of some of the marinas, ramps, and boat rental providers in the area.

Marinas
Patapsco River
ANCHORAGE MARINA
2501 Boston St., Canton
(410) 522-7200
www.anchoragemarina.com
This Canton marina offers slips for a night or a year. It's located near the Promenade and you can easily reach the Inner Harbor or Fell's Point via water taxi. Or just stay in the area; it's an easy stroll to the restaurants of Canton. The daily docking rate is $2.25 per foot plus $10 per night per line for 30 amp electric or $15 per night for 50 or twin 30 amp electric.

THE BALTIMORE INNER HARBOR MARINE CENTER
400 Key Hwy.
(410) 837-5339
www.baltimoreinnerharbormarinecenter.com
The Baltimore Inner Harbor Marine Center has been serving Baltimore boaters and visitors since

1975 with 158 slips, concrete floating piers, and walking access to the Inner Harbor. Overnight and day docking are available with the weekday rate of $2 per foot on weekdays (Monday through Thursday) and $2.50 per foot on weekends. You can also "dock 'n dine" for $20 for up to two hours and $30 for three hours. Over that and the overnight transient rate applies. Electric (50 amp only) starts at $18 per day. Amenities include 24-hour security and customer service, 24-hour dock and pump-out facility, and a 24-hour convenience and marine store. There are also laundry and shower facilities (so you can clean your bod while cleaning your clothes), Wi-Fi, pool and health club access, concierge service, and business center.

BALTIMORE MARINE CENTER
2738 Lighthouse Point East, Inner Harbor
(410) 675-8888
www.baltimoremarinecenter.com
Baltimore Marine Center at Lighthouse Point has 500 slips on the south side of the Inner Harbor, and indoor boat storage, a health club, and a heated pool. Wi-Fi and fuel dock are available. Overnight rates are $2 per foot per day for weekdays and $2.50 for weekends. Cable TV, wireless Internet, and 30 and 50 amp service are $18 a day.

BALTIMORE PUBLIC DOCKING
Patapsco River at Baltimore Harbor and Canton
(410) 396-3174
The city's docks are always crowded, but the locations at the Inner Harbor and Canton can be among the best for sightseers or for those seeking to be seen. High visibility comes at a high price at this 16-foot-deep marina. Electricity and showers are available, along with ice. Other services, including grocery stores, pharmacies, shopping, and restaurants, are near each dock.

INNER HARBOR EAST MARINA
801 Lancaster St.
(410) 625-1700
www.innerharboreast.net
This marina, which has been in the midst of Legg Mason and Four Seasons hotel construction for

much too long, has 188 floating boat slips. It's a 15-minute walk to the Inner Harbor or 10 minutes to Little Italy and Fell's Point. Transients are welcome and slips are $2.10 a foot per night and $2.75 per foot if you need a T-head. An electrical hookup is $16 a night. This is also home of the Canton Kayak Club (www.cantonkayakclub.com).

MIDDLE BRANCH MARINA
3101 Waterview Ave.
(410) 539-2628
www.middlebmarina.com
Under the Hanover Street Bridge, about 1 mile directly across the Patapsco River from the Inner Harbor, this 365-slip marina is one of the most affordable for all the amenities it provides. With a transient rate of $1.50 per foot and facilities for everything from a dinghy to a 60-footer, it's hard to go wrong. The 6-foot-deep, protected cove provides safety, security, and access. Among the amenities are water and electricity ($5 a day) connections to each slip, shower rooms, a full-service repair yard, a ships store, and a do-it-yourself service area, where tools are provided at an hourly rate. Gas and diesel service and pump-out facilities are also available.

Boat Ramps
Baltimore City operates several public boat ramps.

Broening Park Ramp at Harbor Hospital: Four ramps, plenty of parking, no fees, and it's open 24 hours a day.

Boston Street Ramp Inner Harbor: Two ramps, limited parking, no fees, open 24 hours a day.

Fort Armistead Park, Patapsco River/Key Bridge: Two ramps, plenty of parking, no fees, good condition (steep), open 24 hours a day.

Marine Services
DECKELMAN'S BOAT YARD
201 Oak Ave., Middle River
(410) 391-6482, (410) 850-2993 (beeper)
www.chesapeakebayassist.com
If your boat's in need of a tow, Deckelman's is the place to go. They're quick, efficient, and reason-

ably priced. They're also available 24 hours a day. They'll tow your boat where you want it to go and the fees and cost of service depend on your level of membership within the Chesapeake Bay Assist program.

TIDEWATER YACHT SERVICE CENTER
321 East Cromwell St.
(410) 625-4992
www.tysc.com
If you can float it, Tidewater Yacht Service Center can fix it—at a guaranteed rate established before the work begins. Located now at the Port Covington Maritime Center, Tidewater specializes in cleaning and detailing, bottom painting, engine and generator repairs and sales, fiberglass and blister repair, woodworking, awlgrip refinishing, varnishing, air conditioning and refrigeration, electrical service, sail repair, and canvas installation and repair. Since 1965 the facility has provided service to boats weighing as much as 60 tons or with beams as long as 20 feet. Towing services are also available. The fuel dock is still located near the DOMINO SUGAR sign at Key Highway. They are a BoatUS cooperating marina.

Sailing
GETAWAY SAILING
2700 Lighthouse Point (Suite 905)
(410) 342-3110, (888) 342-3709
www.getawaysailing.com
Getaway Sailing offers a fleet of sailboats from 9 feet to 34 feet at the Lighthouse Point Marina, on the Patapsco River in Canton. Rentals vary depending on the size and type of boat and on how long you decide to spend sailing it—so call ahead for details. Baredeck and skippered charters and cruises are available. Owner Dick Mead also offers afternoon and overnight cruises to the Eastern Shore. In addition to rentals, the company provides lessons.

SAIL BALTIMORE
1809 Thames St.
(410) 522-7300
www.sailbaltimore.org

Sail Baltimore is a nonprofit, community service organization that works as a great resource for boating and sailing activities in the area. It was founded as the Mayor's Official Committee on Visiting Ships to host Baltimore's first tall ship gathering in the summer of 1976 and is responsible for coordinating Baltimore's waterfront activities. The organization has been responsible for brining in about two dozen visiting ships (tall ships, military vessels, and education and environmental ships). They have a calendar of ship visits so you can see if and when a particular ship is due to arrive and depart. Sail Baltimore also supports other maritime events, such as the Great Chesapeake Bay Schooner Race, the Fell's Point Yacht Club Lighted Boat Parade, the Blessing of Baltimore's Work Boats, and OpSail Baltimore.

FISHING

Largemouth bass, smallmouth bass, and brown trout, oh my! Baltimoreans are fascinated by marine life, and we enjoy hauling it over the side of a boat just as much as visiting it at the National Aquarium. The Chesapeake Bay and the Susquehanna, Middle, and Patapsco Rivers are great places to drop your line. Gunpowder River is stocked with brown trout every spring and fall offering you, the cunning angler, 150 to 200 fish per acre, and Loch Raven Reservoir has its own fishing center.

Here we've provided information for obtaining a license in Maryland and highlighted some of the charter boats in the area.

Licenses

Maryland's fishing license fees depend on whether you're a state resident or visitor. A license is required for anyone age 16 or older and can be obtained from a number of sports and tackle shops around the state and at several regional service centers operated by the Maryland Department of Natural Resources. For more information, call (410) 260-3220 or visit www.dnr.state.md.us.

Maryland residents pay $20.50 for a nontidal license or $15 for a tidal license, which is applicable to fishing in the Chesapeake Bay and its tidal tributaries. Those hailing from outside Maryland pay their state's fee for a nontidal license or $15 for a tidal license.

All other licenses, stamps, and permits are the same regardless of residency. A short-term nontidal license, which is valid for five days from the date of issuance, is $7. A trout stamp is $5. A pleasure boat decal to fish, which allows fishing from a boat by all the people on board, is $40. No license is required to fish from a charter boat.

Charter Boats

BLUE GOOSE YACHT CHARTER SERVICE
Anchorage Marina
2501 Boston St.
(410) 647-2583
www.bluegoosecharters.com
This charter service, based out of Anchorage Marina in the Baltimore Harbor, has five trawlers in its fleet. The yachts come fully equipped—complete with linens, towels, and utensils. Early boarding is allowed the night before, at no additional charge, if the schedule permits. They like their boats to stay in the upper Bay area. They do not like them to go south of the Choptank River, east of Cambridge on the Eastern Shore, south or west of the Solomons on the Western Shore, or near the C&D Canal. Discounts for charters lasting longer than one week and for repeat customers are offered. Blue Goose operates from late April or early May through the end of October.

CAPTAIN DON'S FISHING CHARTER
Henderson's Wharf Marina
1001 Fell St., Fell's Point
(410) 342-2004
www.captdonscharters.com
The 46-foot *Lady Luck* has room for six passengers and leaves for the Chesapeake Bay from Fell's Point. Fishing tackle and licenses are provided, but bring your own food and beverages. The boat goes on a variety of trips, from eight-hour rock fishing expeditions for $450 to two-hour Inner Harbor cruises for $220. Less-serious fishermen might like the three-hour fishing trip for $250. In the fall the boat goes out on hunting expeditions for sea ducks or Canada geese.

SWIMMING

NORTH BALTIMORE AQUATIC CLUB
5700 Cottonwood Ave.
(410) 433-8300
www.nbac.net
Yes, the NBAC is where Bob Bowman coached Dr. McSwimmy as he swam his way into history. They've formed a partnership to operate this pool, where Phelps began his training at age seven and the Meadowbrook Aquatic Center. If you (your children) want to rub hand paddles with future swimming stars, you can start with lessons here.

OTHER WATER SPORTS

BALTIMORE ROWING CLUB
3301 Waterview Ave.
(410) 355-5659
www.baltimorerowing.org
Get up and go near the Hanover Street Bridge south of the Inner Harbor and you might see the slim rowing boats of the Baltimore Rowing Club—or the sculls of local high school and college teams—breaking the still waters of the Patapsco River. If you've ever seen these graceful vessels and wanted to take your turn at an oar, the Baltimore Rowing Club offers lessons and regattas. You've got to get up early; classes begin at 5 a.m.

CHESAPEAKE PADDLERS ASSOCIATION
P.O. Box 341, Greenbelt, MD 20768
www.cpakayaker.com
With more than 300 members from the Maryland, Delaware, and District of Columbia, the Chesapeake Paddlers Association offers a forum for sea kayakers who'd like to discuss techniques and common interests, improve paddling skills, and experience the beauty of the Chesapeake Bay region's waters. Membership costs $10, and while the organization has no telephone number, you can learn more about it by sending a letter to the listed address or by checking the Web site.

SPECTATOR SPORTS

Sports lovers find a home in Baltimore that could rival almost any sports-crazed city. We have major league baseball and football, Michael Phelps, lacrosse, indoor soccer, horse racing, and just about any other sport you'd like to participate in or watch. Here are some other activities that don't receive quite as much attention.

Lacrosse is to Baltimore as football is to Texas. That is never more evident than at a Hopkins lacrosse game at Homewood Field (3400 N. Charles St.)—especially one against rivals like University of Virginia or University of Maryland. The field's lights shine down on thousands of spectators as the student band peps everyone up. The fast-paced agility of the talented Blue Jays is exciting enough to keep every fan hooked, even when it's not exactly our year.

Then there's the Baltimore Arena, which was called the Baltimore Civic Center when the NBA's Bullets ruled there. The Bullets moved to Washington, D.C., and are now called the Washington Wizards. The civic center is now called an arena. It plays host to indoor soccer but not basketball or hockey because professional teams in these sports have failed here.

Yet we consider ourselves a big-league town, where home football or baseball games can significantly affect sales at the movies, restaurants, and other venues. We drop everything for a Saturday in May when the Preakness, the second jewel in horse racing's Triple Crown, comes to town.

For many of us, Cal Ripken Jr., the Orioles infielder who played in 2,632 consecutive baseball games before ending the streak on September 20, 1998—a major league record—is a symbol of what we demand of ourselves. Through Cal we see ourselves—working hard, playing hard, having fun, getting better and better, facing adversity. It's hard to forget Cal catching the final out as shortstop in the 5-0 victory over the Phillies in Philadelphia on October 16, 1983. The catch, the raised arms, the jumping up and down, the thrill of the moment. Then there's the night time stood still in baseball—September 6, 1995. All the world's sports fans watched as the banner proclaiming 2,131—the record number game—was unfurled on the warehouse past right field. In a scene seemingly out of The Natural, Cal took an impromptu victory lap at Camden Yards, slapping and shaking hands of the fans in the front row, as though each was a close friend.

It's hard to forget the arm of Johnny Unitas launching touchdown passes to Raymond Berry heading down the sidelines toward the closed end of the field at Memorial Stadium more than three decades ago, or when a game between the Pittsburgh Steelers and the Colts or the New York Jets and the Colts practically paralyzed the town all day Sunday.

Then there's more heartbreak. More than 50,000 fans filled Memorial Stadium in 1988 to celebrate the end of a 21-game losing streak for the Baltimore Orioles, a record that brought the city ridicule and attention from local, national, and international sports fans. When the streak ended, the fans were there, another sellout, as if they had been a part of the streak, even though it was something they would have rather forgotten.

We live and breathe with the players—they aren't just the team. They're family, people who would be welcomed with open arms at a family picnic or birthday dinner. To love an athlete is a concept that is all too often thrown around without meaning, but in Baltimore there is truth to the statement that we love our teams. They form a big part of who and what we are—to ourselves, to our friends, and to the world.

FOOTBALL

BALTIMORE RAVENS
M&T Bank Stadium
1101 Russell St.
(410) 230-8000
www.ravenszone.net

Baltimore has a love affair with the Ravens that no Super Bowl trophy (XXXV, January 28, 2001, when the Ravens defeated the New York Giants 34-7, under the leadership of head coach Brian Billick) can overstate or losing seasons can explain. Denied their beloved Baltimore Colts in the midnight raid in 1984 by Ursay to Indianapolis, the local fans were not one bit sympathetic to the cries from the fans when Art Modell moved the Cleveland Browns from their hometown in 1995. The major difference was Baltimore was not allowed to keep the Colts as their image and Cleveland was allowed to keep the Browns. Ergo, we became the Ravens, as in the bird from the Edgar Allan Poe poem.

The story is told that after the first score of the first home game played by the Ravens, an unholy sound like a wounded Raven squeaked over the loud speaker system. It was also the last time. Team colors are purple, black, and gold and you can see purple invade everywhere during the season and sometimes all year.

After decades during which the exploits of the greats—"Golden Arm" Johnny Unitas, Raymond Berry, Lenny Moore, and Bert Jones—cemented fans' love of the team, people are starting to find new heroes to focus their football fandom on.

In 1998 a new era began for the team, as it opened a football-only stadium, built across from Oriole Park at Camden Yards in downtown Baltimore, about 6 blocks from the Inner Harbor. After closing the book on Memorial Stadium—a 60,000-seat grande dame among outdoor stadiums, used by the Colts, Ravens, and the Canadian Football League's now-defunct Baltimore Stallions (not to mention the Baltimore Orioles until 1992)—the team's move to what is now called M&T Bank Stadium has brought more of the historic charm that came with Camden Yards.

The new digs provide the team, its owner, and fans with the state-of-the-art facilities considered so essential to a winning football organization these days.

The 69,300-seat stadium, with 108 luxury suites, is fully ADA compliant, with 700+ seats for the disabled and eight family bathrooms.

The stadium has several unique characteristics, including a distinct upper-seating level with notched corner. There are 62 oversized restrooms located throughout the stadium. The stadium has 245 food and beverage stands. Extra-wide concourses and unobstructed views place this stadium in a class of its own.

The two SmartVision boards, each measuring 25 by 100 feet almost give you the feeling of being right on the field in the middle of the action, minus the bruises and the paycheck. More than 10,000 Phelps Phever fans stayed after the Ravens-Vikings pre-season game (Ravens lost 23-15) to watch Michael Phelps' final Beijing Olympic swim win on August 16, 2008. At least one home-town hero gave them something to rally behind (OK, so Derrick Martin did intercept John David Booty for 22 years that was followed by a 2 point conversion).

Back to the stadium. There are seven levels, including five with seating. The facade has brick arches at its base, aluminum trim at the grid lines, and a frame of concrete supported by pewter structural steel rakers. Throughout the project, dark, rich brick and mortar, manufactured in Maryland and similar in appearance to other buildings in the area, were used.

Training camp for the Ravens has been held at McDaniel College in Westminster since the mid-1960s. The late July practices open with rookies, quarterbacks, and injured veterans reporting first, followed by all veterans, and the first full-squad practices that are open to the public. Pets are not allowed. Players are available for autographs each day after practice. Just line up next to the fences and ropes surrounding the field. No guarantees that your favorite player will sign an autograph. Please park around Bair Stadium. Call (410) 261-RAVE for updated information about practice times.

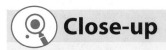# Close-up

Baseball

If you love baseball, you've gotta love Baltimore. The birthplace of Babe Ruth has (we think) the greatest baseball stadium in the world, two museums dedicated to the sport, and a ring of minor league stadiums surrounding it out in the suburbs.

Oriole Park at Camden Yards is the shrine to the majors. So what if the Orioles can't seem to pull out a winning season? As the team of Ironman Cal Ripken and Hall-of-Famers Brooks Robinson, Luis Aparicio, and Eddie Murray, we know they'll win one of these days. Meanwhile, we're proud of our downtown stadium, a retro stadium built as homage to old-fashioned stadiums, with plenty of good seats, a beautiful brick facade, and lots of stands selling crab cakes, hot dogs, and Cracker Jacks. Regulars know the beer man by name, and everyone is happy to stand and sing "Thank God I'm a Country Boy" during the seventh-inning stretch. John Denver even came and led the crowd the year just before he died.

The 16' statue of Babe Ruth, by Susan Luery, outside the Eutaw Street entrance, is the meeting place when you and your friends want to connect before entering the park. Note that the glove hanging from the Babe's belt is a right-handed glove. No one bothered to tell Luery that he was a leftie. Within the courtyard—between the stadium and the Sports Legend Museum are 4' aluminum monuments depicting retired Os uniform numbers including 4 (Earl Weaver), 5 (Brooks Robinson), 8 (Ripken, whose number was stolen and returned in late 2009), 22 (Jim Palmer), and 33 (Eddie Murray).

Tours of Oriole Park are available for groups and individuals. It's a great way to take a seat in the Orioles dugout, see the press box, and see the controls for the scoreboard. You'll be told that the H and E letters in *The Sun* advertisement on the scoreboard light up to indicate whether the officials called a hit or error. While checking out the scoreboard, note the two Oriole birds on either side that are 600-pound wind vanes. There's a video camera on top of the board that makes about a 350° turn around the stadium so you can see the harbor. You'll be told about the 75 miles of beer pipeline that snake through the stadium. They eliminate barrels being rolled back and forth and keep the brew at a constant temperature. Ninety-minute tours run at 11 a.m., noon, and 1 and 2 p.m. Monday through Saturday and Sunday at 12:20 p.m. and 1, 2, and 3 p.m. Tickets are $7 for adult and $5 for children and can be purchased online at baltimore.orioles.mlb.com or at the stadium box office. Call (410) 547-6234.

BALLPARK RULES

The following rules apply at all Orioles home games:

- No alcoholic beverages, cans, or glass can be brought into the park. Containers, including coolers and bags, are checked as spectators enter.

- Food can be brought into the stadium, meaning those peanut and pretzel vendors outside the ballpark make good money. Their prices are lower than what you'll find inside.

- All entrants must pay, except infants sitting on the same seat as parents.

- Smoking is prohibited in all areas, except the concourses outside the playing field and seating area.

- Selling tickets for more than face value is illegal, and undercover police stings targeting offenders are not unusual.

The Baltimore Orioles, routinely referred to as the Os or the Birds, roost in the dugout on the first-base side of the field, even though it gets the afternoon sun. It also offers the team management a "bird's-eye" view into the opponent's bullpen so they can keep an on the opponent's battery.

Getting to/from the stadium is best done via public transit. Take Light Rail to the Hamburg Street stop at the stadium. Take the Subway to Lexington Market North or Charles Center West stations, then walk. Take any local bus (1, 3, 7, 11, 19, 27, 35, and 64). Each costs $1.60 one-way, $3.20 round trip, and $3.50 for a day pass. Check www.mtamaryland.com/sports/Ravens for details and changes. Other options include parking at a local gas station or city lot (figure $10-20 or more).

Stadium Rules

The following rules apply at all Ravens home games:

- No alcoholic beverages, cans, or glass can be brought into the stadium. Fans must be age 21 or older to purchase or consume alcoholic beverages at the stadium. This includes any parking lots designated as tailgating zones.
- Smoking is not permitted in the seating areas or restrooms. Smoking is allowed on open concourses and ramps.
- Umbrellas are not allowed in the stadium so as not to interfere with the sightlines of other guests.
- Cameras and video equipment are permitted in the stadium during Ravens' games but cannot be used to reproduce the game.
- Selling tickets for more than face value is illegal.

STEEPLECHASE SEASON

For most people April means showers and the start of warmer weather. But for many of us in Baltimore it really only means one thing—the

Tailgating with Charlie

Baltimore is passionate about its tailgating parties, particularly when it comes to the Ravens games. Should you not be passionate enough to want to go to the trouble, then stop by the Baltimore City Firefighter's Local #734. It's located at 1202 Ridgely St. (410-234-0734), the former Engine Co. 37 that opened in 1910 and disbanded in 1988 because of budget cuts.

Charles "Charlie" Cieslak, retired from the force and Engine Company 2 at Light and Montgomery Streets, coordinates the food and beverages, with the help of Rick Schluderberg, the recently retired union president. Proceeds benefit the Baltimore City Firefighter's Widows and Orphans Fund with money going to families of firefighters killed in action.

About 700 to 1000 people come through the union hall sometimes starting at 9:30 a.m., mostly about three hours before game time; chatting (no charge); enjoying the pit ham, beef, or turkey ($6 a sandwich) or Italian sausage ($4), hot dogs, and more. Beverages, from mixed drinks to wine to beer to soda and water cost $2 to $4. During the preseason, you'll see a bunch of children and then mostly adults during the regular season.

You're about a block or maybe a 5-minute walk (how much traffic and how much beer might have some impact on that time frame) to the stadium.

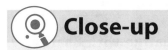

Close-up

Maryland's State Sport—Jousting?!?

Ask most Baltimoreans, and they'll tell you the state sport is lacrosse, a high-speed, bone-crunching sport played by young men and women with webbed sticks. Lacrosse is huge in the northeastern United States, and Johns Hopkins University and the University of Maryland are two local powerhouses.

But the state sport (and Maryland is the only state with a designated state sport) is jousting, a medieval test of bravery and skill that pitted knight against knight in battle, often for the hand of a fair maiden.

In Europe between the 10th and 12th centuries, jousting required that an armor-clad rider on horseback knock another knight from his mount using a long pole. Jousting was an occupation and the widely accepted method throughout Europe for competing knights to prove their mettle to the fair maiden of the day, while making some money for beating an able competitor.

Thankfully, riders don't square off against each other anymore. Instead, they compete in the "running at the rings," the name given to the new approach to the sport created about the time of James I of England. It was this form that Cecil Calvert, the first Lord Baltimore, brought to the colonies in the early 1700s.

Today, as in colonial times, jousting riders take three runs at the rings, which in the first round are an inch in diameter, roughly the size of a quarter. The rider steers toward three small rings with a 5- to 7-foot-long wooden pole, designed specifically for the rider. The pole must be crafted to provide perfect balance when on the rider's arm. Inserted into the end of the pole is a 2-foot lance, handmade of aluminum, stainless steel, or steel. Riders who succeed in collecting nine rings (three in each of three rounds) compete at the next level, where the rings are about the size of a nickel. A subsequent round has rings a quarter-inch in diameter, about the size of a dime.

The rings are suspended from arches 30 yards apart, with a 40-yard starting area for the horse and rider to get their timing and approach perfect. Competitors are given nine seconds to complete a regular round, eight seconds for a championship round. They are timed from when they cross a starting line 20 yards from the first ring until they gather the third ring. Taking more time than allotted eliminates the competitor, regardless of whether the rider succeeds in gathering the rings on his pole.

The winner is crowned at an elaborate closing ceremony, where the winning knight chooses the lady to be crowned "Queen of Love and Beauty." When women win, and they increasingly compete in this skill event, they choose the "King of Love and Beauty."

In keeping with the medieval tradition, riders male and female take names like Knight of One-Thousand Days or Maiden of Misery, often using humor or their real family names as sources for their monikers. These modern-day knights have chosen brightly colored costumes of the period over the medieval armor of centuries past.

Because the rider must focus all attention on the rings, the movements of the horse must be exact. For this reason, horses typically go through at least two years of formal training with riders before entering competitions.

Few formal jousting tournaments are held, though exhibitions are often performed at county fairs and the Maryland Renaissance Festival. A careful eye to the open stretches of farmland in northern Baltimore County can often reveal the telltale arches where would-be lords practice for the opportunity to be Lord of the Rings.

start of steeplechase season. During the first four Saturdays in April a different steeplechase is held on four farms in northern Baltimore and Harford Counties. If you've never experienced a steeplechase, it's an exciting opportunity to view—usually up-close—a traditional point-to-point race. But remember these events are held outside, rain or shine, so be sure to wear proper attire. A few stores in close proximity to the races usually sell steeplechase tickets; a good bet is Butler Store and Liquors (410-771-4383) at 14921 Falls Rd.

One of the first races of the season, held the first Saturday of April, is the **Elkridge Harford,** run over Atlanta Hall Farm in Monkton. This race has served over the past 50-plus years as the testing ground for riders and horse. Its placement on the calendar and its inviting course have attracted such world-renowned horses as Jay Trump and Ben Nevis II, both of whom went on to capture the English Grand National in Liverpool. This is the smallest of the races, so observers can really get in close to the action. There are six races, both timber and flat races. General admission tickets are $25 per carload. To get there, take I-695 to exit 27/Dulaney Valley Road. Cross Loch Raven Reservoir and bear left onto Jarrettsville Pike. Continue through the light at Jacksonville and go 4 miles to Pocock Road. Left on Pocock Road and follow parking signs.

On the second Saturday of April the **My Lady's Manor Steeplechase Races** are held to benefit Ladew Topiary Gardens. Gates open at noon and post time is 2:30 p.m. This is Harford County's largest annual sporting event, with an estimated crowd of anywhere between 2,000 and 6,000 people attending. The day includes three races, 3 miles over timber. People may bring coolers, picnics, or charcoal stoves. Because of danger to the horses, all glass containers should be deposited only in receptacles provided. General admission tickets are $30 and family parking is $35. These are available on race day at the gate or ahead of time at local stores. You can call Ladew Topiary Gardens for more information at (410) 557-9570. To get there take I-695 to exit 27B, then take Dulaney Valley Road, north. Keep left to Jarrettsville Pike. Go to Pocock Road and follow signs.

On the third Saturday in April, the **Grand National Steeplechase** is held starting at 3:15 p.m., with gates opening at noon. This race, second in age only to the Hunt Cup, began as an outgrowth of a boys' race that was instituted in 1898. In 1900 the race, which is restricted to amateur riders, became an annual event. The Grand National has moved four times before finding its present home in Butler. The day includes three races. General admission tickets are $20 per car. Tickets can be obtained by writing to: Grand National Steeplechase, P.O. Box 1, Butler, MD 21023. To get to the race, take I-83 north to Belfast Road west. Follow to Falls Road and make a right. Go less than a mile, making a left onto Butler Road. Go out Butler Road a little over a mile, until you see signs for parking.

On the fourth Saturday in April is the most popular and largest of the races, the **Maryland Hunt Cup.** This race ranks with the English Grand National as one of the two greatest steeplechase races in the world. It was originally run as a rivalry race between the Green Spring and Elkridge hunt clubs but in 1903 opened to any recognized hunt club in the United States and Canada. The race is run over Worthington Farms, a distance of 4 miles, and gates open at 11 p.m. Parking passes must be obtained prior to the day of the race by sending $35 and a self-addressed, stamped envelope to: The Maryland Hunt Cup Association, P.O. Box 3606, Glyndon, MD 21071. No sales are made on race day. The schedule, ticket, and parking information for the steeplechase season can be found at www.marylandsteeplechasing.com. Tickets can also be picked up at many local stores. To get there take I-83 north to Shawan Road. Follow Shawan Road west until you see signs for parking.

Shawan Downs, an equestrian center in Cockeysville, was established to save 300 acres of farmland and preserve the horsey traditions in an area quickly being swallowed up by suburbia. From March through September the center holds a series of equestrian events that benefit local charities. These include the Green Spring Valley Point to Point and the Maryland Junior Hunt Cup for young riders, and horse shows. The course's

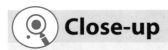# Close-up

Lacrosse

Marylanders love lacrosse, and Baltimore, with its concentration of colleges and universities, is the lacrosse center for the state. Drive by any prep school at 3:30 p.m., and you'll see loads of boys and girls carting their lacrosse sticks and helmets to the fields. Many graduate to play at the collegiate level, and Maryland boasts some of the top schools for NCAA lacrosse. The game is primarily a collegiate sport with nearly 25,000 men playing lacrosse at more than 400 colleges and universities.

The earliest accounts of lacrosse date from the first French missionaries and English explorers who came to the New World around 1630. The Native American tribes playing the stick and ball game intrigued explorers in the Great Lakes area, along the northeastern seaboard, and in Canada. Lacrosse was given its name by early French settlers, using the generic term for any game played with a curved stick (crosse) and a ball. There is no evidence of non–Native Americans taking up the game until the mid-19th century, when English-speakers in Montreal adopted the sport from the Mohawks. For some classic history lessons about lacrosse, you may want to pick up George Beers' book about the Mohawk playing techniques entitled *Lacrosse* (1869) or James Mooney's *American Anthropologist* (1890), which describes in detail the Eastern Cherokee game and its elaborate rituals. *American Indian Lacrosse: Little Brother of War* (1994) by Thomas Vennum Jr. offers a good contemporary look at the history of the game.

The sport of lacrosse is a combination of basketball, soccer, and hockey. Like hockey, a small semicircle called the crease protects the goalie, and offensive players cannot step inside this area (there is a sports bar and grill on York Road in Towson that honors the game with its name, "The Crease"). The cardinal rule of lacrosse is that your hands can never touch the ball. Players handle the ball with a long stick that has a net on the end. Quickness and agility are essential skills for this fast-moving sport. Players frequently sprint down the field making fast precision passes. Men's and women's lacrosse were played under the same rules, with no protective equipment, until the mid-1930s. At that time, men's lacrosse began evolving to the game that exists today, one of more physical contact. Men wear helmets and padding to protect from the occasional stick jab or elbow that comes from an opposing team member.

If you've never watched live lacrosse you are missing an exciting game. The adept skill with which the men and women play the sport coupled with the advances in sports equipment makes for a fast, graceful game that is a thrill to watch. Spring weekends at Homewood Field at the Johns Hopkins University are packed with lacrosse fans cheering the men's lacrosse team. With Loyola, Towson University, and the University of Maryland competing in the same division, hometown rivalries can get fierce. Friendly jabs at opposing team's fans are common, but it's all in good fun. The lacrosse season begins in the spring, and everyone looks forward to enjoying the breezy Baltimore weather, the blue skies, and the sunshine at an afternoon lacrosse game and the inevitable tailgates that go with it. But even the most inclement weather won't keep the diehard fans from braving the elements to watch the game.

If you don't know the rules of the game, don't worry. The uninitiated are sure to find a friendly lacrosse fan willing to share the details of the game. If you really want to do your homework and know what you're watching before you get to the game, visit the U.S. Lacrosse National Hall of Fame and Museum located on the Johns Hopkins University campus. There you can get a crash course in the history and glories of lacrosse. You'll learn that lacrosse is considered one of the quickest growing team sports in the United States today.

Collegiate lacrosse is attracting major league-sized crowds. M&T Bank Stadium in Baltimore hosted the 2003 and 2004 NCAA Lacrosse Finals and Championship over Memorial Day Weekend, attracting a record-breaking 108,000 people from around the country. The Finals were also played at M&T Bank Stadium in 2007, and the games attracted even larger numbers of attendees.

premier event is its final event of the season, the **Legacy Chase,** held in late September. The event combines the steeplechase with country fair and events for children—even a stick horse race. Tickets go on sale in the summer. Check www .shawandowns.org for the schedule and ticket prices. Or call (410) 666-3676 to order. Ticket prices range from $10 to $30 per carload.

INDOOR SOCCER

BALTIMORE BLAST
Baltimore Arena
201 West Baltimore St.
(410) 732-5278
www.baltimoreblast.com
The Baltimore Blast may be a top-scoring soccer team but Baltimoreans often don't seem to notice. Usually disappointed by the Baltimore Orioles or engrossed by the Baltimore Ravens, city residents don't seem to notice that right there in the Baltimore Arena, the local franchise of the National Professional Soccer League is winning games—and they're making it look like a lot of fun. This is a championship franchise that topped the rest in 1984, 2003, 2004, and 2006. Baltimore has had a professional indoor soccer team since 1980. Indoor soccer is played November through March on a modified hockey rink covered with artificial turf.

The team features mostly American players, often drafting players from college. While the team is international, a couple of local boys are on the roster. One of the top scorers on the team, Giuliano Celenza (#4), holds the University of Maryland Baltimore County's record as the number two scorer in school history. A graduate of UMBC and Archbishop Curley High School, he lives with his family in Perry Hall. Billy Nelson (#2) hails from Bel Air, a northern suburb, and played for UMBC before joining the Blast in 2003. He even coaches for Boys Latin, taking the team there to the local championship in 2006. And Mike Lookingland (#24) is from Fallston, Maryland, and played for Loyola High School, winning the team's MVP award his junior and senior years.

The Baltimore Blast fans can rock the Baltimore Arena, which has room for 11,400 fans. Unfortunately, average game attendance fills about half the seats. So there's usually space available for those who want to join in the fun at the last minute.

Home games start at 7:35 p.m. Tickets are available at the arena box office, (410) 732-5278, or through Ticketmaster at (410) 547-SEAT. They are available online at www.ticketmaster.com. Tickets are $20 for prime seats, $17 for upper levels, and $14 behind the goal line. Games are broadcast on WCBM (680AM) radio.

COLLEGE SPORTS

Baltimore is a hotbed of college sports action, where you can often find good competition at family rates. Several area teams garner national attention for their exploits.

Johns Hopkins University (410-516-7490, www.hopkinssports.cstv.com) plays a variety of sports but is best known for men's lacrosse, in which it frequently competes with other powerhouses including Syracuse, Rutgers, Towson, and the universities of Maryland, Virginia, and North Carolina. The school's outdoor field features artificial turf with concrete grandstands on both sides of the playing surface. The Bluejays rarely miss the NCAA lacrosse tournament, and they won the 2007 title right here in Baltimore.

Morgan State University (443-885-1522, www.morganstatebears.com) fields teams in most college athletics. Morgan's best sports include football, track and field, and basketball.

University of Maryland, Baltimore County (UMBC, 410-455-1000, www.umbc.com), is part of the University of Maryland system. The ACC-affiliated Terrapins in College Park, outside Washington, gain national attention for basketball and lacrosse play. UMBC competes in Division I, fielding good teams in basketball, including a top-notch women's basketball team, baseball, soccer, and lacrosse. The men's lacrosse team reached the NCAA finals held in Baltimore in 2007.

DAY TRIPS

Maryland is called America in Miniature because the state goes from sea level at the Atlantic Ocean to the 3,360' Backbone Mountain in the Allegheny Mountains. Yes, you can snow ski in the morning and water ski in the afternoon, or vice versa.

At the approximate center of all this lies Baltimore. Depending on the traffic, of course, in three hours you can be in Ocean City to the east, or the Cumberland Gap to the west. In a little more than an hour, you can find the Mason-Dixon Line to the north and the Virginia border to the south, Baltimore makes an excellent jumping-off point for day trips and weekend getaways in the mid-Atlantic.

If you'd rather not hit the highways, just head a little east or west to find the original older roads that will take you to the same place and more often than not offer a more scenic drive. Interstate 83, for instance, runs almost parallel to York Road—actually in sight of it for most of the ride. If you'd rather go through small towns, drive more slowly, and stop when you feel like it, these roads are an attractive alternative.

All of the trips noted in this chapter can be taken in a day, although you may want to stay longer. Two take you into Pennsylvania. Maryland, as the 42nd largest state, is relatively small. The destinations offer history, shopping, relaxation, sporting activities, culture, and I'm sure you'll find other attractions beyond what's listed.

YORK, PENNSYLVANIA
Exit 9 off I-83
52 miles from Baltimore

York's big boast (at least one of them) is its factory tours. The options include the Bluett Bros. Violins, Bube's Brewery, Family Heir-Loom Weavers, First Capital Federal Credit Union (showing you how they have made their building green – sorry, no monetary samples), George's Woodcrafts, Harley-Davidson Motor Company, Martin's Potato Chips, Naylor Wine Cellars, Painted Spring Farm Alpacas, Perrydell Farm Dairy, Revonah Pretzels, Snyder's of Hanover, Susquehanna Glass, Utz Quality Foods, Wolfgang Candy Company, and the York Time Institute (do you want the job of changing the clocks for daylight saving time and back again?).

Obviously, the big suggestion is to go hungry or, if you're watching your snack food intake, go after you've eaten lunch. Some of these tours request reservations or have some restrictions. Check the Web site for details. **York County,** Pennsylvania, Factory Tour Capital of the World (888-858-YORK; www.yorkpa.org).

HERSHEY, PENNSYLVANIA
100 West Hersheypark Drive
Hershey, PA
(800) HERSHEY
www.hersheypa.com
I-83 north to U.S. Highway 322
90 miles from Baltimore

Hersheypark, "The sweetest place on earth" is a seasonal theme park (generally opening May 1) is a theme park with 11 roller coasters, 9 wild water attractions (Memorial Day through Labor Day weekend), 20 rides for little ones, daily entertainment, strolling performers, life-sized Hershey product characters, food, souvenirs, and more. Arrive the night before, use the preview plan and you can be in the park for two and a half hours before closing and then come back for the full day on the next day. They also have two day and three day flex passes (visit the park for any two or three days during the season), consecutive days admission, sunset admission (when you come later in the day, just for that day), You can buy discounted tickets at some grocery stores, fast food restaurants, drug stores and gas stations. Combine a ticket with a trip to Dutch Wonderland, 30 miles away, and it's another $18 for adults.

When you decide this little town with Hershey kisses for street lamp tops deserves more of your time, stay at the **Hotel Hershey, Hershey Lodge,** or **Hershey Highmeadow Campground,** the official resorts of Hersheypark. As a guest, you'll receive complimentary shuttle service, admission to attractions, and other VIP benefits, including early access to select rides at the park. When you're through with the park, you can play golf or indulge at the Chocolate Spa. One other attraction is worth its weight in rose petals and that's the 23 acres of display gardens and the outdoor butterfly house (www.hershey gardens.com).

LADEW TOPIARY GARDENS
3535 Jarrettsville Pike,
Monkton, 2111
(410) 557-9570.
www.ladewgardens.com
20 miles from Baltimore

Ladew Topiary Gardens, created by Harvey S. Ladew (1887-1976), a self-taught gardener, is known around the world for its topiary and flower gardens. He made 15 thematic "garden rooms" that are devoted to a single color, plant, or theme. Every season features different blooms from the tulips, daffodils, candytuft, andromedia, Virginia bluebells, early azaleas, and crab apples in April to roses, asters, Mexican sage, Japanese anemone, and annuals in September. Visit the gardens, walk the nature walk, tour the manor house, and enjoy a lot of the outdoors less than an hour from Baltimore. Concerts and special events are presented regularly,

ANNAPOLIS
I-97 South to US 50
23 miles from Baltimore

Maryland's capital city is situated at the mouth of the Severn River, which makes it our political and historical capital, and our sailing capital.

Oh, the wonders you can enjoy in this town that lays claim to already having the buildings and history that the Rockefeller people had to create in Williamsburg. Stop here for great food (particularly the seafood and shellfish), a tour of the Naval Academy, soak in African American history, walk the cobblestone streets, and let the sea breeze blow through your hair on a variety of boat rides. The main focus starts at the City Dock and Ego Alley (the pricey yachts "parade" through Ego Alley so you can see how nice the boats are) and shop for some delightful souvenirs. Admittedly, there are more chain stores than there used to be, but you can still find an idiosyncratic shop or two. Try the **City Dock Café** (www.city dockcafe.com) for coffee and news about what's happening in town.

One of the most fascinating exhibits in Annapolis is the display of model ships at the **U.S. Naval Academy Museum.** (118 Maryland Ave.; 410-293-2108; www.usna.edu/Museum/visitor .htm) on the ground floor of Preble Hall. My mind is totally boggled every time I visit this exhibit. In the collection are ship models from about the time the pilgrims landed in America to just after the War of 1812. Although some of these models may have been created after the ship was built, many of them were built prior to blueprints so shipbuilders could use the models to build the ships, only real-life size. The big (100-gun) ships took one person from four to six years to build, plus another year for the rigging. More likely than one person doing all the work, there would have been a master model maker supervising a crew of workers or apprentices, thus speeding up the process. You'll also want to see Bone Ships, which were crafted by prisoners of war on frigates from meat bones. They are intricate and accurate portrayals of the fighting ships of the times. Other exhibits include Academy class rings, silverware from naval vessels, flags, uniforms, medals, weapons, navigational instruments, documents, and the stories of several naval heroes, including John Paul Jones. The museum is open Monday through Saturday from 9 a.m. to 5 p.m. and Sunday from 11 a.m. to 5 p.m.

For more information about **Annapolis and Anne Arundel County,** stop by the visitor center (26 West St., Annapolis; 410-974-8188; www .visitannapolis.org).

CALVERT COUNTY
US 50 to US 301 to Highway 4 South
Approximately 81 miles from Baltimore

For a great day or two away, head south to Calvert County for shell collecting, camping, boating, golf, historic churches, science, nature, fresh-catch dining, wineries, lighthouses, and sculpture gardens.

When you're looking for something unusual to do, try the **Biplane Air Tours out of St. Mary's County Airport.** The open cockpit sightseeing rides in a restored 1944 biplane are offered from April through October and cost $55 for 15 minutes, $100 for 30 minutes. 605 Patuxent Reach Drive, Prince Frederick; (410) 535-4136. www .biplaneairtours.com.

Water, water everywhere, particularly at the **Chesapeake Beach Water Park** where you'll find a children's pool, activity pool, 12' floating gator, 12' floating snake, seashell slide, and well, you can enjoy the rest. All pools are heated during cooler weather. The park has a snack party and is great for birthday parties. Prices vary according to age, time of day, residency (county and non-county prices), and day of the week. 4079 Gordon Stinnett Avenue, Chesapeake Beach; (410) 257-1404 or (301) 855-3803; www .chesapeake-beach.md.us.

Another water option is a fishing trip for the famed state fish, striped bass (a.k.a. rockfish) or other seafood, check with Captain Ed O'Brien, an active member of the Maryland Charter Boat Captain Association and the National Association of Charter Boat Operators. Call Semper Fidelas III Charters, Chesapeake Beach; (410) 741-5609.

Accommodations range from bed and breakfast establishments to cabins to hotels and motels and campgrounds. For specific **Calvert County tourism information,** call (800) 331-9771; www.eclavert.com.

As mentioned, you can reach any part of the state within a few hours of Baltimore, so aim east to Ocean City and the beach or west to Deep Creek Lake and the mountains. Head south a little and you're in the middle of Washington, D.C. with more than a dozen free Smithsonian Institution museums and north a little to Philadelphia. Baltimore definitely is in the middle of everything.

ST. MARY'S COUNTY
Route 4 to Route 5 South
Approximately 85 miles

St. Mary's City was the state's first capital until the locals thought that the waterfront exposure might be too dangerous in case of a foreign attack. The move to Annapolis also put the capital in a more central location. The original capital is gone (although the city's been under archeological restoration for years), the welcoming spirit of the first 140 settlers who landed in 1634 is still warm and strong. The area is well nestled between the arms of the Chesapeake Bay, and the Patuxent and Potomac Rivers.

The Barnwood to Beach Glass Trail is something you probably won't find anyplace else. And the sailing accomplishments of the students at **St. Mary's Honors College of Maryland** (www .smcm.edu) is almost as legendary as their scholastic achievements.

For accommodations, you can pick from a half-dozen or so motels or enjoy the modern adaptation of **Woodlawn Bed & Breakfast** (301-872-0555; www.woodlawn-farm.com) in Ridge, a late eighteenth-century manor with cottages. Jim Grube and help provide a gourmet breakfast that may make you wonder why you don't just move in permanently.

Michael and Lisa Kelley invite you to stay at the **Brome-Howard Inn** (301-866-0656; www .bromehowardinn.com.

in St. Mary's City in their 1840 farmhouse, complete with breakfast and afternoon tea. Bicycles are available so you can ride through the neighboring woods and trails. One solution to the problem of where to do what is stay at Wood-lawn and enjoy an extraordinary dinner (Thursday through Sunday) at Brome-Howard.

ROCKY GAP LODGE & GOLF RESORT
16701 Lakeview Road, Northeast
Flintstone, MD
(800) 724-0828
www.rockygapresort.com.
1-70 West
125 miles
Rocky Gap Lodge is out in the mountains in the western part of the state. It has been awarded the AAA Four Diamond award and you might think you have to catch a flight to a remote island to enjoy all it has to offer. It has an 18-hole Jack Nicklaus Signature golf course, a spa, and what seems to be a gazillion activities that include geocaching, bike and boat rental, horseback riding, sporting clays, rock climbing and rappelling. If that's not enough to work up an appetite, think about local and regional ingredients, farm fresh eggs, and locally produced fish and meats. When you like an organized approach to your visit, check the resort's calendar for wine dinners, murder mystery events, live music, and holiday specials.

Appendix

LIVING HERE

In this section we feature specific information for residents or those planning to
relocate here. Topics include real estate,
education, health care, and much more.

RELOCATION

O nce upon a time . . . Baltimore City was a little pocket of industry and commerce nestled near the Patapsco River and surrounded by vast estates. Large spurts of growth occurred after the Civil War, after the turn of the 20th century, and in concert with World Wars I and II. By the 1950s most of the inner and midtown areas of the city had been filled in.

Baltimore is bracing for new growth in the next few years, too. With the Base Realignment and Closure (BRAC) bringing thousands of new jobs to Maryland, the city expects many families to move here. Military jobs are being reassigned from Virginia and New Jersey to nearby bases, including Fort Meade in Anne Arundel County, Aberdeen Proving Ground in Harford County, and Fort Detrick in Frederick. Expansion of supporting services and defense contractors has followed the growth of the military in the past—and that is expected here, too.

If you're moving to Baltimore, relocating to this city is easy. Many services help newcomers get acclimated. **Live Baltimore Home Center** is an independent, nonprofit organization founded in 1997 to promote the benefits of city living. It produces an extensive relocation kit with up-to-date information including the latest home buying incentives. You can order a package for $15 by contacting Live Baltimore Home Center at 343 North Charles St., 1st Floor, (410) 637-3750. You can also visit the Web site, www.livebaltimore.com, which offers a comprehensive list of neighborhoods, home values, real estate contact information, and more.

In this chapter we focus on greater Baltimore and a few of the neighborhoods that are particularly interesting for one reason or six others.

Newcomers to the area often talk about Baltimore's quality of life, about what a pleasant, easy place it is to live. The great thing is that, unlike some small towns where distrust among the natives runs high toward newcomers, Baltimore tends to open its arms. We are always happy to have newcomers embrace the city and its way of life.

In the city and the counties, schools and churches are important neighborhood fixtures, with solid outreach into the community. They are the institutions we look to to provide day care, after-school care, and places for bazaars, dances, and meetings.

Within the city limits, we try to "buy neighborhood." If there's a good drugstore on the corner, we don't go to one 3 blocks away, and if there's a good bakery 3 blocks away, we don't drive a mile to find another. This may account for the continuing success of our neighborhood grocery stores and restaurants.

We've tried to provide a range of housing prices, but, as with other cities, they have been jumping all over the place. Perhaps the best thing to do is create a matrix of the kind of housing you want (inner city, back-yard suburban), what price range, how far it should be from your work, and neighborhood services and then decide what area best fits those needs and desires.

Real Estate Firms

Baltimore has some well-respected local and national real estate agents, and most have multiple locations. What follows is just a small sampling of those available.

ALLEN REALTY
8314 Liberty Rd., Randallstown
(410) 496-6700
www.allenrealty.net
This is a small, independently owned business formed in 1996. The Realtors focus on simplifying the process of homeownership to help low- to middle-income families find and select the best loan programs available. They specialize in HUD, VA, and foreclosures.

i When you find yourself at the foot of Broadway in Fell's Point, look east. You will see the old Recreation Pier, which you may recognize as the outside set for the police station on *Homicide: Life on the Street,* the former NBC detective show filmed in Baltimore and produced by one of Baltimore's own, Barry Levinson.

CENTURY 21 HORIZON REALTY
3117 East Joppa Rd., Parkville
(410) 882-0021
www.c21horizon.com
Century 21 has been selling homes in the Baltimore community for 35 years. Part of the largest real estate organization in the world, there are 27 agents selling property in northern Baltimore, and in the Parkville-White Marsh, northern Baltimore County area; a sister office in Dundalk has 45 agents. It serves the eastern part of the city and county.

CHASE FITZGERALD & COMPANY, INC.
1 Village Sq., Suite 131, Cross Keys
(410) 323-6000
www.chasefitzgerald.com
Chase Fitzgerald is a Baltimore company that traces its roots back to the Roland Park Company. The focus is in Roland Park, Guilford, Hampden,

and points north. It's neither a high-end or low-end real estate company, selling row houses for $246,000 and country estates for $2.5 million. They also specialize in north Baltimore condominiums and have 20 agents.

COLDWELL BANKER RESIDENTIAL BROKERAGE
3301 Boston St.
(410) 563-7601
www.coldwellbankermove.com
With more than 2,800 agents throughout Maryland, Coldwell Banker has Realtors in most neighborhoods throughout Baltimore City, including Fell's Point, Federal Hill, and Roland Park. The agency also covers the Eastern Shore and the Maryland suburbs around Washington, D.C. Coldwell Banker provides services ranging from concierge and relocation services to mortgage and insurance advice. The firm handles a wide range of housing prices and options, and also services the bustling rental market downtown.

O'CONOR & MOONEY REALTORS
1414 Key Hwy., Suite 101
(410) 385-8800
www.oconorhomes.com
This real estate company with 52 agents has offices in Baltimore City and northern Baltimore County. Although the names keep changing, the O'Conor name has been part of the real estate scene in Baltimore for more than 40 years. Locally owned by Sean O'Conor and Tom Mooney, the company's listings range from mid-town town houses listed in the mid $100,000s to mansions in horse country for $2.5 million.

OTIS WARREN AND COMPANY
10 South Howard St., Suite 110
(410) 539-1010
www.otiswarren.com
When Otis Warren started out nearly half a century ago, he managed rental properties and then expanded to sell real estate in his west Baltimore neighborhood. Now he is also a developer with new residential and commercial projects dotting Baltimore City, including the $40 million City

 **Close-up**

Mount Vernon Cultural District

Mount Vernon is one of Baltimore's culturally rich neighborhoods, with some of the best architecture, culture, housing, food, and fun in the downtown area. The center of Mount Vernon is the Washington Monument on Charles Street, so much a part of the city that it is featured on Baltimore's seal. The 178-foot Doric column that supports a statue of George Washington can be seen from many spots around town. American author Herman Melville once wrote, "Great Washington stands aloft on his towering mainmast in Baltimore, and like one of Hercules' pillars, his column marks that point of human grandeur beyond which few mortals will go."

Baltimore's statue was our country's first monument to George Washington, predating the one in Washington, D.C., by 55 years (designed by Robert Mills, the same architect). The base of the monument offers an exhibit detailing the construction of the neoclassic sculpture begun in 1815. You may wind your way up the dizzying 228 steps to the top of the monument for a bird's-eye view of the city. Conservation sometimes prohibits visitors from climbing the column, but the exhibit on the ground floor usually remains open.

Around the statue is Mount Vernon Square, a primarily 19th-century neighborhood founded by Baltimore's elite. When the monument was first constructed, Mount Vernon lay far north of the burgeoning city, but by 1840 the city expanded to encompass the neighborhood. The houses that border the Washington Monument range from Greek Revival to Italian Renaissance and Gothic Revival, with the oldest house in the square standing at 8 West Mount Vernon Place. These homes were the place to live in the 1800s, and urban revival has put them back in high demand. There are only four buildings built after 1900 in the square. A series of landscaped parks punctuated by sculptures and fountains add to the charm of this urban setting.

The circle of cobblestone and the adjoining parks that surround the Washington Monument are the site of many annual festivals and parades. Each winter the city kicks off the holiday by stringing strands of twinkling lights around the monument. Each May the Flower Mart ushers in spring and every September the Book Festival takes over the square with books, music, and visits from famous authors.

Within 3 blocks of the monument are the Maryland Historical Society Museum, the Contemporary Museum, the Walters Art Museum, the Enoch Pratt Free Library, and the Peabody Institute. You will also find commercial galleries, fine food, cafes, and unique shops. In recent years many cultural organizations and businesses in the neighborhood gelled to create the Mount Vernon Cultural District (MVCD), whose cooperative goal is to improve the physical amenities in the area and to help spread the word about the many cultural, historic, and social attractions. The organization touts that Mount Vernon is "one neighborhood with 100 things to do." The MVCD is a good stepping-off point for a tour of the Mount Vernon area. Its Web site has a map with links to member organizations at www.mvcd.org.

The MVCD is housed in the same building as the Downtown Partnership, a nonprofit corporation dedicated to making Downtown Baltimore a great place to invest, work, live, and play. Stop by the Downtown Partnership, 217 North Charles St., for brochures, general information, and friendly advice from the informed staff.

Crescent Office Building. Still family-owned, the company continues to sell and lease residential properties.

RE/MAX REALTORS
22 West Rd., #100, Towson
(410) 337-9300
http://greatermetro.maryland.remax.com

The Enterprise Foundation

The Rouse Company that Jim Rouse created has been a fixture in Maryland for more than 30 years. A major developer in Maryland generally, the Rouse Company has been responsible for some of Baltimore's more impressive development, including Harborplace, which serves as the centerpiece for Baltimore's Inner Harbor Development. The Enterprise Foundation (www.enterprisefoundation.org), a nonprofit housing and community development organization begun in 1982 by Jim and Patty Rouse, supports an entirely different kind of development—the development of neighborhoods. They call the process "Neighborhood Transformation." Its goal is to literally transform neighborhoods from urban decay into safe, livable, cohesive communities.

Foundation funds go to support public housing redevelopment, assisted-living programs for low-income seniors, inner-city child-care facilities, neighborhood planning, job creation, neighborhood safety programs, and more.

As of 2007, The Enterprise Foundation had raised and invested more than $8 billion in grants, loans, and equity to the process of neighborhood transformation. In 2006 alone, the foundation raised $1.2 billion and built or rehabilitated apartments and homes for 23,000 families.

Though begun in Baltimore, The Enterprise Foundation is not being stingy with its expertise. Projects as far away as Texas have had the benefit of The Enterprise Foundation's direct intervention. Its outreach extends to just about anywhere people need help and right now that includes scores of networking organizations in 41 states.

Through an online site, Enterprise OnLine, the foundation shares practical how-to and model program information with other nonprofit organizations who seek to do the same nationwide.

A measure of its success is the fact that since its inception in 1982, the foundation has helped create some 200,000 homes for low-income people, including the development of "green" communities and new homes for Gulf Coast families affected by Hurricane Katrina. The Enterprise Foundation has a network of local organizations that stretches across the country. It maintains local offices in 16 areas of the country, including New York, Texas, and California.

RE/MAX is the largest franchised real estate broker in the world, with more than 50,000 agents in the United States and Canada alone—1,100 of whom are in the state of Maryland. Broker Mary Lou Kaestner has been in the real estate business since 1970. She opened her own office in 1981 and became affiliated with RE/MAX in 1994. She and her 14 full-time independent agents list and sell properties in Baltimore City and Baltimore, Anne Arundel, Howard, Harford, and Carroll Counties. One of the perks of being associated with a worldwide agency is the ability to reach people on the other side of the globe—real people with a name, a face, and a bio—and work with them to help clients who are looking to relocate or need to move people and companies. The bulk of the company's business, however, is home sales. Agents handle properties in all price ranges, from $30,000 to $2 million and more.

RENTER'S RESOURCES

Baltimore has many renting options, and it doesn't have the pressure-cooker issues of major metropolises like New York and Boston. It's not unreasonable to find a listing, see a place, and rent it on a handshake. Most places do require a one-year lease and a security deposit. Like every city, Baltimore has its share of dubious landlords, the ones who take advantage of newcomers and their need to find a place fast. Tenant-landlord information resources are available and are worth consulting before signing any agreement. Baltimore Neighborhoods, Inc. provides a counseling hotline at (410) 243-6007.

Landlords also frequently require their tenants to carry renters' insurance. You can usually procure insurance through your auto insurance company and tack it on to your car premiums for a minimal monthly cost.

ZONING

Remember to call the Zoning Commission in whatever area you want to settle down in, have an office in, or do business in. You may think that because you are a done-by-computer business that has no clients visit and has no need to hang out a shingle that you need not worry about zoning. And, you may not. New regulations are being written all the time in all divisions. So it's better to be sure.

Baltimore City Zoning Commission, (410) 396-4301, www.ci.baltimore.md.us

Baltimore County Zoning Commission, (410) 887-3391, www.co.ba.md.us

Howard County Planning and Zoning, (410) 313-2393, www.co.ho.md.us

Anne Arundel Zoning Enforcement, (410) 222-7446, www.aacounty.org

EDUCATION

Baltimore is chock-full of schools. In fact, institutions of higher learning are one of Baltimore's main draws. Such names as the Johns Hopkins University, Goucher College, Loyola College, and the University of Maryland, Baltimore are known worldwide for the quality of the education. Our private and parochial school systems are widespread as well, and our public schools offer some surprises in vocational training and the arts.

Outside of these traditional educational institutions, the Baltimore area lays claim to specialty schools that run the gamut from institutions for physically challenged children to courses that specialize in haute cuisine.

All public and private elementary and secondary systems across the state have advanced courses for academics, usually known as gifted and talented or honors programs. Most systems also offer some kind of technical course or a school-to-work program. The Maryland State Department of Education requires all students take high school assessments in core subjects to receive a Maryland diploma. Students must also complete service-learning hours and attendance requirements. Some of the public high schools, such as the Baltimore City School for the Arts that offers an intensive training in visual arts, music, theater, or dance with regular college preparatory classes, are known for the specialization. The Polytechnic Institute specializes in engineering, offering courses for future engineers who enjoy doing integral calculus or for students who just want a college-prep environment with an emphasis in math and science. And the Kenwood High School Sports Science Academy is for those who want to coach and those who are considering a career in sports medicine.

To be honest, many (maybe most) locals identify themselves by the high school they attended. They remain Poly boys and Western girls essentially forever. Gilman vs. McDonogh, Calvert Hall vs. Loyola, Poly (Polytechnic Institute) vs. City (Baltimore City College), Dunbar vs. Lake Clifton, IND (the Institute of Notre Dame) vs. Mercy—all are historic rivalries known citywide. Though we love a good game, Baltimore has always placed more emphasis on academics than sports. Many of our Baltimore Firsts have been in education. The first parochial school to educate African-American children was opened here, as were the first parochial schools for girls.

OVERVIEW

In this chapter we provide a thumbnail picture of the public school systems, some of the popular private and specialty schools, community colleges, and four-year institutions.

Among the information presented, you will occasionally find student-teacher ratios. It is important to note that these are average figures that do not necessarily reflect exact class size. For instance, in a school with an average ratio of 22 to 1, you may find some seminar classes for seniors

that have only 10 students and a science class with 35. However, the ratios provide a general idea of class size, which is why they're included.

Tuition for private schools varies considerably, depending on the school and courses selected, financial aid eligibility, etc. Therefore, the rates are not included. Most schools (not all) list tuition on their Web sites. Generally, expect to pay between $2,000 and $6,000 for Catholic elementary school and up to $20,000 for other private elementary schools. The rates go up to about $10,000 for Catholic high school and hover near $20,000 for other private high schools.

All private and parochial schools have a dress code or a required uniform. Many public schools, particularly elementary schools, have uniform options, and most public high schools have some rules about acceptable attire. Call the individual school to resolve questions about uniforms and costs.

When you visit a prospective school stop by the admissions and administration offices and if you're allowed, hang around to talk to the faculty and students about curricula, after-school programs and activities, and the school's approach to academic and social discipline. Their enthusiasm or lack thereof gives the best insight into what the school is really like.

PUBLIC SCHOOLS

Public education in the greater Baltimore area, as in Maryland generally, is supported by our property taxes. According to Maryland policy, these tax funds are distributed to some extent based on need so a portion of the Howard County (third richest in the country) taxes will help fund Baltimore City schools.

Maryland recently adopted a new set of standards for marking a school's performance, and it also issues an annual School Performance Report, which takes a comprehensive look at individual schools' success in meeting basic educational requirements. These reports can be downloaded from the Web site, www.mdreportcard.org.

BALTIMORE PUBLIC SCHOOLS
Baltimore City Department of Education
200 East North Ave.
(443) 984-2000
www.bcps.k12.md.us
Baltimore City's schools are in the process of a rebirth. Test scores and measured skill levels are rising among the city's children, and it is expected that this trend will continue. The class of 2009 met state criteria for graduation by meeting first ever high school exit tests or passing Bridge projects.

The city has about 82,200 students attending 69 extended elementary schools (elementary/middle schools with grades K through 8), 12 middle/high schools (grades 6-12), and 20 citywide schools.

Among the citywide schools are some specialty schools including the Baltimore City School for the Arts, the Polytechnic Institute, the Merganthaler Vocational Technical Center, and the Carver Vocational Technical Center.

Although the names are probably self-explanatory, the School for the Arts prepares students to play for the Baltimore Symphony or head for Broadway. Polytechnic grounds college-bound engineering students in the basics of their field, and the vo-tech schools offer a focus in commercial trades as diverse as carpentry and commercial art. The Occupation Prep program deals with such skills as cosmetology and drafting.

Other classes allow students to pursue a more specialized path at nonspecialty schools. The Tech Prep program permits high school students to take courses in biotechnology, business technology, electronics/computer repair technology, child care, travel and tourism, and machine tool technology in addition to their regular coursework. Tech Prep was created in conjunction with Baltimore City Community College and is meant to help a student take college-level courses relating to a chosen career as early as the ninth grade.

ROTC and CollegeBound also are offered at the high school level. The individual school listings book, *Planning Your High School Program,* is available free from Baltimore City Schools. It can tell you which schools offer what. Contact the Department of Education for a copy to be sent to you.

Although there may have been some staffing adjustments with the tanking economy, the basic staffing of Baltimore's schools includes more than 6,600 teachers and nearly 1,000 school-based support staff and school-based administrators. Overall, student-teacher ratios are 25 to 1. The late 1990s saw significant betterment in the Baltimore City School System. Several national foundations, including the Bill and Melinda Gates

Foundation, contributed almost $21 million, fueling the transformation of nine large Baltimore city neighborhood high schools into smaller learning communities. The city's Master Plan II developed goals, through the 2008 school year, for improving student achievement with clean, safe schools; more parent involvement; and better instruction.

Communities have the go-ahead to institute programs that they feel are needed for their children, and they're acting quickly to put new elements into play for their children. Elementary schools, for instance, have created after-school enrichment and/or tutoring programs that extend the school day, thereby helping out with child care and also creating another avenue to improve student performance. Nearly all of Baltimore City's elementary schools have such programs, and their success is helping test results move upward—sometimes in double digits.

BALTIMORE COUNTY PUBLIC SCHOOLS
6901 North Charles St., Towson
(410) 887-5555
www.bcps.org
The Baltimore County Public School System is the 26th-largest in the United States. It serves 103,643 students (as of 9/30/2008). Choices of study include many options outside traditional academic areas, from carpentry to quilting and everything in between.

The county uses a program called Values Education and Ethical Behavior that seeks to address values and ethics issues in the curricula and to speak to their practical application. The program is not a laundry list of values and ethics, but, as the county schools' yearly report noted, a "process of inquiry to help students pose and understand . . . ethical questions and dilemmas." A relatively unusual program, it covers everything from encouraging students to be honest and compassionate to questions about scientific discovery and what constitutes responsible citizenship.

Of the county's 172 schools, programs, and centers, 29 are magnet schools (7 each at the elementary and middle school levels, and 15 at the high school level). These magnet schools offer special programs that draw students from a particular geographic area. At the elementary levels, it is area alone that determines if your child may enter a particular magnet school. At the middle school level, entrance is determined by prior academic achievement, student interest, and geographic location. At the high school level, geographic area still plays a part in most cases, but that area is either countywide or a large general area, such as northern Baltimore County. And if for some reason the student is not in the chosen area but has the qualifications and desire for the education offered at the site, then he or she may be admitted by special permission. Magnet programs of study at the high school level include the Lansdowne Academy of Finance, the Kenwood High School Sports Science Academy, and the Towson High School Law and Public Policy Program.

The county also has five alternative schools for students with special needs including one that serves students between the ages of 3 years and 21 years who have multiple disabilities.

Academically, Baltimore County offers a relatively competitive environment, which includes advanced placement courses and testing. Using the state standards for performance, Baltimore County matched or exceeded state standards in 97 percent of the areas measured.

Baltimore County spends $9,500 on each pupil annually, and the student-teacher ratio is 22 to 1. The average dropout rate is 4.1 percent.

PRIVATE SCHOOLS

Baltimore has an extensive system of private and parochial institutions. This list includes high schools and K-12 institutions. If you want information on a parochial elementary school in your area, it is best to contact your house of worship or simply look under private schools on the Internet.

ARCHBISHOP CURLEY HIGH SCHOOL
3701 Sinclair Lane
(410) 485-5000
www.archbishopcurley.org

Choosing Maryland

Maryland is the center of the Boston-Atlanta Corridor on the Atlantic seaboard and about 40 miles northeast of Washington, D.C., the nation's capital. Among the 50 states, Maryland ranks 42nd in size and 20th in population. Its per capita income is the fourth highest in the United States. Of Maryland's population age 25 and older, about 87 percent hold a bachelor's degree or higher, which is the third highest percentage among the states. Professional and technical workers constitute 25 percent of the state's workforce, the second highest concentration among states in the nation. In Baltimore there is increasing interest in recycling waterfront industrial buildings to house technology firms, as part of Baltimore's new "Digital Harbor." The Can Company in Canton, for example, is an old manufacturing plant transformed into a mixed-use space that couples high-end retail and restaurants with digitally wired office space for high-tech companies.

Whether you already live here or are thinking about moving here, here are some reasons that the State Department of Business and Economic Development thinks should make your decision sound extremely solid:

* Top-rated public school system in the nation
* Number two ranking among the states in science and technology assets
* Proximity to Washington, D.C., the nation's capital, and more than 50 federal agencies
* First in the nation in R&D obligations on a per capita basis
* Highly educated workforce—second in the United States in the percentage of professional and technical workers
* Member of the Regional Greenhouse Initiatives—committed to reducing carbon emissions 20 percent by 2022
* A cluster of nearly 400 bioscience companies
* Bio 2020 Initiative—providing an investment of $1.3 billion over the next 10 years
* The longest-running Triple-A bond rating in the United States since 1961
* Export growth that outpaces the nation—$11.4 billion in 2008—a 28 percent increase over 2007

—Excerpted from the State Department of Business and Economic Development Web site, www.choosemaryland.org

"Curley" is an all-male college preparatory high school with a well-developed arts program. The school opened on its 33-acre site in 1961 to serve its surrounding, then densely Catholic, neighborhoods, but it now accepts students from all over the state. For a student who wants to study math and play trumpet, Curley is made to order. The school has professional-quality orchestra, dance, and jazz bands. They rock the house! There are also newer visual arts programs for budding painters, photographers, and other artists. The school encourages parent involvement and is proud of the fact that many of its parents continue to work with and for the school long after their own boys have graduated.

BETH TFILOH DAHAN COMMUNITY SCHOOL
3300 Old Court Rd.
(410) 486-1900
www.btfiloh.org
Beth Tfiloh Community School opened on its 20-acre campus in west Baltimore County in 1942 with five students in kindergarten. Currently, the school provides the only coeducational college preparatory curriculum in greater Baltimore for Jewish study in grades pre-K through 12. Beth Tfiloh is affiliated with a Modern Orthodox synagogue, however, membership is not required to attend the school. Students and their families belong to Orthodox, Conservative, Reform, and Reconstructionist synagogues and some of the students are unaffiliated. Because of its comprehensive course of Jewish study, the school has never had a student of another faith attend, but it does not prohibit such attendance, and it openly encourages participation of all Jewish denominations. Beth Tfiloh offers advanced-placement classes and an honors track for its high school students and some interesting internships and study opportunities, including Senior Seminars in Israel.

BOYS LATIN SCHOOL OF MARYLAND
822 West Lake Ave.
(410) 377-5192
www.boyslatinmd.com
Boys Latin School, a college preparatory day school, began in the mind of Evert Marsh Topping, a professor of long-standing at Princeton University, who over time had come to believe that standard teaching methods of the time did not teach students to think and understand, and that only through understanding did children truly learn. This revolutionary idea prompted him to come to Baltimore and open his own private school in 1846, the oldest, non-sectarian school for boys in Maryland. The current Boys Latin School, which straddles the city-county line just west of the east/west dividing line of

How to Apply to Private Schools

Private and Catholic schools schedule school fairs to give prospective students an informal look at a variety of schools at one time. The Association of Independent Maryland Schools, a group of more than 100 private college preparatory schools, holds their school fair in early fall. They recommend starting the process of selecting a private school the year before your child intends to enter school. For the actual date and listing of schools, visit www.aimsmd.org.

The Archdiocese of Baltimore's Division of Catholic Schools holds two high school fairs in September. The first is held the Sunday after Labor Day at the University of Maryland Baltimore County west of Baltimore city from 3 to 5 p.m. The second is usually held the next Sunday at another location, frequently at the College of Notre Dame, on the northern edges of the city. In the fall, each high school holds an open house on a weekend day

During the summer, schools that still have openings for the upcoming year take part in a school fair held at Archbishop Curley High School in east Baltimore. It is usually held on a weekday in mid-July from 6 to 8 p.m.

All of the Catholic high schools coordinate their placement test date so prospective students may take the test at any school the second Saturday in December at 8:30 a.m. The test comes just before applications are due to the schools. For details, visit www.archbalt.org schools or call (800) 5-CATHOLIC.

Charles Street, has more than 640 boys in grades K through 12. The school's educational focus is to build on each boy's strengths and not harp on any weaknesses. The median SAT score is 1,120.

BRYN MAWR SCHOOL
109 West Melrose Ave.
(410) 323-8800
www.brynmawr.pvt.k12.md.us
Bryn Mawr was founded in 1885 on the belief that women were entitled to the same classical education as boys. The school has a competitive college preparatory curriculum, while still providing its girls with extensive opportunities in art, music, and athletics. Bryn Mawr has a comprehensive language department and all students learn Latin in grades seven and eight. The school believes the close study of Latin words helps to expand and enrich students' English vocabulary, just as the study of Latin grammar helps students to understand the structure of English and other languages. Once in the upper grades, students may take Spanish, French, Greek, German, Russian, Arabic, and Chinese. Enrollment is close to 800 in grades K through 12 and in a coed preschool group and day care. Just around the corner from Roland Park Country and Gilman schools, Bryn Mawr coordinates some classes with both schools in grades 9 through 12, where, potentially, students could take classes at all three schools.

CALVERT HALL COLLEGE
8102 Lasalle Rd., Towson
(410) 825-4266
www.calverthall.com
Calvert Hall College was the first Christian Brothers school in the country, established in 1845 by the first American Christian Brother who was himself barely out of seminary at 17 years old. The first year it was in operation, the school had 100 students. In operation for more than 150 years and at its 33-acre campus in Towson for about 40 years, this all-boys college preparatory school serves approximately 1,200 students today. Academically competitive, Calvert Hall also has a full complement of arts and athletics. The Activities Center, for instance, houses art studios, learning

resource center, and its swimming pool and weight training room. Calvert Hall's marching band is as well known as its football team.

THE CATHOLIC HIGH SCHOOL OF BALTIMORE
2800 Edison Hwy.
(410) 732-6200
www.thecatholichighschool.org
Catholic High, begun in 1939 and currently serving 325 students, is an area-wide college preparatory school for girls. The school offers two primary focuses: technology and the arts. Fine-arts offerings include advanced-placement opportunities in art and chorus, and the technology side boasts state-of-the-art equipment and teachers. Every week teachers are trained in the latest technological offerings, so that students in their turn receive up-to-the-minute knowledge. This unique competitive curriculum offers a McCafferty Honors Program; Science, Technology, Engineering and Mathematics (STEM) Program; Archangel Program; Distance Learning, Advanced Placement Courses; and online courses. What is most interesting about the school is its individualized approach. Courses are mixed and matched depending on the ability of the student, so that a freshman with talent in math could be placed in pre-calculus, rather than having to wade through the typical freshman math.

CRISTO REY JESUIT HIGH SCHOOL
420 South Chester St.
(410) 727-3255
www.cristoreybalt.org
Cristo Rey Jesuit, the latest initiative of the Maryland Jesuits, is located in Fell's Point, three blocks from Patterson Park. The school is one of 24 schools in the Cristo Rey Network nationwide and opened in August 2007 with 110 students. As of 2009 enrollment had swelled to 273 students and they plan to have a total student capacity of 360 to 400. Cristo Rey Jesuit is a unique Baltimore high school providing affordable, Catholic, college preparatory education to students from low-income families in Baltimore City. The tuition is around $2,500 annually and to help offset

Close-up

Learning in the Midst of Ghosts and History

The Institute of Notre Dame (IND) has ghosts. A Union soldier is seen walking his post in an upstairs hall. In the old dormitories, a 40-year-old candle left on a side table by its last occupant spontaneously erupts into flame. A mother trying to find the school offices gets lost and is shown the way by a soft voice that comes from the direction of a large statue of the Virgin Mary. No one else is there.

IND's history began when Mother Theresa of Jesus Gerhardinger, who helped found the School Sisters of Notre Dame (SSND) in her native Germany, crossed the Atlantic with four others intent on educating immigrant girls. The school's original mission included only German immigrants, but it quickly reached out to serve all Catholic girls and has, for many years now, focused simply on girls regardless to race or faith. A typical class at IND is an eclectic mix: 4 percent from the city and the remainder from surrounding areas as far as an hour's drive.

When the site for the school was chosen in 1847, it was outside the city's limits, surrounded by rolling hills and ancient trees. The Baltimore & Ohio Railroad was still laying new track when the modern marvel of the telegraph had just been discovered, and the United States of America was only 60 years old.

The initial buildings for the school were little more than large cabins, which between 1852 and 1925 were changed and added on as growth demanded, to become the blocklong complex of buildings that is used today. SSND sisters still reside in the original brick convent, with its stunning stained-glass windows and tongue-in-groove wainscot. Students are no longer permitted access to the original underground catacombs and stables.

The student dormitories were rehabilitated in 1996 and 1997 to become the Caroline Center, a job training center for neighborhood women in East Baltimore.

IND was one of Baltimore's many stops on the Underground Railroad, in which former slaves on their way to freedom were housed, fed, and clothed, then passed on to those who could see them to safety.

When Civil War battles raged, the catacombs beneath the school served as an infirmary, where nuns nursed Union and Confederate soldiers back to health or, if that was not possible, buried them.

As the city grew up around it, IND surmounted city problems. The school suffered through the Great Baltimore Fire of 1904, which destroyed the area all around it but left the school unscathed. It also survived the Depression and was left untouched by the riots of 1968.

the cost of tuition, students spend five days per month in a work-study program. The school offers a challenging traditional curriculum focusing on core academic subjects and a program in the arts, athletics, service, and spiritual formation.

FRIENDS SCHOOL
5114 North Charles St.
(410) 649-3200
www.friendsbalt.org
Founded in 1784 by the Quakers, it moved several times before settling in its present location

in 1925. Halfway between Towson and the Inner Harbor on a well-traveled stretch of North Charles Street, it is now nonsectarian and the school has a large campus that includes woods and a stream and the use of the Roland Park swimming pool for its summer camp. The school and the camp make good use of the dance studio, fitness room, two gymnasiums, outdoor tennis courts, five playing fields, and two practice fields. Students attend Meetings on a regular basis and are encouraged in critical thinking and problem solving and academics. The Upper School (grades

9-12) offers a challenging college preparatory program in an environment where individual differences and perspectives are respected and encouraged. Students generally take five major courses: English, history, mathematics, science, and a foreign language (Russian, Latin, French, or Spanish). Additionally, seniors gain real-life work experiences in month-long professional internships in the spring of the 12th grade year. About 960 students attend the school, pre-K through 12 (with almost 400 in grades 9-12). Friends School students' average SAT scores over the past several years have been 1,280 on the 1,600 point scale. The average score for the Friends class of 2006 was 1,906 on the new 2,400 point scale.

GARRISON FOREST SCHOOL
300 Garrison Forest Rd., Owings Mills
(410) 363-1500
www.gfs.org
Garrison Forest was founded in 1910 as a day school for the girls of families living in Greenspring Valley, which at that time was far away from city schools. By 1912 the school had established a boarding program, and it still offers boarding for girls in grades 8 through 12 and day school for girls K through 12 and a coeducational pre-K for students from age two. Their motto is *Esse Quam Videri*—To Be Rather Than To Seem, and their academic program balances exceedingly high standards within a welcoming, spirited atmosphere that enables each student to flourish intellectually and individually. Approximately 270 students are in grades 9-12 and come from all over the world, including the Pacific Rim, Latin and Central America, the Caribbean, and parts of Europe. The school has a new performing arts center, new lower school, and new riding and athletic facilities. Garrison Forrest students are involved in the arts and the school has a 401-seat Garland Theater as well as a Dance Studio in the modern, collegiate-level Campus Center. Additionally, students from the school have worked professionally on national television shows for HBO. Notable graduates from Garrison include Jamie O'Brien, Miss Teen Maryland of 2006 (class of 2006) and Beth Botsford, 1996

Olympic gold medalist (class of 1999), Garrison Forest underwent a campus-wide rewiring that allows students to access the school's computers from anywhere, dorm to classroom.

GILMAN SCHOOL
5407 Roland Ave.
(410) 323-3800
www.gilman.edu
Gilman School, the first country day school in the United States, turned 100 years old in 1997. The school was conceived by Anne Galbraith Carey, who also founded the Women's Civic League in Baltimore and worked to help found the Girl Scouts in Maryland. At the time Carey was simply looking for a healthy educational environment in which to place her eight-year-old son that was not attached to a military or religious discipline. Approximately 1,015 boys attend Gilman (460 in grades 9-12) on its 64-acre campus in Roland Park. Because of the country school concept, which seeks to educate the body, the mind, and spirit, athletics at Gilman are almost as important as the academics. Gilman is a rigorous academic program, as evidenced by the number of seniors moving on to top colleges and universities and the hours the students put in each day, 8 a.m. to 5 p.m. for the Upper School (interscholastic teams stay later). Main entry points at Gilman are the sixth and ninth grades. There are a limited number of spaces in seventh, eighth, and tenth grades. Only under special conditions are eleventh and twelfth grade admissions considered. All Upper School students have the opportunity to take courses through the tri-school coordination program allowing Gilman students to take classes at Roland Park Country School and Bryn Mawr School.

INSTITUTE OF NOTRE DAME (IND)
901 North Aisquith St.
(410) 522-7800
www.indofmd.org
IND is a college preparatory high school (grade 9-12) for girls run by the School Sisters of Notre Dame. The school offers general academic, college preparatory, and Theresian Honors pro-

grams. Advanced placement courses are available. Basketball, crew, soccer, softball, theater, chorus, and many more extracurricular activities and service clubs tend to keep the girls way past their normal school hours, but there are few complaints. The school consistently achieves the statistic of 100 percent of IND graduates moving on to additional education. IND is the only all-girls school in the country that can count two members of United States Congress among its alumnae: Senator Barbara Mikulski (class of 1954) and Speaker of the House Nancy D'Alesandro Pelosi (class of 1958). Additionally, Lauren Parkes, Miss Black Delaware USA 2007, Miss Maryland Galaxy 2008; was a 2005 graduate. (For more information on IND, see the Close-up in this chapter.) IND has recently increased its scholarship program.

MARYVALE PREPARATORY SCHOOL FOR GIRLS
11300 Falls Rd., Brooklandville
(410) 252-3366
www.maryvale.com
Begun in 1945 by the Sisters of Notre Dame De Namur as a boarding school, Maryvale had only 12 students when it opened. That was OK by the sisters, however, whose mission was to set up a school that was small by design so each girl would receive a lot of individual attention. Staying true to the sisters' mission, only 380 day students are enrolled in grades 6 through 12. The campus, on 115 acres with sprawling woods, nature trails, streams, and waterfalls, is an idyllic setting for a school. Citing a competitive college preparatory curriculum, Maryvale's academic focus encourages girls in mathematics and the sciences. A Science and Student Center was completed in 1997 and houses computer and science labs. Maryvale boasts a championship-winning athletic department, strong in field hockey, basketball, volleyball, lacrosse, and softball. Its choruses produce two musicals each year. Community service is an important part of every Maryvale girl's life, with ample opportunities to take part in fund-raising for breast cancer research, foreign missions, and other charities. Girls also serve meals at a Fell's Point soup kitchen at least once a month. Parent involvement is strong in this school along with traditions such as the Mother/Daughter Liturgy and the Father/Daughter Dinner Dance.

MCDONOGH SCHOOL
8600 McDonogh Rd., McDonogh
(410) 363-0600
www.mcdonogh.org
The American Civil War orphaned thousands of children and destroyed much of the South, including its schools. Philanthropist John McDonogh must have had this on his mind, for when he died, he willed money to fund a public school system in Louisiana and the McDonogh Farm School for orphaned boys in Maryland. McDonogh opened in 1873 on its 800-acre campus with a multiracial student body that worked the farm, growing vegetables, raising pigs, and milking cows. The original headmaster, Col. William Allen, who had fought with the Confederacy under Stonewall Jackson, imposed a military discipline and the military uniforms the boys wore were Confederate gray. Today, the school's original mandate to serve students in need is still much in evidence, but the school has changed a lot over the years. Now coed, with just over 1,300 students from kindergarten though 12th grade, the semi-military atmosphere was dropped in 1971, and the farm no longer exists, save for the horse barn and riding facilities. Every McDonogh student learns to ride, and horsey amenities include riding rings and yearly horse shows. Other athletic pursuits include the more conventional football, lacrosse, tennis, golf, and swimming. Teachers, and students, live on campus, eat in the dining hall, and take part in campus life. The college preparatory curriculum is competitive, and 100 percent of McDonogh's graduates go on to further education.

MERCY HIGH SCHOOL
1300 East Northern Parkway
(410) 433-8880
www.mercyhighschool.com
Mercy High School, run by the Sisters of Mercy, was built in 1960 to serve a burgeoning Northeast city population. On a campus that takes up

most of the large block between Loch Raven Boulevard and The Alameda, Mercy serves 539 female students (known as Mercy Girls) with a college preparatory curriculum. One of Mercy's offerings is the Adviser Program, in which the school has created a new relationship between adviser and student. In Mercy's Adviser Program, an adviser is attached to only 15 or so students whom she follows through the four years at the school. She acts as homeroom contact, mentor, and sometimes mediator, and becomes a vested part of each girl's success. In the past Mercy's graduating seniors received close to $4.2 million in scholarships and grants, and 99 percent entered college.

MOUNT DE SALES ACADEMY
700 Academy Rd.
(410) 744-8498
www.mountdesales.org/testindex.php
Mount de Sales is an all-girl Catholic school established in 1852 that believes in "Academic Excellence in the Catholic Tradition." Four levels of classes are offered: College Preparatory Level 1, College Preparatory Level 2, Honors, and Advanced Placement, and these levels and commitment to education excellence show in the honors this school has received. It has been named to the Catholic High School Honor Roll as a Top 50 Catholic High School in the nation for four years in a row. In 2008 they had three National Merit Commended Students, 17 National AP Scholars, 13 Maryland Distinguished Scholars, and 72 percent of the class of 2008 received scholarships totaling $9.7 million. Admission preference is given to daughters/granddaughters of alumnae and sisters of current students and alumnae and then to Catholic students attending Catholic elementary/middle schools, and then Catholic students who are home schooled.

MOUNT SAINT JOSEPH HIGH SCHOOL
4403 Frederick Ave.
(410) 644-3300
www.msjnet.edu
St. Joe's, as it is lovingly called, is also referred to as "The Mount" and began in 1876 on the

prayer of one Brother Bernardine, who asked for the intervention of Saint Joseph to help him and his Xaverian Brothers find the money to start the school. Although St. Joe's has a balanced college preparatory curriculum, the focus in its advanced-placement courses is on science. The school recently added a 30,000-square-foot, state-of-the-art media and technology building to its pastoral 31-acre campus and is set to upgrade its athletic facilities.

NOTRE DAME PREPARATORY SCHOOL (NDP)
815 Hampton Lane, Towson
(410) 825-6202
www.notredameprep.com
Founded in 1873 by the School Sisters of Notre Dame to complement the Institute of Notre Dame, NDP opened in 1874 as the Notre Dame Collegiate Institute for Young Ladies on what was then wilderness acreage where the College of Notre Dame now stands. At its current campus on Hampton Lane, NDP offers a competitive, college preparatory curriculum to more than 740 girls in grades 6 through 12. NDP boasts an active social service program that includes the students' working with abused children at Villa Maria, spending time with patients at AIDS hospices, and working with Habitat for Humanity, among other projects. Religious study is required for all students in all grades. College preparatory, including more than 160 courses (25 advanced placement) are offered in grades 9-12.

OUR LADY OF MOUNT CARMEL HIGH SCHOOL
1706 Old Eastern Ave.
(410) 686-1023
www.olmcmd.org
Founded in 1959, Our Lady of Mount Carmel is a Catholic co-educational college preparatory school serving the students of Our Lady of Mount Carmel Parish and other local parishes. The average SAT school is 1,435 on the new scale, and they received a Character Education Award from the Maryland Center for Character Education.

The award distinguishes Mt. Carmel High School for its innovative efforts in the area of Academic Integrity Policy and Procedures. They also have lots of sports with 13 athletic teams. The school serves approximately 230 students.

THE PARK SCHOOL
2425 Old Court Rd., Brooklandville
(410) 339-7070
www.parkschool.net

The Park School was founded in 1912 as a progressive school, located on a 100-acre tract of land, and is one in which children are guided toward moral behavior, self-discipline, and intellectual achievement. Park is a nonsectarian, independent, coeducational day school. A 27,000-square-foot science, math, and technology center opened in 1997, and the middle and upper schools have been renovated to better support Park's seminar style of teaching. Park students have a record of achievement in advanced level mathematics. Enrollment in upper level math courses is high: 45 percent of Park's current senior class has taken or is taking an AP calculus course; 99 percent elect to take four years of math. Park placed first in Maryland Mathematics League contests over the last 10 years; Park placed first among private schools in the Baltimore area for eight years and second for the other two years.

ROLAND PARK COUNTRY SCHOOL
5204 Roland Ave.
(410) 323-5500
www.rpcs.org

Roland Park Country School (RPCS) began in 1894 as a neighborhood school housed in a private home. By 1901 it had won sponsorship from the Roland Park Company and eventually became the first fully accredited independent school for girls in Baltimore city. RPCS places emphasis on academic achievement and athletic accomplishment. It fields teams in field hockey, lacrosse, and crew. RPCS also has a laptop policy. Beginning in kindergarten, girls take computer courses as part of the curriculum. All students in grades 7

to 12 must purchase a laptop computer and are trained in the use of that computer. The entire school is wirelessly connected to the Internet. There are 700 girls in grades K through 12, who are, according to *U.S. News & World Report*, consistently admitted into the nation's 25 most selective liberal arts colleges and universities. The student-faculty ratio is 6 to 1 in the Upper School, and Middle and Upper School have average class sizes of 14 to 16 girls. RPCS is also part of the tri-school coordination program. All Upper School students have the opportunity to take courses at Gilman School and Bryn Mawr School.

ST. FRANCES ACADEMY
501 East Chase St.
(410) 539-5794
www.sfacademy.org

St. Frances Academy was founded in 1828 by Mother Mary Lange, foundress of the Oblate Sisters of Providence, who is currently being considered for sainthood by the Roman Catholic Church. The school building once served as the mother house for the Oblate Sisters and an orphanage and a boarding school for young women. St. Frances was the first parochial school to be created to educate African-American children and currently serves a coeducational student body of about 280 in a college preparatory curriculum in grades 9 through 12. St. Frances serves what's deemed the "disenfranchised" student, e.g., the student who has not been performing up to his or her intellectual or social potential. The school's instructional success is shown by the fact that more than 90 percent of its graduates go on to post-secondary education. Though a historically African-American school, the school is open to students of all races and economic backgrounds.

ST. TIMOTHY'S SCHOOL
8400 Greenspring Ave., Stevenson
(410) 486-7400
www.sttims-school.org

St. Timothy's was founded in 1882 and merged with the Hannah More Academy, the oldest Episcopal girls' boarding school in the country, in 1974, Today, the expanded St. Timothy's offers boarding and day school from grades 9 through 12. With 70 percent of its students living on campus and a student-to-faculty ratio of 5 to 1, St. Timothy's girls receive close attention in a community atmosphere that seeks to "develop each person's ability to live thoughtfully in a community of diverse and unique individuals."

Academically, St. Tim's is competitive, with 100 percent of its graduates heading for higher education. St. Timothy's also offers The Global Immersion Program that explores world issues through unforgettable learning experiences by understanding relationships between cultures, showing sensitivity to others in the world, and possessing global awareness. Throughout the students' tenure, the school offers off-campus experiences through a program called Connections, in which students study the political, social, economic, and cultural aspects of Baltimore, Annapolis, and Washington, D.C. And in the senior year, students perform three weeks of independent study in which they become corporate interns.

Students interested in athletics can participate in eight interscholastic sports, including tennis and riding. The school has a theater, complete with costume shop, dance studio, music practice rooms, and the art barn with darkrooms and kilns.

SETON KEOUGH HIGH SCHOOL
1201 South Caton Ave.
(410) 646-4444
www.setonkeough.com
Seton Keough is a hybrid that was created in 1988 when Seton High School, a midtown city high school for girls founded by the Daughters of Charity in 1865, merged with Archbishop Keough High School and moved out to its 30-acre campus where Keough had been since its founding by the School Sisters of Notre Dame in 1965. Seton Keough offers a comprehensive college preparatory program for all its girls that includes advanced-placement classes, and the Marillac Program for students with special needs, and the Focus program for students who enter the school achieving below their grade level in major subject areas. New in the fall of 2009 was Project Lead the Way in Engineering and Biomedical Science. The science and engineering curriculum is partnered with St. Agnes Hospital, Northrop Grumman, the Knott Foundation, and the France-Merrick Foundation. The curriculum has two tracks Engineering and Biomedical Sciences. This dynamic program uses hands-on experiences, and real-world problems to engage and challenge students. To be accepted into the program, students must demonstrate aptitude in mathematics and science and be recommended by their teachers. The program begins in freshmen year with introductory courses in engineering and biomedical science. Additionally, Seton Keough offers the Parallel Enrollment Program (PEP), a program that provides college courses on campus at Seton Keough. The course offerings are in business management, business law, psychology, and sociology. More than 500 students are enrolled at Seton Keough.

TALMUDICAL ACADEMY OF BALTIMORE
4445 Old Court Rd., Pikesville
(410) 484-6600
www.talmudicalacademy.org
Talmudical Academy is the oldest Jewish day school in the United States outside of New York. Founded in 1917, it provides young Jewish boys with an Orthodox environment in which they can receive a secular and a religious education. Boys in pre-K through grade 12 spend mornings in study of the Hebrew alphabet, the Torah, and other sacred Hebrew texts. In the afternoon, they pursue the reading, writing, and arithmetic part of their education.

COLLEGES AND UNIVERSITIES

GOUCHER COLLEGE
1021 Dulaney Valley Rd., Towson
(410) 337-6000
www.goucher.edu
Goucher was founded in 1885 as a liberal arts college for women in midtown Baltimore. It moved to its 287-acre Towson campus in 1953 and began accepting male students in 1986. Goucher counts among its student body about 1,350 undergraduates and 1,000 graduate students

from all over the United States and 20 foreign countries. In the fall of 2006, Goucher College launched a new liberal education curriculum and all incoming first-year students—and some transfer students—are subject to its new requirements. This curriculum states what the college believes every student should know by the time he or she graduates. Each student must study abroad before being graduated. Goucher offers 31 undergraduate majors and 6 interdisciplinary areas and students can also design their own majors. Most classes have fewer than 20 students. Internships and independent study and research are encouraged and in some cases required for graduation. Master's degrees in education, teaching, historic preservation, and creative nonfiction and a post-baccalaureate premedical program are available. In September 2009, the college opened Athenaeum, a $48 million "green" structure described as a 24/7 technologically superior library, spacious open forum for public events, café, art gallery, community center, group study rooms; and spaces for exercise, conversation, and reflection.

THE JOHNS HOPKINS UNIVERSITY
Charles and 34th Streets
(410) 516-8000
www.jhu.edu

The Johns Hopkins University (JHU) was founded in 1876 when, upon his death, Johns Hopkins willed $7 million to create it and The Johns Hopkins Hospital. Then, as now, the hospital and the university work hand in hand, so that research, instruction, and practical application are all put together in one neat package. JHU was the first university in the United States to employ this all-encompassing method of teaching that was modeled after the European research teaching methods of the time.

Originally an all-white male facility, JHU admitted its first African-American student in 1887, but admitted women only sparingly over the years until 1970, when it officially became a coeducational facility. More than 16,000 full- and part-time students are enrolled at its three major mid-Atlantic campuses and campuses in China and Italy. The

4,700 undergraduate students on the Homewood campus choose from 50 majors in the humanities, social sciences, natural sciences, and engineering. The East Baltimore campus where the hospital is located also houses the schools of medicine, nursing, and hygiene and public health.

Some of Hopkins' special divisions include the Paul H. Nitze School of Advanced International Studies and the Applied Physics Laboratory, and Hopkins also now runs the Peabody Institute.

A highly competitive private university that received 16,011 applications of which 1,235 actually enrolled, JHU has extensive community outreach. Intercollegiate sports are well attended, particularly lacrosse and football, and the annual Hopkins Fair is always crowded. JHU, which is the largest private employer in Baltimore, has its fingers in many pies, including building and renovating city buildings in cooperation with Habitat for Humanity on the volunteer level and through Dome Corporation, a Hopkins subsidiary, on the corporate level.

LOYOLA UNIVERSITY MARYLAND & LOYOLA COLLEGE
4501 North Charles St.
(800) 221-9107
www.loyola.edu

Loyola College in Maryland was founded in 1852 by the Jesuit order as an all-male post-secondary institution. In 1971 it merged with Mount St. Agnes College (an all-women's college) and became a coeducational facility. In August 2008, the college requested to have the name changed to University as it felt it better reflected its comprehensive array of academic fields. With the approval of the Maryland Higher Education Commission, and a fee for the name change, the official name change to Loyola University Maryland took effect in August 2009. This name change applies to the undergraduate school only with the post-graduate school now known as simply Loyola College. Loyola offers three main areas of concentration for undergraduate degrees, bachelor of arts, science and business administration Post-graduate degrees include finance and business degrees from their Sellinger School of Business and Management, education related degrees from their School of Education, and Computer Science. Loyola has more than 3,500 undergraduates on-campus and 68 percent of the students study abroad.

Loyola also offers classes at campuses in Columbia and Hunt Valley, Maryland; Belgium; Thailand; and England. Classes are also offered through community colleges in Anne Arundel, Harford, and Cecil Counties, and graduate classes are accessible through a site in Timonium. The school has a student-teacher ratio of 12 to 1 with an average class size of 25. Notable alumni include Tom Clancy, author of *The Hunt for Red October*, and Mark Bowden, author of *Black Hawk Down*.

MORGAN STATE UNIVERSITY
1700 East Cold Spring Lane
(410) 885-3333
www.morgan.edu
Morgan State University was founded in 1867 by members of the Baltimore Methodist Episcopal Church to educate African Americans and prepare them for the Methodist clergy. Its mission quickly expanded to include educating teachers. For almost a century, Morgan functioned as a private college, but in 1968 it was accepted under the umbrella of the University System of Maryland, and with its resources became a university in 1975. Enrollment dwindled to 2,000 students until 1984 when in an effort to save itself, the school once again became independent. With current enrollments at 6,000 and a full-time faculty of 300, it has become one of the fastest growing campuses in the state. Morgan offers more than 60 academic programs that lead to the Bachelor of Science or Bachelor of Arts degree, and specialized programs at the master's and doctoral levels. Morgan's range of academic programs includes business, engineering, education, architecture, social work, hospitality management, and arts and sciences. Morgan also offers a University Honors Program that consists of accelerated and intensified math, science, and humanities courses that are especially suited for highly motivated, high-ability students. Morgan also offers a unique study and research opportunity for its Marine Biology students through its Estuarine Research Center in southern Maryland on the Chesapeake watershed. It is home to the well-regarded new Carl Murphy Fine Arts Center.

ST. MARY'S SEMINARY AND UNIVERSITY
5400 Roland Ave.
(410) 864-4000
www.stmarys.edu
This private university began in 1791 by the Society of St. Sulpice to educate students for the priesthood and was the first Catholic seminary in the United States. The equivalent of a high school and community college by today's standards, it grew in importance when the Sulpicians were granted recognition as a Pontifical Theological Faculty in 1822 by Pope Pius VII and gained the ability to grant pontifical degrees. St. Mary's Seminary is one of only six seminaries in the United States that are allowed to grant such degrees. The Ecumenical Institute of Theology, which opened in 1968 to persons of all faiths, continues to provide a platform for investigation and argument of religious and philosophical topics and awards master's degrees in theology and religious education. Within its School of Theology, St. Mary's opened the Center for Continuing Formation in 1995, which hosts priests on sabbatical and provides learning opportunities in religion and philosophy for the general public.

The University System of Maryland
The University System of Maryland (USM) comprises previously independent schools that have come under its umbrella and schools that have historically been branches or campuses of the University of Maryland. There are 11 universities, 2 research institutions, and 2 regional centers enrolling some 114,800 undergraduate students and 41,000 graduate students worldwide in 6,000 bachelor's, master's, doctoral, and professional academic programs.

COPPIN STATE UNIVERSITY
2500 West North Ave.
(410) 951-3000
www.coppin.edu

Coppin State University is a historically African-American college that was established in 1900 as a private normal school to train elementary school teachers. Coppin, which became a part of the university system in 1988, currently offers degrees and certification programs in dentistry, engineering, pharmacy, criminal justice, and social work and teaching. It also offers graduate degrees in the arts and sciences, including nursing and teacher education. Originally a day school, most of Coppin's 3,300 students are day-trippers, but a new 300-bed residence hall attracts students from out of state to the 52-acre campus.

TOWSON UNIVERSITY
8000 York Rd., Towson
(410) 704-2000
www.towson.edu

Towson University began as the State Normal School, a state-sponsored teaching school in Baltimore city. It moved to its Towson campus in 1915, and the majestic building in which it was housed is still used by the university. Since then, the school has gone through many incarnations, ending up as the current Towson University, sitting on 328 acres, the second-largest university in Maryland. The university grants baccalaureate degrees in 63 majors, 39 masters degrees, and 4 doctorial programs through its eight colleges: the College of Business and Economics; the College of Education; the College of Fine Arts and Communication; the College of Graduate and Extended Education; the College of Health Professions; the College of Liberal Arts; the College of Natural and Mathematical Sciences; and the Honors College. Approximately 21,177 full- and part-time students attend Towson, with an 18:1 student-teacher ratio. There's residential space for 4,500. The school boasts state-of-the-art facilities in radio and TV and a growing reputation in the mass-media industry.

UNIVERSITY OF BALTIMORE
1420 North Charles St.
(410) 837-4200
www.ubalt.edu

The University of Baltimore (UB) began in 1925 as a private, coeducational, two-year school of business. In 1975 it went public and became part of the Maryland system. UB awards 4-year baccalaureate degrees. Today, UB is a "green school" and there are three schools within the University of Baltimore: the Yale Gordon College of Liberal Arts, Merrick School of Business, and School of Law offering more than 50 undergraduate, graduate, and professional degrees program. It is also well-known for its School of Law, which offers day and evening classes. UB is the largest law school in Maryland, with approximately 1,000 students in attendance. The staff to student ratio in the law school is 1:20. UB has also been reaching out to more distant sites to centers in Harford and Howard Counties, and it also offers a virtual degree. You can get your bachelor's degree by studying with UB online from anywhere in the world. Currently, there are just over 3,000 undergraduate students at UB. In 2006, the 38,000-square-foot, five-story student center opened and features a 200-seat theater with panoramic city views, retail shops, student organization offices, and areas for group study, recreation, and quiet reflection.

UNIVERSITY OF MARYLAND, BALTIMORE
737 West Lombard St.
(410) 706-3100
www.umaryland.edu

Although the University of Maryland's main campus is in College Park, Maryland, the university began here in Baltimore in 1807 with the founding of the School of Medicine. Davidge Hall, a lecture hall and operating theater built in 1812 and now a National Historic Landmark, is the oldest building in the United States in continuous use for medical teaching. In 1816 a School of Law was added. In 1840 the Baltimore College of Dental Surgery, Dental School opened as the first dental college in the world. In 1841, the Maryland College of Pharmacy was begun; and in 1889, the School of Nursing opened. The most recent addition was the School of Social Work, in 1961. Today, this 61-acre campus for research and technology encompasses 62 buildings in West Baltimore near the Inner Harbor. The university is Maryland's only public academic health, human services, and law center. Seven professional and graduate schools train the majority of the state's physicians, nurses, dentists, lawyers, social workers, and pharmacists. The university community gives more than 2 million hours a year in service to the public. It has close to 6,100 students served by more than 1,600 faculty members. There are 42 graduate programs offered.

UNIVERSITY OF MARYLAND, BALTIMORE COUNTY
1000 Hillltop Circle
(410) 455-1000
www.umbc.edu

The University of Maryland, Baltimore County (UMBC) was founded in 1966. A separate school from the University of Maryland, College Park, UMBC has more than 12,870 undergraduate and graduate students studying in the liberal arts and sciences at its 500-acre campus. The focus is on cutting-edge science and technology and the visual and performing arts while billing itself a "public research university." In this regard, UMBC offers 54 majors and 45 minors and 20 certificate programs in the physical and biological sciences, social and behavioral sciences, engineering, mathematics, information technology, humanities, and visual and performing arts. UMBC also offers the Joint Center for Earth Systems Technology, a NASA Goddard Space Flight Center (GSFC)/UMBC JCET's research focuses on themes that align with NASA's earth science interests: engineering, mesoscale atmospheric processes, climate and radiation, atmospheric chemistry and dynamics, hydrospheric and biospheric sciences, and solar system science including geodesy and geophysics.

Community Colleges

BALTIMORE CITY COMMUNITY COLLEGE
600 East Lombard St.
(410) 986-5599

2901 Liberty Heights Ave.
(410) 462-8000
www.bccc.edu

Baltimore City Community College (BCCC) has two main campuses in the city. Its Downtown campus, whose center is only a few blocks from the Inner Harbor, is convenient and well used by downtown residents and workers. Its Liberty Road campus was the original site of the school when it was known as Baltimore Junior College, and its popular radio station, WBJC, still bears the original acronym. The school, however, has come a long way since the BJC days. More than 15,000 students pursue credit and noncredit courses in 35 degree and 31 certificate programs in such varied fields as allied health, nursing, human services, business, and information technology. Additionally, their college offers adult education, GED, and English as a Second Language courses in over 80 communities throughout the city. BCCC is the largest provider of literacy services in the city of Baltimore.

The only state-sponsored, two-year college in Maryland, BCCC enrolls more city residents than any other college in Baltimore. BCCC offers an Apparel Technology Program, which was cited by the American Textile Manufacturers Institute for its innovative curriculum design and teaching excellence.

One of BCCC's most interesting features is that its education comes with a guarantee. "First, if a graduate of a career program who is seeking employment does not have a full-time job within 90 days after graduation, the College will provide an additional 12 credits of course work and other support services at no cost to the student. Second, if an employer is not satisfied with the quality of job performance of a career program graduate, BCCC will provide an additional 12 credits of instruction at no charge to the student or the employer."

THE COMMUNITY COLLEGES OF BALTIMORE COUNTY
www.ccbcmd.edu

There are three community colleges in Baltimore County, each of which grew up separately, responding to the needs of their respective communities. Within the last few years, they have been bundled under the umbrella name and administration of a new entity, The Community Colleges of Baltimore County (CCBC). Through this act of centralization, Baltimore County hopes to be able to enhance offerings while reducing overall costs through reorganization. The three original schools that now serve as CCBC's main campuses are at 800 South Rolling Rd., Catonsville, (410) 455-6050; 7200 Sollers Point Rd., Dundalk, (410) 282-6700; and 7201 Rossville Blvd., Essex, (410) 682-6000. The CCBC also offers classes through neighborhood centers in Owings Mills and Hunt Valley.

Through all its campuses and centers, CCBC serves more than 70,000 students and offers 6,600 credit courses and 7,000 continuing education courses, including employee training courses that the county offers to employers in the area at more than 90 locations. Various certificates of completion are available for specific course offerings, but, overwhelmingly, students seek associate of arts degrees and transfer to a four-year institution.

Associate degrees and certificates are offered in more than 100 programs in the arts and sciences, business administration, computer sciences, engineering, general studies, and teacher education. Certificate programs include such options as computer graphics and visual communications, printing management technology, environmental technology, chemical dependency counseling, retail floristry, and varied allied health programs. CCBC offers a student to teacher ratio of 17:1.

SPECIALTY SCHOOLS

BALTIMORE ACTORS' THEATRE AND CONSERVATORY
300 Dumbarton Rd.
(410) 337-8519
www.baltimoreactorstheatre.org
If you have a five-year-old who can really belt out a song or a 15-year-old who can make you believe he's Hamlet, then you might want to consider approaching Baltimore Actors' Theatre

and Conservatory to see if your child can become one of the select few who are admitted every year. The K-12 student body at the conservatory numbers only 30, with an equal number of students pursuing a three-year baccalaureate degree and postgraduate studies. These 60 students work hand-in-hand with the resident professional performance company of 100 to produce a minimum of 12 plays per year, while pursuing a rigorous academic curriculum. High school degrees are accredited by the state of Maryland, but the baccalaureate and master's degrees offered are through Trinity College in London, although students do not study abroad.

The Baltimore Actors' Theatre and Conservatory is less expensive than many traditional private K-12 institutions and many area colleges because much of the school's expenses are paid for through performance receipts.

BALTIMORE INTERNATIONAL COLLEGE (BIC)
17 Commerce St.
(410) 752-4710
www.bic.edu

BIC was founded in 1972 to offer certificates in culinary arts. It has grown to include bachelor's and associate's degrees in culinary arts and hospitality business and management. Graduate degrees in hospitality are also available. Classes are hands-on for all students, who can be seen heading to class in their chef's jackets and carrying their knife cases. They get to test their skills every weekday at lunchtime during the semester—and we get to see how good they are. The Bay Atlantic Club is staffed by students and open Monday through Friday 11:30 a.m. to 2 p.m. at 206 East Redwood St. Call ahead if you want to go, for a reservation and to be sure the restaurant is open. They close for school holidays. The Bay Atlantic Club's phone number is (410) 752-1448 ext. 24

THE MARYLAND INSTITUTE, COLLEGE OF ART (MICA
1300 West Mount Royal Ave.
(410) 669-9200
www.mica.edu

The Maryland Institute, selected by *U.S. News & World Report* as one of the top four graduate programs in visual arts in the nation, was established in 1826 and has the distinction of being the oldest independent, degree-granting, fully accredited art college in the United States. The campus is made up of 16 buildings, most of which line Mount Royal Avenue from North Avenue to Park Avenue, adjacent to Mount Royal Terrace. Two of the buildings—the main building at 1300 and Mount Royal Station, a historic train station that the institute renovated for gallery and workspace—are on the National Register of Historic Places. In the winter of 2004–2005, MICA opened its new Brown Center, filled with classrooms, labs, and an auditorium. In 2008, the Gateway Building, housing dorms and a performing arts center opened.

But what is really most important about the institute is the education it offers its students. The college enrolls 1,714 undergraduate and 218 graduate students from 48 states and 52 foreign countries, offering programs of study leading to the bachelor of fine arts (B.F.A.), master of arts (M.A.), and master of fine arts (M.F.A.) degrees, post-baccalaureate certificate programs, and a full slate of credit and noncredit courses for adults, college-bound students, and children. Undergraduate majors in 14 studio areas and art history lead to the bachelor of fine arts degree. Students in any major can use the generous number of studio electives to create a unique program of study to support their career goals and interests through the addition of 11 studio concentrations; in addition, MICA offers liberal arts minors in art history, creative writing, critical theory, culture and politics, gender studies, and literary studies. A five-year BFA/MAT capstone program prepares art educators for certification in 48 states—graduates of this program have a 100 percent placement rate. Undergraduate degrees are available in all major 11 internationally renowned graduate programs and lead to the master of fine arts, master of arts, and post-baccalaureate certificate in a full array of studio disciplines, community arts, and art education (teaching and research). MICA administers the most study-abroad programs of any art college in the United States.

The institute also offers a plethora of options for continuing studies in everything from interior design to computer art, for those seeking degrees and those simply wanting to learn.

MARYLAND SCHOOL FOR THE BLIND
3501 Taylor Ave.
(410) 444-5000
www.mdschblind.org

The Maryland School for the Blind was founded in 1853 and moved from the city to its current location in 1906 because the children needed a place to run that had no obstacles. From its inception until the 1970s, the school served primarily blind and visually impaired students with a basic academic curriculum and specialized courses in Braille and orientation mobility. Daily living skills, such as personal hygiene, food preparation, and table etiquette, were also taught.

Since the 1970s when the federal government mandated that all states provide education for handicapped children, the Maryland School has adapted its curriculum and services to include children that have visual, physical, and emotional disparities.

More than 300 professionals and 140 volunteers help the Maryland School's 185 children and youth from infancy to age 21 with visual impairments, including those with multiple disabilities, for functional independence learn how to lead normal lives. Some 140 students live on campus five days a week and are supported by house parents, who live with them, and a 24-hour nursing staff on campus.

Students who are residents of Maryland pay nothing for their room, board, and tuition. Students from outside the state pay tuition and fees, but these are often picked up by their respective states that may have no facilities that fulfill the federal mandate. The Maryland School also helps public school systems develop programs within their schools for children with visual and/or physical handicaps and boasts an outreach program to an additional 800 students across Maryland. The school has also begun working with babies and toddlers in basic skills to give them a head start.

THE PEABODY INSTITUTE
1 East Mount Vernon Place
(410) 659-8100
www.peabody.jhu.edu

The Peabody Conservatory of Music, now the Peabody Institute of the Johns Hopkins University, was founded in 1857 with a bequest from George Peabody. It has become one of the premier music schools in the country. The Peabody has a preparatory division in music and dance that is open to people of all ages. The conservatory offers high school, college, and advanced degrees in music. Close to 600 full-time and 40 part-time students are accepted into the conservatory versus the almost 6,400 students in the preparatory school. Faculty size is about 150, making the student to faculty ratio less than 5:1 and the average class size 7 to 18. The Peabody is performance oriented, and its students stage almost 60 public concerts every year. Peabody focuses on "classical" music and jazz. All Peabody undergraduates—even the ones majoring in music education or recording arts and sciences—must complete the same performance curriculum as those majoring in performance. Auditions for the conservatory are specific and you should review the instructions on their Web site.

HEALTH CARE

If you have to be sick or have a medical problem, Baltimore is just about the greatest place to live. Cutting-edge work is being done at the world-renowned Johns Hopkins Hospital in East Baltimore. The University of Maryland Medical Center near the Inner Harbor and Mercy Medical Center are two centers that are outstanding in their fields. Most specifically, the R. Adams Cowley Shock Trauma Center at the University of Maryland Medical Center has been a leader in caring for critically injured people since the 1970s.

Dr. Ben Carson, a neurosurgeon at Johns Hopkins Hospital, has saved hundreds of children through his surgical skills and is particularly well-known for separations of conjoined twins.

Dr. Robert Gallo, a scientist and leader in the research of AIDS, opened a facility at the Institute of Human Virology at the University of Maryland School of Medicine in 1996, bringing to Baltimore a first-rate warrior against one of the era's most fatal and devastating diseases.

While advertisements and promotional materials make it seem as if there's great competition among the hospitals, a good deal of their success is in working together to help patients. Patients are routinely sent from one hospital to another for consultations, second opinions, and surgeries. The hospitals in the area play host to thousands of patients from all over the world, who come to the area seeking the best care possible.

Beyond the traditional forms of medicine practiced in hospitals, the area has seen growth in the holistic approaches to health care, including such alternative healing methods as acupuncture, aromatherapy, and other forms of care practiced for centuries elsewhere and only now gaining wider acceptance in this country.

HOSPITALS

BALTIMORE VA MEDICAL CENTER
10 North Greene St.
(410) 605-7000, (800) 463-6295
www.maryland.va.gov
Part of the Veterans Affairs Maryland Health Care System, the Baltimore VA Medical Center offers veterans some of the most state-of-the-art facilities available through the military. The 221-bed medical center is home to the world's first film-less radiology department, which allows doctors nearly instant access to patient imaging from throughout the facility.

Conveniently located near the Inner Harbor and next door to the University of Maryland Medical System, the center offers a full range of inpatient, outpatient, and research programs for veterans. The Geriatric Research, Education and Clinical Center, offering research on strokes and cardiovascular disease prevention through exercise, smoking cessation, and nutrition therapy for older veterans, is one of only 21 VA system providers of these services in the country.

The hospital has one of two MS Centers of Excellence centers for the growing population of multiple sclerosis patients and one of the VA's eight Mental Illness Research Education and Clinical Centers.

The center in Baltimore offers a wide range of specialties, including a state-of-the-art endoscopic suite; inpatient and outpatient mental health services; MRI, mammography, and CAT scan facilities; a home-based primary-care program; a refractory congestive heart failure program; an outpatient spinal cord injury support clinic; and a senior exercise rehabilitation facility.

The medical center offers free parking for outpatients only in its parking lot below the facility on Greene Street. A shuttle service takes patients to and from Perry Point and Fort Howard medical centers, separate facilities that are part of the same network of veterans' services, on weekdays.

BALTIMORE WASHINGTON MEDICAL CENTER
301 Hospital Dr., Glen Burnie
(410) 787-4000
www.mybwmc.org
Part of the University of Maryland Medical System, this 311-bed facility in Anne Arundel County employs about 2,600 people and 600 physicians. Specialties include orthopedics, psychiatry, cardiology, and emergency medicine. The Tate Cancer Center, an outpatient facility, opened in 2003. It also has the Joslin Diabetes Center, Aiello Breast Center, Maryland Vascular Center, Joint Replacement Center and other specialty departments. The emergency room sees about 95,000 patients a year. A new women's health center with obstetrics opened in October 2009, offering a family-like atmosphere to welcome the new arrival.

BON SECOURS HOSPITAL
2000 West Baltimore St.
(410) 362-3000
http://bonsecoursbaltimore.com
Cardinal James Gibbons, the ninth archbishop of Baltimore, asked the Sisters of Bon Secours to come from Paris in 1881 to provide health care to the sick in their homes. Through the financial support of philanthropist George Jenkins, they opened the first Bon Secours Hospital in Baltimore in 1919. Now, with 208 beds and 973 employees, that mission has spread to include 10 primary-care centers around West Baltimore; the largest outpatient renal dialysis program in the city; the New Hope Treatment Center, offering drug treatment and counseling; and Operation Reach-Out, a community development program. The hospital merged in 1996 with Liberty Health System to form Bon Secours Medical System. Among Bon Secours Hospital's specialties are

---

Selected Baltimore Firsts

The first Department of Public Health was established here in 1793.

Granville Stanley Hall established the first psychology laboratory at Johns Hopkins University in 1881.

In 1894 Dr. Williams Halsted, chief surgeon at Johns Hopkins Hospital, was the first to use rubber gloves for surgery.

In 1942 Johns Hopkins Hospital was the first to identify the polio virus.

The first intensive care unit was established at Johns Hopkins in 1955; the first shock-trauma unit, at the University of Maryland Hospital in 1961.

—Excerpted from *Baltimore—America's City of Firsts,* a pamphlet published by Baltimore Bicentennial Celebration, Inc.

---

cardiology, podiatry, surgery, substance abuse services, and home health.

FRANKLIN SQUARE HOSPITAL CENTER
9000 Franklin Square Dr., Essex
(410) 777-7000
www.franklinsquare.org
The founding hospital in the growing MedStar Health System, this 357-bed facility is the third largest in Baltimore, offering subacute and acute care to eastern Baltimore County residents. A teaching hospital, Franklin Square has more than 750 physicians and 2,800 employees. Students at Essex Community College, located next door, receive clinical training in radiography and respiratory therapy. Its heart center is the third-largest, in terms of cases handled, in the area, while its OBTLC (Obstetrics Tender Loving Care) program, featuring home-like accommodations for

birthing, makes it one of the busiest obstetrics programs in the area. Its Psychology and Behavioral Medicine section handles inpatient adult, adolescent, and child psychiatric care services. Specialties include cardiology, oncology, emergency medicine, labor and delivery, and general medicine. A new 356,000-square-foot patient care tower is scheduled to open in late 2010. The seven-story building will have 291 private rooms, an expanded emergency department, a dedicated pediatric emergency department and inpatient suite, four medical and surgical units, and an expanded 50-bed critical care unit.

GOOD SAMARITAN HOSPITAL OF MARYLAND
5601 Loch Raven Blvd.
(443) 444-8000
www.goodsam-md.org
Good Samaritan was founded in 1968 through a gift from Thomas O'Neill, a local merchant and philanthropist. O'Neill set the condition that all activities at the hospital conform to the Catholic Principles, as set by the U.S. National Conference of Catholic Bishops. This means that abortions and in vitro fertilizations are not performed here. Through an arrangement with Johns Hopkins School of Medicine, the hospital provides orthopedics, rehabilitation medicine, and rheumatology. A MedStar hospital, it is located on a 43-acre site in northeastern Baltimore City, where its 346 beds and 2,300 employees provide care to northern Baltimore City and the greater Towson area. The Emergency Department sees more than 23,000 patients a year, and the hospital's Good Health Center offers free and low-cost preventive medical services. The hospital also offers 69 rehabilitation beds and a 24-station renal dialysis unit. Specialties include medical/surgical care, obstetrics and gynecology, pediatric care, and emergency care. Good Samaritan is one of the top 10 hospitals for complex knee surgery.

GREATER BALTIMORE MEDICAL CENTER
6701 North Charles St., Towson
(443) 849-2000
www.gbmc.org

Formed from the Presbyterian Eye, Ear and Throat Hospital and the Women's Hospital of Maryland, both of which opened in the 1880s, GBMC opened on its 106-acre wooded campus in 1965. The 300-bed medical center (acute and subacute care) handles more than 26,700 inpatient cases and approximately 60,000 emergency room visits annually. The nonprofit community hospital performs more surgeries—44,000—than any other hospital in the state. Its obstetrics wing delivers the most babies in the region. Recognized nationally for its gynecological surgeries, the hospital was the first to bring laser surgery to Maryland in the mid-1970s and has continued to revolutionize the use of lasers in laparoscopic surgical techniques. The hospital has also been active in breast cancer awareness and care, providing all services—from consultation to X-rays to treatment—through its Comprehensive Breast Care Center. It's a one-stop approach to breast health. The F. Barton Harvey Institute of Human Genetics, endowed with a $1 million gift and directed by nationally known geneticist Maimon Cohen, is working to bring practical applications of genetic research, especially on the adult onset of Alzheimer's and Parkinson's diseases, to patients. Through its GBMC HealthCare program, it offers all levels of medical care, including hospice through its Hospice of Baltimore center and the Gilchrest Center.

Specialties include emergency care, obstetrics and gynecological services, cancer care, ophthalmology, otolaryngology, and laparoscopic surgery.

HARBOR HOSPITAL
3001 South Hanover St.
(410) 350-3200
www.harborhospital.org
Another member of the MedStar System, Harbor Hospital Center started when Dr. Harry Peterman founded the South Baltimore Eye, Ear, Nose and Throat Clinic in the industrial area of South Baltimore in 1901. Two years later, a growing population serving the industrial area, especially Bethlehem Steel shipyard, turned his clinic into a hospital that by 1918 had "an accident room" for

Shock Trauma—"The Golden Hour"

Dr. R. Adams Cowley theorized in the 1970s that if a person suffering a serious trauma could reach specially trained doctors within an hour of suffering a life-threatening injury, the chances of survival would increase greatly.

With the support of Maryland officials, Cowley created the first of its kind, critical-care system. The result of his groundbreaking work is a trauma center in Baltimore that now bears his name.

The R. Adams Cowley Shock Trauma Center, which is part of the University of Maryland System, has been responsible for saving the lives of thousands of people who probably would otherwise have died from injuries received in car crashes, violence, or other traumas to the brain and body.

More than 6,000 patients are treated at the center every year, about a third of them arriving by helicopter.

Most of these patients have been injured in vehicle crashes, falls, and violence. The majority of them are between 20 and 40 years of age and three-quarters of them are male.

Medevac pilots, many of whom have served in the armed forces, staff the high-speed helicopters that are kept in strategic locations around the state. The multimillion-dollar helicopters have specially equipped compartments with room for stretchers, emergency medicine personnel, and medical equipment.

Amazingly enough, in spite of their terrible injuries, some 97 percent of patients who arrive at Shock Trauma survive.

Because of this success rate, Baltimoreans are justly proud of—and thankful for—the work of so many dedicated men and women at the R. Adams Cowley Shock Trauma Center.

---

sudden injuries, many resulting from workplace accidents. Fifty years later, in 1968, South Baltimore General Hospital moved from its home on Light Street to South Hanover Street, looking over the Patapsco River, where it continues today. Now called Harbor Hospital, the 222-bed teaching hospital offers about 30 specialties, which are provided by more than 1,500 employees, many of whom are affiliated with the University of Maryland School of Medicine. Their primary centers of excellence are cancer care, orthopedic specialty care, women's care, and community education and family wellness. The facility offers numerous free classes and support groups to help people understand such medical concerns as joint replacement, yoga, or dinner with the doctor discussing coping with a hernia. The classes are held at the waterfront campus and in Anne Arundel, Baltimore, and Howard Counties

JOHNS HOPKINS BAYVIEW
MEDICAL CENTER
4940 Eastern Ave.
(410) 550-0100
www.hopkinsbayview.org
Formerly known as Francis Scott Key Medical Center, this 700-bed community teaching hospital has evolved, since 1773, from an alms house to an asylum to a municipal hospital before having its ownership transferred from the city to Johns Hopkins Hospital and University in 1984. Staffed by physicians who are primarily full-time faculty

Important Numbers and Web Sites to Know

Police, fire, ambulance, or other emergencies, 911 (in Baltimore City, call 311 for nonemergency matters)
Maryland Natural Resources Police (maritime emergencies), (410) 260-8888, (877) 620-8367, www.dnr.state.md.us
Poison Control, (410) 706-7701, (800) 222-1222, www.mdpoison.com

Departments of Mental Health and Hygiene
These numbers will lead you to people who can make referrals to specialists ranging from community health centers to centers dealing with specific types of care.
State of Maryland, (410) 767-5300, www.mdpublichealth.org
Anne Arundel County, (410) 222-7095, www.aahealth.org
Baltimore City, (410) 396-4398, www.baltimorehealth.org
Baltimore County, (410) 887-3740, www.co.ba.md.us
Howard County, (410) 313-6300, www.co.ho.md.us

Other Aid Agencies
Associated Black Charities, (888) 450-5836, www.abc-md.org
Associated Catholic Charities, (410) 547-5490, www.catholiccharities-md.org
Episcopal Community Services, (410) 467-1264, www.ecsm.org
Jewish Family Services, (410) 466-9200, www.jirs.org
Lutheran Social Services in Maryland, (410) 558-3168, www.lssnca.org

Crisis Intervention
Family Crisis Center, (410) 828-6390, www.familycrisiscenter.net
First Step (suicide intervention), (410) 521-3800 or (800) SUICIDE, www.suicidehotlines.com/maryland
House of Ruth (domestic violence), (410) 889-0840; 24-hour hotline: (410) 889-7884, www.hruth.org
Maryland Network Against Domestic Violence, (800) MDHELPS, www.mnadv.org
Maryland Youth Crisis Hotline, (800) 784-2433, (800) 273-8255, http://suicidehotlines.com/maryland.html
Family Stress Line, 24-hour hotline, (800) 243-7337, www.familytreemd.org

Referral Sources
Maryland Psychiatric Society, (410) 625-0232, www.mdpsych.org
Maryland Psychological Association, (410) 992-4258, www.marylandpsychology.org

Substance Abuse
Al-Anon and Alateen, (410) 766-1984, www.md-al-anon.org
Alcoholics Anonymous, (410) 663-1922, www.baltimoreaa.org
Narcotics Anonymous, (410) 566-4022; hotline, (800) 317-3222, www.freestatena.org

at Johns Hopkins University School of Medicine, the hospital serves as a satellite to the bigger Hopkins hospital campus, although it has its own areas of specialty, too. Bayview's employees work on a beautiful and growing 130-acre campus, featuring jogging trails and a community park-like environment. The hospital's Francis Scott Key Burn Center does amazing work for people suffering from serious burns. The hospital is home to one of Maryland's most comprehensive neonatal intensive care units, a sleep disorder center, an area-wide trauma center, and a geriatrics center.

THE JOHNS HOPKINS HOSPITAL
600 North Wolfe St.
(410) 955-5000
www.hopkinsmedicine.org
The hospital opened in 1889, and since that time its recognition and groundbreaking work have grown with the years. Established as part of philanthropist Johns Hopkins' gift to form Johns Hopkins University, the school of medicine and hospital revolutionized American higher education, medical education, and health care by establishing an intense teaching and learning environment where doctors, teachers, and students work hand in hand. Hopkins was the first medical school to require an undergraduate degree for admission and the first to combine science learning and intensive clinical mentoring, thus creating a model for medical education that remains in use throughout the world today. Among the firsts the hospital can claim is the first major medical school in the country to admit women, the first to use rubber gloves during surgery, and the first to develop renal dialysis and CPR.

The hospital has 982 beds and draws patients from all over the world who seek the cures for which Hopkins is renowned. The hospital features marvelous accommodations for those having to spend time in the hospital. Travel agents, concierges, several types of dining, and other amenities ease the tough times, and the hospital is located on the city's subway system, meaning transportation from the train station or airport doesn't require a taxicab ride.

Its children's ward features games, movies, and a giant stuffed animal zoo that makes kids feel like they're not so far away from home. Among its specialties are AIDS care, anesthesiology, critical care, asthma and allergies, cancer, cardiology and cardiac surgery, dermatology, digestive disorders, emergency medicine, endocrinology, immunology and infectious diseases, kidney disorders, neurology and neurosurgery, pediatrics, pulmonary medicine, reconstructive and plastic surgery, transplant surgery, and urology.

KERNAN ORTHOPAEDICS AND REHABILITATION
2200 Kernan Dr.
(888) 4KERNAN, (800) 492-5538
www.umm.edu/kernan
Part of the University of Maryland Medical System, the 152-bed hospital began more than a century ago as a home for children with orthopedic deficits. The hospital has evolved into a site for innovative orthopedic and rehabilitation services for children and adults. Located on the border of Baltimore City and Baltimore County on a 90-acre wooded site, where founder James Kernan's original Victorian mansion still stands, the hospital, employing about 500 people, treats patients suffering from a variety of orthopedic and neurological conditions, including spinal cord and brain injury rehabilitation and sports medicine. The pediatric orthopedics department focuses on the wide variety of growing children's problems, such as scoliosis and club feet. It is the largest inpatient rehabilitation hospital and provider of rehabilitation services in Maryland.

LEVINDALE HEBREW GERIATRIC CENTER AND HOSPITAL
2434 West Belvedere Ave.
(410) 601-2400
www.lifebridgehealth.org/Levindale
Started as the Hebrew Friendly Inn for the Old in the 1890s, the 172-bed facility is now a specialty hospital. Named after Louis H. Levin, executive director of the Associated Jewish Charities from 1921 until his death in 1923, the hospital observes all Jewish laws and rituals and is strictly

kosher. Now part of the Lifebridge Health System, of which Sinai Hospital is also a part, Levindale has 202 nursing home beds, 50 specialty long-term-stay beds, 20 psychiatric-rehab beds, and 16 comprehensive rehabilitation beds. Employing about 600 people, the hospital also provides subacute care.

MARYLAND GENERAL HOSPITAL
827 Linden Ave.
(410) 225-8000
www.marylandgeneral.org
Founded in 1881 by a group of Baltimore doctors as a university-affiliated teaching hospital, the Baltimore Medical College, as it was called back then, became Maryland General after becoming affiliated with the University of Maryland School of Medicine. In 1965 it again merged, this time with the Baltimore Eye and Ear Hospital to become the premier teaching hospital for eye, ear, nose, and throat problems. Now, the 243-bed hospital, with more than 500 doctors and 30 different specialties, provides those services, and rehabilitation, transitional care, mental health, and obstetrics and gynecological services. In 1997 the hospital opened its Obstetrical Center, which allows each mother to remain in her one, well-furnished, home-like room throughout the entire childbirthing process. The hospital's rehabilitation facility provides subacute services, and has a unique brain injury program.

MERCY MEDICAL CENTER
301 St. Paul Place
(410) 332-9000
www.mdmercy.com
The 285-bed hospital started as a 20-bed clinic for the poor and indigent of Baltimore. It was run by one doctor and a couple of medical students in an abandoned schoolhouse in 1867. At that time, the hospital was part of Washington University School of Medicine. In 1874 City Hospital, named for the nearby City Springs, a public fountain and park, was taken over by six Sisters of Mercy, who continued to care for the city's poor, while opening the Mercy Hospital School of Nursing in 1899. Since that time, the hospital has continued

to grow into one of the area's larger hospitals, employing 2,033 people and having an operating budget of about $147 million.

The Weinberg Center for Women's Health and Medicine is headed by world-class gynecologic oncologist Dr. Neil Rosenshein, and breast cancer surgeon Dr. Neil B. Freidman heads the Hoffberger Breast Center. The newest additions are institutes for surgical oncology and foot and ankle reconstruction. In recent years the hospital has been making arrangements with a number of area businesses and government agencies to provide first-line health care to injured workers, giving it a new niche to fill in the Downtown area. The hospital provides care in internal medicine, surgery, obstetrics, pediatrics, urology, cardiology, oncology, cosmetic surgery, hospice, transitional care, and emergency medicine. The Cardinal Shehan Center/Stella Maris geriatric care facility and Mercy Ridge retirement community, both in Timonium, are Mercy affiliates.

MOUNT WASHINGTON PEDIATRIC HOSPITAL
1708 West Rogers Ave.
(410) 578-8600
www.mwph.org
Founded in 1922, the 70-bed nonprofit facility provides long-term pediatric care for children with complex needs. In 2006, it came under the joint control of the Johns Hopkins and University of Maryland Medical System. Employing about 500 people, the hospital's specialties include inpatient and outpatient care for infants and children with rehabilitation and special medical needs, including asthma and obesity.

NORTHWEST HOSPITAL CENTER
5401 Old Court Rd., Randallstown
(410) 521-2200
www.lifebridgehealth.org/northwesthospital
This 242-bed hospital employs about 600 doctors and serves Northwest Baltimore and the Randallstown and Pikesville areas. Specialties are minimally invasive surgery, general medical/surgical, cardiology, gynecology, internal medicine, and hospice patients. Its facilities are designed around

the Friesen concept where nursing alcoves are outside the patients' rooms in smaller 20-bed units. This system eliminates nursing stations and places supplies, medications, and charts near the patients. It is part of the Lifebridge Health System.

ST. AGNES HOSPITAL
900 Caton Ave.
(410) 368-6000
ww.stagnes.org
The first Catholic hospital in Baltimore, St. Agnes was founded by the Daughters of Charity in 1823 so they could provide nursing care to the poor. The 307-bed hospital moved to its current location, Caton Avenue at Wilkens Avenue, in 1876 and reorganized into a full-service hospital in 1906. Part of St. Agnes HealthCare, an integrated delivery system for all levels of medical care with numerous off-site centers, the hospital's 3,086 employees are part of the Maryland Health Network that provides health services to about three million residents of Maryland and the Washington suburbs. The full-service teaching hospital has residency programs in a number of surgical specialties including a cancer center, bariatric center, blood disorders, chest pain emergency center, and cardiovascular services. The emergency department includes pediatric, adult, and urgent care.

ST. JOSEPH MEDICAL CENTER
7601 Osler Dr., Towson
(410) 337-1000
www.sjmcmd.org
Operated by the Sisters of St. Francis of Philadelphia, this Catholic hospital in Towson is an acute care, regional medical center with 365 acute and 26 transitional beds. With more than 1,100 physicians and 2,400 nurses and other employees, it is known for its outstanding cardiac care. It is also famed for its Orthopaedic Institute. Its primary service area is Baltimore County, from Towson north to the Pennsylvania line. Other specialties include cardiovascular services, open-heart surgery, obstetrics, women's services, and minimally invasive surgery.

SINAI HOSPITAL
2401 West Belvedere Ave.
(410) 601-9000
www.lifebridgehealth.org/sinaihospital
Founded in 1866 as the Hebrew Hospital and Asylum, the hospital is now part of the Lifebridge Health System. It is Maryland's largest community hospital and the third-largest teaching hospital in the state. With 467 beds and 2,543 employees, the hospital's residency program includes doctors from Johns Hopkins University School of Medicine and other schools in Baltimore and elsewhere. Among its accomplishments are the introduction of a procedure to heal corneal epithelial glaucoma, showing the benefits of administering magnesium to speed recovery times after open-heart surgery, development of a Minimally Invasive Direct Cardiac Artery Bypass, and the invention of Automatic Implantable Cardioverter Defibrillator, both of which improve a patient's success after heart problems. The hospital has opened a state-of-the-art Emergency Center, called ER7, which offers seven separate patient-care centers under one roof. The goal of the center is to reduce the anxiety of patients and their families while delivering the necessary and best care possible, including concierge service, 24-hour valet parking, and 22 private waiting rooms. An agency of the Jewish Community Federation of Baltimore, the hospital's specialties include heart services, cancer care, neurosciences, rehabilitation services, and women's and children's health care.

UNIVERSITY OF MARYLAND MEDICAL SYSTEM
22 South Green St.
(410) 328-8667, (800) 492-5538
www.umm.edu
Calling itself "Maryland's other great hospital" in deference to the more widely recognized Johns Hopkins Hospital, Maryland's largest hospital serves more than 250,000 patients a year. Established in 1807, the affiliated University of Maryland School of Medicine is the nation's fifth-oldest medical school. In 1823 the medical school built the Baltimore Infirmary, which later became

University Hospital. Just blocks from Camden Yards and the Inner Harbor, the hospital has 747 beds, served by 5,500 employees.

A private, nonprofit teaching hospital, the first teaching hospital in the state, the University of Maryland Medical Center often assists with referrals and the handling of difficult cases from the region's doctors and smaller hospitals. The R. Adams Cowley Shock Trauma Center was the first of its kind for providing critical care to those in immediate need of medical attention, using state police helicopters and the region's ambulance systems. The Greenebaum Cancer Center opened in 1996 and serves thousands of people in the region suffering from all types of cancer. The Gudelsky Building, featuring a unique 12-story atrium to provide comfort and solace to patients and their loved ones, transcends the typical hospital environment, while rooms in the building are mostly private. Specialties include neurosurgical care, cardiac care, transplant surgery, and cutting-edge research and surgical advancements, including pioneering work in transplants, video-assisted surgery, and the Gamma Knife, a radiological procedure that requires no surgery to destroy brain tumors and repair vascular malformations. The hospital made news and history in November 2009 by completing a four-way kidney exchange involving eight patients from four states.

UNION MEMORIAL HOSPITAL
201 East University Parkway
(410) 554-2000
www.unionmemorial.org
The Union Protestant Infirmary was founded in 1854 to provide shelter and medical care to the sick, poor, and disabled. In 1923 its name was changed to honor the people who contributed to its founding and development. One of the first community hospitals in the nation to support graduate medical education, the hospital supports about 85 residents and fellows in areas ranging from sports medicine and orthopedics to foot surgery and obstetrics and gynecology. The hospital is nationally known for its orthopedic

program, including the Curtis National Hand Center and the Sports Medicine Program. It's also the Baltimore Raven's official medical team. Union Memorial's more than 2,000 employees serve the people of northern Baltimore and greater Towson. The hospital is close to Johns Hopkins University and the other colleges in the area. Specialties include mental health services, oncology, cardiac and surgery services, and women's services at the Calvert Women's Group Center.

SPECIALTY FACILITIES

KENNEDY KRIEGER INSTITUTE
707 North Broadway
(443) 923-9400, (888) 554-2080
www.kennedykrieger.org
Next door to Johns Hopkins Hospital, this facility serves more than 12,000 children annually, specializing in the needs of children and adolescents with disorders of the brain, spinal cord, and musculoskeletal systems to they can achieve their potential and participate as fully as possible in family, school, and community life. They provide multiple-day, home-based, and outpatient services, treating those with congenital onset or acquired problems through injury or illness. They have an internationally renowned neurogenics program that draws children from all over the world. With specialists in more than 14 disciplines, the center's scientists have identified the genes responsible for disorders including Tay-Sachs disease and adrenoleukodystrophy (ALD). In recent years the center has been a leader in lead-paint poisoning prevention and treatment and infant eating disorders. Valet parking is available.

SHEPPARD PRATT HEALTH SYSTEM
6501 North Charles St., Towson
(410) 938-3000
www.sheppardpratt.org
Moses Sheppard bequeathed his entire estate to start the Sheppard Asylum in 1862. Several years later, Enoch Pratt, who gave more than $1 million to create the free library in Baltimore

bearing his name, asked that the 322-bed facility be changed to the Sheppard and Enoch Pratt Hospital after giving $1.6 million to complete the building. Today, the facility provides inpatient and outpatient behavior health, addiction services, crisis intervention, special education schools, and employee assistance programs. Through a partnership with the University of Maryland Medical Center, the facility operates a fellowship program in child and adolescent psychiatry. Its alcohol and drug addiction services have drawn notables from all over the world who seek help at the sprawling campus in Towson in anonymity. Sheppard Pratt employs 2,100 people and has programs in numerous counties of Maryland and Prince William County, Virginia. The Towson campus is home to several unique art and history installations with the works of nearly 100 professionally trained artists whose life experiences have been impacted by mental illness or addiction.

UNIVERSITY SPECIALTY HOSPITAL
601 South Charles St.
(410) 547-8500
www.specialtyhospital.org
Part of the University of Maryland Medical System, this 380-bed facility provides specialty care for the chronically ill, with programs in wound management, traumatic brain injury, respiratory care, terminal care, clinical diatetics, and IV therapy. Their specialty is caring for patients who require continued hospitalization beyond an acute care setting It was formerly Deaton Specialty Hospital and Home.

HOSPICE CARE

As the population in general ages, there is an increased need for hospice care, and once again, the Baltimore area is blessed with caring people. Hospice care enables people with terminal illnesses to remain in their natural settings during the final days of their lives. Instead of measures to prolong their lives with machines and technology, hospice care focuses on providing people with the medicines and services to make them as comfortable as possible. The benefits, according to proponents, are more peaceful experiences for the ill person and for family members and friends, who can share the final, important days of someone's life in the safety, protection, and security of a familiar surrounding.

Nurses, aides, and others who can ease the experience for these patients and for their families are available through the following agencies, all of which have been certified by the state and the Hospice Network of Maryland. To find out more information on hospice care in Maryland, contact the Hospice & Palliative Care Network of Maryland, 408 Headquarters Dr., Suite 3-H, Millersville, Maryland 12208 or by calling (410) 729-4571 or visiting the Web site at www.hnmd.org.

GILCHRIST HOSPICE CARE
11311 McCormick Rd., Suite 350, Hunt Valley
(443) 849-8200
www.gilchristhospice.org
Formerly Hospice of Baltimore and Howard County, they are committed to providing comfort-oriented care with a holistic approach. They coordinate the administration of medical care, nursing care, social work, home health and volunteer assistance, and spiritual and grief counseling and support. They have a home-based care office in Columbia and a center in Towson.

JOHNS HOPKINS HOME CARE GROUP
5901 Holabird Ave., Suite A
(410) 288-8100
www.hopkinsmedicine.org/homecare
Full home care services are available in Cecil, Harford, Baltimore, Carroll, Howard, and Anne Arundel Counties and Baltimore City. Some services are provided in Frederick, Montgomery, and Prince George's Counties. A few services are available in Calvert, Charles, and St. Mary's Counties.

JOSEPH RICHEY HOSPICE INC.
838 North Eutaw St.
(410) 523-2150
www.josephricheyhospice.org
Located in downtown Baltimore, this 20-bed inpatient unit also provides home care. They

are building Dr. Bob's Place, the first hospice for children in Maryland. It will have 10 private rooms and provide hospice services to children at home.

LEVINDALE HEBREW GERIATRIC CENTER AND HOSPITAL
2434 West Belvedere Ave.
(410) 601-2400
www.lifebridgehealth.org
Levindale has created a PALS program for end-of-life and pain management care. It stands for Patient-centered ways of Anticipating the needs of residents, patients, and their families and Listening when patients and residents share their desires and Serving them so their wishes are met.

STELLA MARIS HOSPICE CARE PROGRAM
2300 Dulaney Valley Rd., Timonium
(410) 252-4500 ext 7307
www.stellamarisinc.com
Stella Maris has a 20-bed inpatient hospice unit with private rooms, family areas, a country kitchen, a children's playroom, outdoor deck,

and sleep-over facilities for families. They also provide hospice care at nursing homes and in private homes.

ST. AGNES HOME CARE AND HOSPICE
3421 Benson Ave.
(410) 368-2825
www.stagnes.org/svc_hope.html
The HOPE Palliative Care Services Program is available to anyone with a chronic or life-threatening illness. It provides holistic support to ensure a better quality of life for their patients.

ALTERNATIVE HEALTH CARE

As is true of most of this country's traditional professional health care community, alternative healing methods are making some inroads and winning converts. New offices for holistic health providers, acupuncturists, and aromatherapists are opening all the time. For a fairly comprehensive list of alternative providers, check the listings at www.marylandinfo.com/Medical_and_Health.

MEDIA

Baltimore's media, like the city itself, has an international and a neighborhood focus. On the same local TV news broadcast, you're likely to hear how neighbors are taking up a collection to help a family whose home was destroyed by fire and coverage of the latest developments in China and the bills that were passed in Washington that day. Newspapers will run 2-inch headlines about a local high school's football victory right next to a story about the recent meat or toy recall. Their focus is what's happening that has the most impact on the lives of the people who read, listen, or watch them. After that, they'll approach national or international news.

Baltimore has always been big on rock 'n' roll. Back in the 1950s and '60s, we had local dance-party shows on radio and TV. Buddy Dean and his teenage committee were the ones to watch when you got home from school every day. We watched and learned all the new dances so that at the weekend's record hop we would be in the know. (John Waters spoofed this semi-religious dedication to *The Buddy Dean Show* in his movie and Broadway musical *Hairspray*.) Baltimore stations carried *Dance Party* and other national dance shows on radio, but the local show on Friday nights was *Lee Case and the HiFi Club,* on WCBM and sponsored by Coca-Cola. Children could go down to the studio and be part of the show; they'd talk about local high school functions and dances and then win prizes. On Saturday nights there was always a HiFi Club record hop somewhere in town.

Print media is one of Baltimore's true passions. We have some large publishing houses, many of which are book publishers and oriented toward educational or medical publishing. ,

Baltimore has only two daily newspapers, the *Baltimore Sun,* and the tabloid-sized *Examiner* that started in 2006. There is also one main business daily, the *Daily Record*. A few free citywide weeklies and monthlies tend to make up for the loss a few years ago of the *Baltimore News American* and the *Baltimore Evening Sun*. Baltimore also boasts newspapers that focus on specific neighborhoods, such as the *Dundalk Eagle* and the *Charles Villager,* or even a specific religion, such as the *Catholic Review* and *Jewish Times.*

We also have two monthly four-color magazines that are Baltimore-centric, *Baltimore* and *Style,* and some area-specific ones, such as *The Urbanite,* which chats about urban living. Baltimore's active arts and culture scene is covered in two publications, *Link* and *radar.*

Subsequently we've listed some of the major players in the Baltimore media market.

NEWSPAPERS

Dailies

THE BALTIMORE EXAMINER
400 East Pratt St.
www.examiner.com
Since April 2006, Baltimore has been a two-daily town again. The *Examiner,* which also has newspapers in San Francisco, Washington, D.C., and Denver, was started by Qwest founder Philip Anschutz to tap into the huge population that doesn't read the *Sun.* The *Examiner* is distributed in affluent neighborhoods in parts of Baltimore City, and Baltimore, Anne Arundel, and Howard Counties for free. Some 250,000 newspapers are delivered Monday through Saturday. Local news and sports coverage, with a number of Baltimore-based columnists, are emphasized, though there are plenty of pages devoted to national and inter-

national news. Scoops are a big thing with the tabloid-size *Examiner,* which tries to find stories the *Sun* isn't covering.

THE BALTIMORE SUN
501 North Calvert St.
(410) 332-6000
www.baltimoresun.com
A. S. Abell originally created the *Sun* in 1837 as a penny paper to appeal to and serve Baltimore's middle class. The *Sun's* first foreign correspondent left the harbor in 1887, and its in-depth coverage of the international scene continues today with firsthand accounts from its five foreign bureaus and through the Associated Press, of which it was a founding member. Over the years the *Sun's* journalism has won more than 15 Pulitzer Prizes .

From 1920 to 1995 A. S. Abell Company also published the *Evening Sun,* which many Baltimoreans still mourn. Its focus was more community-oriented and its tone slightly more irreverent—a legacy of H. L. Mencken, Baltimore's most famous curmudgeon and founder of the *Evening Sun's* editorial page.

The *Sun,* bought by a private investor in 2007, enjoys a circulation of nearly a half million for its Sunday editions. The *Sun* has daily circulation of 210,098 (as of 2007) and Sunday of 351,243 and it offers county-specific editions for Anne Arundel, Howard, Carroll, and Baltimore Counties and also owns Patuxent Publishing (see the listing under Weeklies in this chapter). Weekly tabs include Thursday's "Live," a pullout that lists Baltimore happenings, while Sunday's edition has real estate and employment sections. As the print readership declined, it's online (www.baltimoresun.com) readership has zoomed since its launch in 1996 to more than 3.5 million unique visitors a month. About three dozen blogs are created by its staff members, covering such topics as restaurants, pets, and sports.

With the death of so many print newspapers, and the *Sun* seemingly joining them in bleeding money, the paper has been redesigned twice, thinned the staff and the number of pages. Although decried by purists, the paper seems to spend more time and space on what readers want to know rather than what editors want them to know. It makes for a fast, fun, and still educational read.

The daily paper is 50 cents a copy; 25 cents if you buy it late in the day from a street vendor and $1.66 on Sundays. One-year subscription is $176.80, but look for special offers that can reduce that amount.

THE DAILY RECORD
11 East Saratoga St.
(410) 752-3849
www.mddailyrecord.com
In business since 1888, the *Daily Record* delivers business and legal news to 30,000 professionals and the general public Monday through Friday. Founded by Edwin Warfield, who was the governor of Maryland in the early 1900s, the *Daily Record* continued as a family-run printing and publishing company until 1994, when Edwin Warfield IV sold the company. Not much has changed, although a Saturday publication, the *New Daily Record,* which hits the high spots of the week's events, has been added. The *Daily Record* has been in the same building for 70 years. The paper can be received through the mail by subscription ($199 per year), received online ($79 a year), or bought at a newsstand for 75 cents.

Weeklies

THE AFRO-AMERICAN
2519 North Charles St.
(410) 554-8200
www.afro.com
The *Afro-American* has been a family-run publication for more than 100 years. The *Afro's* first owner, John Henry Murphy Sr., was a former slave who gained his freedom with the Emancipation Proclamation of 1863. The original *Afro* was a church paper produced by the Rev. William Alexander for members of Sharon Baptist Church. John Murphy bought the name and equipment in 1882 so that he could publish church information for the Hagerstown District of the AME Church, of which he was Sunday

School Superintendent. In 1900 he joined with St. James Episcopal Church to begin publishing the *Afro-American Ledger.* By 1907 the paper was incorporated into the Afro-American Company of Baltimore City. The paper has a distinguished history of challenging racial and political issues in its editorial pages. Today the *Afro* enjoys a weekly circulation of 100,000 and is the best source for what's happening in the black community, locally and nationally. Look for it every Wednesday. Newsstand price is 50 cents and an annual subscription is $30.

THE BALTIMORE BUSINESS JOURNAL
1 East Pratt St., Suite 205
(410) 576-1161
www.bizjournals.com/baltimore
The *Baltimore Business Journal (BBJ)* has been in business since the mid-1980s. It publishes a weekly newspaper-print magazine about business happenings in Baltimore and business guides that may be purchased separately, such as its *Book of Lists,* an indispensable guide to the top companies and their decision makers. *BBJ* is owned by American City Business Journals, which publishes similar journals for 41 other cities, including Washington, D.C.

Individual copies of the *BBJ* can be purchased for $1.25, or subscriptions are available for $90.57 for 56 issues.

THE BALTIMORE JEWISH TIMES
1040 Park Ave., Suite 200
(410) 752-3504
www.jewishtimes.com
The *Baltimore Jewish Times* has been published every Friday since 1919. The paper covers general national and local news and issues pertaining to Baltimore's Jewish community. This is where 20,000 subscribers are reminded about the current candle lighting time, births and deaths, and other social, political, educational, and sports topics. It takes pride in being able to touch all members of the Jewish population from reformed to conservative. The *Jewish Times* is sold mostly by subscription ($46.59 per year). Newsboxes can be found around Pikesville and Mount Washington.

The *Jewish Times* also publishes the full-color magazines *Style* and *Chesapeake Life* and frequently offers free copies with a subscription to the newspaper.

One lifestyle topic they covered in 2009 is the release of David Sax's book, *Save the Deli: In Search of Perfect Pastrami, Crusty Rye, and the Heart of Jewish Delicatessen* that explores the life and death of Jewish delicatessens around the country. The review notes that Sax mentions Attman's in East Baltimore and Miller's in Pikesville.

THE CATHOLIC REVIEW
880 Park Ave.
(443) 524-3150, (888) 768-9555
www.catholicreview.org
The *Catholic Review* provides the Catholic perspective on local and national news. The most popular section is "Spotlight," which features a different regional archdiocesan parish or school each week. The *Catholic Review* has been published by the Cathedral Foundation Press since 1913; its precursor, the *Catholic Mirror,* began in 1833. Individual copies are available at many 7-11 stores for 75 cents a copy. Subscriptions are available for $45 a year or you can request that a single copy be mailed to you for $1.75. The paper comes out every Thursday.

CITY PAPER
812 Park Ave.
(410) 523-2300
www.citypaper.com
City Paper was started in 1977 by two students at Johns Hopkins University. Their goal was to create a liberal alternative to the mainstream papers in Baltimore, and they were successful. Successful enough that the paper was bought by Times-Shamrock Communications in 1987. The paper is currently owned by the Scranton Times. *City Paper* still keeps a young voice, but it speaks honestly to the whole city and is the place Baltimoreans go to learn what's happening this week. Its calendar of events is pages and pages in length and covers everything from arts galas to movie times to yard sales. The paper prides itself on its in-depth investigative reporting and its arts

coverage. The personals listings are also extensive. The paper has a circulation of 91,000 and is
distributed free at more than 1,800 locations in
the metropolitan area. New editions come out
Wednesdays; look for copies in the bright yellow
boxes, at some corner stores, and at magazine
stands. Subscriptions for home delivery are $75
per year. Individual copies are free.

PATUXENT PUBLISHING COMPANY
10750 Little Patuxent Parkway
(410) 730-3990
www.patuxent.com
Patuxent Publishing creates area-specific newspapers in the greater Baltimore area that are delivered
free right to your door once a week. The *Messenger*
is for residents who live in the northern neighborhoods of Baltimore City, including Roland Park,
Homeland, and Guilford. Towsonians receive the
Towson Times; in Owings Mills residents receive the
Owings Mills Times. Howard County has the *Howard
County Times* and the *Columbia Flier.*

Monthlies

BALTIMORE'S CHILD
11 Dutton Court
(410) 367-5884
www.baltimoreschild.com
Baltimore's Child is a free newspaper that's been
in business since the early 1980s. It covers topics on children from the diaper set to teens
and focuses on the dissemination of practical,
usable information through 52,000 copies. An
issue might cover a round up of birthday party
resources and several stories on moms who work
from home or own their businesses. *Baltimore's
Child* publishes annual schools, summer camp,
and parents' guides. You can find *Baltimore's Child*
at newsstands, in grocery stores, street boxes, all
area libraries, and other places where free papers
are available.

GAY LIFE
241 West Chase St.
(410) 837-7748
www.baltimoregaylife.com

Gay Life, part of the Mid-Atlantic Gay Life Newspaper, is the oldest gay paper in the region,
serving the needs of this community for more
than two decades. It is published by the Gay and
Lesbian Community Center of Baltimore and
includes breaking news, in-depth cover stories,
entertainment and music information, classifieds,
and regular columns written by local activists. It is
published on alternate Fridays.

MAGAZINES

BALTIMORE
Inner Harbor East
1000 Lancaster St., Suite 400
(410) 752-4200, (800) 935-0838
www.baltimoremag.com
Started in 1907, *Baltimore* magazine is the oldest
continuing city magazine in the country. It has
information that runs the gamut from who wore
what at the latest charity gala to feature information about Baltimore personalities and places. A
yearly subscription is $12, or you can purchase
individual copies for $3.95.

CHESAPEAKE LIFE MAGAZINE
1040 Park Ave., Suite 200
(443) 451-6023
www.chesapeakelifemag.com
This magazine was purchased by the *Jewish Times*
and *Style* magazine in 2001, and the editorial
content and graphic layout are much improved.
A lifestyles magazine that focuses on food, travel,
home and garden, architecture, waterfront recreation, and the arts, this is the dominant upscale
magazine for the Chesapeake Bay region. It costs
$4.95 an issue; a yearly subscription (seven issues)
is $15.

MARYLAND FAMILY
501 North Calvert St.
(410) 332-6932
www.marylandfamilymagazine.com
Maryland Family covers topics of interest to the
average young family. For instance, a recent
issue had articles on the H1N1 flu shots and

skateboarding injuries. Pick up a free copy at area grocery stores or your local doctor's office. Subscriptions are $19.95.

MASON DIXON ARRIVE
1242 Paper Mill Rd., Cockeysville
(410) 584-9960
www.mdarrive.com
This bright little tourism magazine covers all kinds of things to do around the state, and nearby states. Special events, such as art shows, concerts, historical commemorations, and festivals, are listed in the calendar. Features focus on antiques, food and wine, tourist destinations, and shopping. The magazine is free and available at lots of antiques shops, coffee shops and restaurants, libraries, and tourism offices in Baltimore and the northeast part of the state. If you don't want to look for it, get a year's subscription for $28.

RADAR
209 B Oak Ave., Pikesville
www.radarreview.org
Produced through the support of local arts organizations, *radar* is a free, pocket-sized print publication reviewing the arts and culture in Baltimore. *Radar* comes out six times a year, and local artists and journalists write the content. The publication is available at area arts venues, coffee shops, restaurants, bookstores, and Visit Baltimore. Subscriptions are $8 a year.

STYLE
1040 Park Ave., Suite 200
(410) 332-1951
www.baltimorestyle.com
Style magazine is well named. The monthly itself has glitz. It is published monthly by the *Baltimore Jewish Times* and features comprehensive articles about living in Baltimore. In fact its subtitle is "Smart Living in Baltimore." Issues are $3.95 apiece. Yearly subscription is $15.90 for seven issues.

THE URBANITE
2002 Clipper Park Rd., 4th Floor
(410) 243-2050
www.urbanitebaltimore.com
The *Urbanite* isn't like other magazines. The editors pick a theme and look for talented wordsmiths to address the theme in their own way. Readers have their own spot in the magazine for essays, too. The ideas are fresh—so you won't find yet another photo spread of pretty clothes on tired, thin women. Local arts, environmentalism, the city's future, and the effects of Baltimore's latest wave of immigration were the themes of recent issues. The magazine is free, and it's available at coffee shops, restaurants, and lots of local businesses.

TELEVISION

Baltimore is considered a medium-size market with a city population of 637,000. We get all the main network channels, including Fox and Warner Brothers. Baltimore has been the launch pad for many nationally recognized talents, such as Gary Moore, Jim McKay, and Oprah Winfrey. Just as writer Anne Tyler, producer/director Barry Levinson, and writer/producer John Waters are still just neighbors to us, many remember Oprah reading the news on Channel 13.

If that sounds like downhome sentimentality, it is. Baltimore's full of sentimental shtick—just watch the morning news on any of the stations and you will see people who have been in this town for the better part of their careers, if not their lives. We've watched Denise Koch and Vic Carter (WJZ), Rod Daniels and Donna Hamilton (WBAL), Jennifer Gilbert (WBFF), and Mary Beth Marsden, Jamie Costello, and Norm Lewis (WMAR) for decades. Sally Thorner, who spent 10 years at WMAR before joining WJZ in 1993, announced her retirement as of the end of 2009. She set off a flood of good wishes from across the city and perhaps a little dismay at the thought of one of Baltimore's most familiar faces leaving the airways.

Local Stations
WJZ Channel 13 (CBS)
WBAL Channel 11 (NBC)
WMAR Channel 2 (ABC)
WBFF Channel 45 (FOX)

WNUV Channel 54 (CW)
WMPT Channel 22 (Maryland Public
 Television)
WMPB Channel 67 (Maryland Public
 Television)

Cable Services

Baltimore City and Baltimore County are served by Comcast Cable. Cable services have been getting a run for their money from the burgeoning satellite TV trend. Call Comcast Communications at (410) 649-9000. DirectTV's phone number for satellite dish service is (410) 727-9580.

RADIO

Baltimoreans still listen heavily to radio in our cars, while we work, while we hold on the telephone, and while we eat. For talk, the public radio programs are available on WYPR all day, and more pointed political commentary is on WBAL and WCBM.

Every music station in Baltimore has a specialty. In the old days of radio, all stations did what they called "block" programming, in which each block of time was programmed separately with music, talk, game shows, or dramatic programs. Now, it's as if each station is a block of its own. We've noted the local stations under a particular format. Remember radio stations can change format faster than our local weather. At least, this is a start.

Adult Contemporary
101.9 FM - WLIF
102.7 FM - WQSR

Classical
91.5 FM - WBJC

Contemporary Hit Radio
104.3 FM - WCHH

Country
93.1 FM - WPOC

Hot Adult Contemporary
106.5 FM - WWMX

Jazz/Ethnic/Talk
88.9 FM - WEAA

News Talk
680 AM - WCBM
1090 AM - WBAL

Religious
95.1 FM - WRBS
600 AM - WCAO
750 AM - WBMD
860 AM - WBGR
1230 AM - WRBS
1400 AM - WWIN

Rock
97.9 FM - WIYY

Sports Talk
1300 AM - WJZ

Talk/News/Various NPR
88.1 FM - WYPR

Urban Contemporary
92.3 FM - WERQ

Urban Talk
1010 AM - WOLB

INDEX